Life Is Like a Kudu Horn

Life Is Like a Kudu Horn

Margaret Jacobsohn

First published by Jacana Media (Pty) Ltd in 2019

10 Orange Street
Sunnyside
Auckland Park 2092
South Africa
+2711 628 3200
www.jacana.co.za

ISBN 978-1-4314-2866-3

Cover design by publicide
Set in Stempel Garamond 10.5/15pt
Printed by ABC Press, Cape Town
Job no. 003517

See a complete list of Jacana titles at www.jacana.co.za

We need to develop an intelligence that is ecological . . .
a way of understanding and articulating our evolutionary
links with all living things, the debt we owe to the earth and
the contribution of wild things to the evolution of human
consciousness – Ian McCallum, *Ecological Intelligence:*
Rediscovering Ourselves in Nature

One person can make a difference, but a community is
unstoppable – LeeAnne Walters, 2018 Goldman Grassroots
Environmental Prize winner for North America

Contents

Preface

THIS BOOK'S TITLE – *Life Is Like a Kudu Horn* – is a proverb used by the semi-nomadic Ovahimba herding people in Namibia and Angola. It means life is full of unexpected twists and turns: a great description of my life in the last nearly six decades. I have been a journalist, an underwater documentary film-maker and an academic, working as an archaeologist and an anthropological field researcher, before finally these strands merged into 35 years in community-based conservation, with a bit of community tourism mixed in. This type of conservation was regarded as lunatic fringe when we started in the 1980s but is today fairly mainstream across the world.

Born a South African, now a Namibian, I was privileged, quite apart from my middle-class background and good education, to live an early life which included spending meaningful time with fellow South Africans whose skin was not the same hue as mine. One of my earliest memories in the 1950s in the Transkei is my small pale hand reaching into a pot of umphokoqo (mealie meal) alongside several small darker hands.

Apartheid's evils have been well chronicled but one of the most pernicious impacts it had on people was that it literally kept us apart – which is why I regard myself as so fortunate to have escaped some of this legal separateness. My world view was enriched and broadened by a circle of friends and acquaintances that was wider than it might have been, had I been born into another family at that time. I grew up – in Pretoria, with regular stays in the Transkei – with gratitude that my forbears had moved from Europe to Africa 100 years earlier and thus enabled me to be born African on an amazing continent that was starting to emerge from the shadows of the past 300 years.

Most of my life choices can be traced back to experiences in my formative years. Writing was a passion from the time I could wield a pen; the only pastime I loved as much was reading. My father, in particular, was an eclectic reader and our home had books of every kind which we were encouraged to read once we were too old to be read to by my mother. Aged about 11, I can still recall the shock of reading Karen Blixen's 1937 *Out of Africa* and realising that a version of what she wrote about in Kenya was also happening in South Africa. Postcolonial critics have since vilified Blixen as romanticising colonialism at best and being a racist or even a white supremacist at worst. Be that as it may, what I took from her book as a child-reader, was a moral awakening about discrimination on the basis of skin colour.

A first career choice – journalism – was driven by a fervent belief in the public's right to know – naively thinking that if enough white readers knew how bad it was for the majority of South Africans, they would change political direction.

My long-suffering mother, weary of my political ranting at the dinner table, once told a 19-year-old me I should have been born black. Yes, I should have been, and you deserve to be blown up in a supermarket, I retorted. My mother, who had been a captain in the South African Defence Force during the Second World War, looked at me and said quietly, 'Your father and I went to war against fascism to ensure freedom for your generation.' She left the table and did not return. Later I cringed with shame at my cruelty toward this warm, caring and thoroughly decent human being.

We didn't speak for many months after that. My only excuse was youthful arrogance and deep frustration that there seemed so little ordinary people like me could do to change the unjust world we'd inherited. I had to do quite a few more years of growing up before I started seeing people as people and not as symbols.

Matriculating at 16, I had gone straight into the newsroom of *Pretoria News*, the city's English daily paper. University was briefly considered, especially after Mrs Nelson, the brilliant headmistress of Pretoria Girls High, called in my parents and told them I was wasting my academic potential by going to work for a newspaper. But as my parents had not taken out a university investment policy for me, as the sole daughter born between two sons (for both of whom a policy existed), lack of money was an easy excuse not to study further. I was keen to get on with real life. In retrospect, I am grateful I only went to university much later as a mature adult and that I paid for it myself.

Women's liberation was a distant rumour in the Pretoria of the 1960s. It would be another few years – September 1968 – before, on the other side of the world, a small group of civil rights activists unfurled a women's liberation banner at a Miss America beauty pageant. So, the by-line at my first newspaper was 'By Our Woman Reporter' and I was supposed to specialise in human interest stories. There was no place for an inexperienced youngster's half-baked reporting in the political arena: I recall the tone of the paper as acknowledging in a gently anguished way that apartheid was not right. I was lucky that three or four tough old former Fleet Street sub-editors ensured that I honed my writing skills over the next two years.

At 19, now a fairly seasoned young news reporter, I moved to a Cape Town morning paper – *The Cape Times* – where I spent more than ten life-enriching years, in different positions, mostly feeling that in a very small way I was contributing to change in South Africa.

By now the other passion in my life – the natural environment including the ocean – was combining with my zeal for human rights. From time to time, an adventurous spirit took me on incredible deviations, such as 18 months in Mozambique making an underwater documentary, using ingeniously homemade Perspex waterproof housings for our two 16 mm Bolex cameras.

We had to flee the country in September 1974 shortly after Portugal signed an agreement with the Front for Liberation of Mozambique (FRELIMO) agreeing to the colony's independence the following year. We'd been hoping to stay on: the coastal area where we – three young white South African scuba divers – were camping and filming was calm, and we were well integrated into local communities. But our stay came to an abrupt end one night after about 20 hostile and unruly men claiming to be Frelimo soldiers, a few of them rather drunk, came to our Vilanculos camp. Be gone by morning, they warned us. We packed and left.

When we finally got to Lorenço Marques, soon to become Maputo, we had to search for an open fuel station to be able to reach the border into South Africa. Unbeknown to us, a group of ex-Portuguese soldiers and other whites had attempted to stage a pre-emptive coup, demanding independence without Frelimo's involvement. The day before we arrived in Lorenço Marques, this group had taken over Radio Mozambique and stormed the main prison, freeing a few hundred members of the disbanded secret police. There had been clashes in the streets between pro-Frelimo and anti-Frelimo crowds.

Our main concern up till then had been getting to the border that evening before it closed. But as we drove into the town, we saw many empty shops with smashed windows, their goods presumably looted. There were few other cars on the road and no people in sight. After passing some burnt out vehicles and dodging still-smoking tyre barriers across streets, we turned a corner to find ourselves engulfed by hundreds of excited pro-Frelimo men and women. I was driving a small, blue, open beach buggy with Capetonian Lyndall Buchanan as passenger and there were moments when we doubted we would survive. But luck and good humour prevailed. We needn't have worried about being too late to cross the border into South Africa – it was kept open all night to accommodate thousands of people fleeing the city.

Back in Cape Town, we made a total of three documentaries – the first set in Mozambique, one off the Cape Peninsula coast and a third exploring the dolomite sink-hole lakes, one of them underground, in the Tsumeb–Grootfontein-Otavi triangle in what was then South West Africa. All were screened on nascent SATV. Then we pitched an idea for a full-length underwater film called *Neptune's People*. A Cape Town film-maker agreed to back us; we hired a small team of divers and went to work. Sadly, in the third month, our backer went bankrupt when another of his films bombed, and we used our own money to give our team decent notice. Broke, I went back to the *Cape Times*, a paper whose values-driven politics I admired.

Spending a few hours on an archaeological dig while on holiday in Cyprus had rekindled a childhood dream – although at eight or nine years old I thought I would access archaeology by marrying an archaeologist and going with him to Egypt! By now I was embracing feminism and knew I didn't need to marry anyone to follow my heart. So I enrolled at the University of Cape Town and over the next few years completed my first two degrees. I funded myself by working at night and very early in the mornings as a foreign correspondent for a Dutch newspaper group. In the afternoons, after my morning lectures, I worked for Professor Andrew B Smith, as his research assistant. On his digs – excavating prehistoric pastoralist remains in the Western Cape – I was site supervisor.

I remember not having much time to sleep during that period of my life. Nevertheless, Andy and I managed to make a few minor political waves together, such as discovering that although the ISBN number of official history texts used in South African schools in the '70s was the same, the books infamously gave three different versions of history – one for black pupils, one for so-called coloured children and another for those with white skins. We wrote an article revealing this for the *Cape Times* and went on to hold several weekend workshops for history teachers. We exposed them to more factual accounts of what was then known about early hunter-gathers and then black occupations – agriculturalists and stock herders – of the Eastern and Western Cape, and also the first contact between them and people from Europe. We presented current interpretations of the archaeological record, rather than the politically expedient line the apartheid government was feeding school pupils – and the populace.

History has always been a point of view – usually the perspective of the dominant ruling group of the time – but at least we were underpinning the views we presented with some facts, literally from the ground.

My disenchantment with academe probably started then, when Andy was accused by certain university colleagues of being a publicity seeker, as well as being unscholarly, because he had lead-authored a popular newspaper article. I also had a run-in with people at the psychology department who refused to sign a powerful petition that solitary confinement was, by its nature, torture. Some of them wanted academic definitions and qualifications added to this document! I recall telling a psychology lecturer and some postgraduate students that real people were suffering in solitary confinement as we spoke and that the lecturer's pedantic issues about the petition language were disgraceful academic pretention.

In the late '70s I went to neighbouring Namibia (then called South West Africa) for the second time. I returned for holidays twice more in the early '80s before making the decision in 1984/85 to focus my postgraduate research in north-western Namibia, known as the Kaokoveld. This would mean working and living on the edge of the liberation war. With laughable naivety in hindsight, I thought I would probably be safe even if I encountered Swapo (South West African People's Organisation which was leading the armed struggle for Namibian independence) because I carried the names and phone numbers of some South African ANC (African National Congress) leaders, including that of a rising young ANC star – future president, Thabo Mbeki.

It is here where my story, as told in this book, begins. I met the Tjipomba's, my first Ovahimba family. I explored north-western Namibia, skirting the war zones, with Blythe Loutit, founder of the Save the Rhino Trust, and later with Garth Owen-Smith who had lost his funding and therefore his job at the Namibia Wildlife Trust in March 1985 because the colonial authorities claimed he was 'a dangerous Swapo supporter who was confusing the communities'.

Hearing from him how he and local black leaders were pioneering a radical new approach to conservation that gave black rural people on communal land the same rights to wildlife that white farmers on freehold land already enjoyed was a turning point in my life. Nature conservation and rural development were almost always in opposition, yet here was a way that wildlife conservation could be linked to post-apartheid economic and social transformation.

The people and landscapes I encountered made relocating to Namibia feel inevitable.

I was sick of endless talk about southern African politics and hearing others mouthing opinions, all of us with glasses of fine wine in our hands. I felt hypocritical. A state of emergency in South Africa meant South Africans could not read what I wrote as a foreign correspondent. So my readers in the Netherlands knew more about what was happening in South Africa than my fellow SA citizens. I longed to engage with people as people.

In 1986 I started my field research in north-west Namibia, being hosted by Ovahimba and Ovaherero families, and never really left, apart from brief returns to my university in Cape Town to fulfil academic requirements.

In 1990, as soon as I had lived in the country for the required five years, I applied for Namibian citizenship. Even though Nelson Mandela had just been released from prison, my beloved South Africa seemed mired in political turmoil whereas newly independent Namibia was alive with idealism and hope. Would I have chosen to remain a South African had I known that South Africa would change far more rapidly than expected? Probably not, as by the '90s, Garth Owen-Smith, by then my life and work partner, and I were several years down the road of helping to pioneer community-based conservation, with me trying to complete my PhD research at the same time (which I finally did in 1995). It was compelling and fulfilling work, which is not yet over.

At my mother's funeral in 1995 I had occasion yet again to feel ashamed of what I once said to her – and to be uplifted at the same time. The last two rows in the Methodist church where the service was held were filled by black women, none of whom I knew. Afterwards, I asked how they knew my mother. Warm stories poured out. For decades, my mom, an avid and expert knitter, had been running a knitting circle with domestic workers in her Pretoria neighbourhood. Scores of women thus learnt to knit and crochet. Hundreds of warm winter garments had been produced over the years for their families and friends or sold to supplement these women's meagre wages. The circle met once a week at my mom's home to knit and share patterns. 'And we talked about everything and anything,' a woman told me. 'We ate ice cream and fruit salad and knitted and talked,' another said, adding: 'Your mother had space in her heart for us all.'

I guess, in her own way, she saw people as people.

To help the reader navigate my kudu horn of a story, the following explanatory notes may be useful.

Firstly, on the use of Otjiherero: because I am writing in English, I have mainly used the English version (Himba) of, for example, Ovahimba (plural) and Omuhimba (singular), except where I am directly quoting from Otjiherero. I have also tried to stay true to the Otjiherero dialect that I encountered in rural north-west Namibia, as spoken by Ovahimba and north-western Ovaherero people in the '80s and early '90s – before the language was more extensively written down and scholars of the language made decisions about correct grammar and usage.

Namibia has two main types of land tenure systems – freehold, which includes plots in declared urban areas and so-called commercial or freehold farms, and customary tenure. Depending on which record one consults, about half of Namibia's population – about 1.5 million people – live on the 40 per cent of the rural land, which is under customary or communal tenure. Community conservation work has focused on these communal areas and in one national park – Bwabwata – where people are living.

Communal lands are under increasing pressure as wealthier Namibians illegally fence off 'farms' for their exclusive use and have the resources to move their cattle into areas used by other communities in times of pasture scarcity. So far, where such non-local cattle have been brought into the core wildlife and tourism areas of some communal conservancies, the Namibian courts have upheld the rights of the conservancy members, not the cattle barons. Independent Namibia inherited a situation where most freehold land was owned by white people. Although this has slightly changed in the past nearly 30 years of independence as thousands of the more affluent black citizens, many of them politicians, have obtained freehold land including farms, the balance is still skewed. Only when we have a more equitable distribution of wealth will our transformation into a just and democratic state be complete.

Readers may also find a definition of community-based natural resource management (or community conservation) useful. Community conservation means rural people viably managing their natural resources, including wildlife and high-value plants, to generate local social, cultural and economic benefits. Conservancies, community forests, communal fish reserves and other community conservation initiatives create the necessary legal framework in Namibia. By choosing to live with wildlife, rural communities are broadening their livelihood options as well as enabling a healthier environment. Through wise management and balanced use, natural resources are conserved for future generations while providing significant returns today. When an idealistic early Swapo government passed enabling legislation for communal conservancies in 1998, it headed off what has happened in many other independent African countries: a black elite mimic the previous white economic dominance and capture tourism concessions and other valuable natural resource income streams, widening the gap between the poor and the wealthy.

The Namibian conservancy programme is a work in progress and full of challenges. While some conservancies are doing well, a minority are still struggling with governance and accountability issues. However, land for wildlife has more than doubled (by 166 276 square km) since 1998, more than 5 300 new rural jobs have been created in remote areas, returns to conservancies, from almost nothing before 1998, have totalled hundreds of millions of Namibian dollars. Since 1990 community conservation has contributed an estimated N$7.11 billion to Namibia's net national income. Above all, the programme facilitates what no other conservation approach has achieved in Africa: it empowers ordinary rural people. Many would argue that the single greatest transformation since independence has been in the conservation sector.

A Namibian communal conservancy is not a wildlife reserve. It can be described as a community-defined geographic area on communal land which residents themselves zone for different uses – farming, mixed farming and wildlife, core wildlife and tourism, hunting etc. The community defines itself as well as the boundaries of their conservancy area which must be agreed with any neighbouring communities. Legal requirements include a democratic constitution, a democratically elected leadership body, a land-use plan to the regional land board, a wildlife management plan to the Ministry of Environment and Tourism (MET) and an equitable benefit distribution plan indicative of how conservancy income will be used and shared. The conservancy employs staff such as conservancy game guards, field officers, conservancy rhino rangers and lion guards, community activators (usually women) and people to run the conservancy's management and administration.

In return for sound management of wildlife, government grants the conservancy rights over wildlife and tourism. The conservancy can thus legally benefit from tourism contracts with private sector and obtain tourism concessions, including inside national parks. Conservancies and their members also set up and run their own natural resource-related businesses. Conservancies can work together in what are called conservancy complexes to address bigger landscape ecological concerns.

I have to convey my thanks to the scores of co-workers in IRDNC and other NACSO (Namibian Association of Community-based Natural Resource Management Support Organisations) partners who continue to support the work being done by rural people to manage and benefit from their valuable natural resources. Without them, such resources – and its income – would have been captured by the elite and the rural poor further disadvantaged.

I am grateful to the Namibian government for its idealism and leadership of a democratic new way of doing conservation. *Aluta continua!*

Thanks too to the Jacana team, a class act, who have been a pleasure every step of the way – Publisher Carol Broomhall who 'gets' community-based conservation, Lara Jacob, an insightful and light-touch editor, and the others in production and marketing.

Finally, thank you to my remarkable partner Garth Owen-Smith. May you continue to challenge the status quo and see the other's point of view for many more years.

ONE

Not all tourists are the same

We can learn a lot about ourselves from the wild. And we can learn something else . . . we can learn how to give back. We can rediscover the meaning of relationships – Ian McCallum, *Untamed: Poems from the Wild*

I AM ON THE BANKS of a dry river bed in remote north-west Namibia with a New York appellate judge. We're both quite wet, not from the sudden heavy cloud-burst that has more or less petered out but from the drenched mopane trees above us. Flurries of wind, remnants of the fierce gale that herded dark rain clouds to this harshly beautiful valley, sporadically shake the branches so that heavy drops of water plop from emerald-green leaves onto us. Like the leaves, the landscape is sluiced green – quartz stones strewn on tawny gravel plains gleam like chips of ice in the soft late-afternoon light; dark grey rocks newly polished in the muted ochre washes and gullies.

The small river bed snaking below us is a tributary to the Khumib River, also usually dry for most of the year. I had gone to fetch Judge Ellen, sheltering from the rain in her tent, when we realised that the river, next to where we were camping for the night, was coming down in flood.

We could hear it, like a train rumbling and rushing towards us. So much noise as the approaching water tumbles rocks and branches that we take a step back from the bank's edge. You can smell the water – a humid gust redolent of herbs and leaves and soil. Then it's here – hurrying round a bend, ankle-deep, then suddenly knee-deep and more, tossing sticks and leaves in its turbulence. The mud-red foamy water swallows up the damp pale sand in front of it and turns into a real river. A powerful un-swimmable river that would sweep away a 4x4 vehicle had we been inexperienced enough to make our mobile camp on its invitingly soft sandy bed.

By now all of our party – members of Ellen's extended family and our camp staff – are on the bank. Everyone is riveted, some taking pictures, some of us just feasting our eyes on this banquet of water in an arid land.

Anyone who has watched a dry river come down in a flash flood knows the visceral excitement: you feel it in the solar plexus. For me, it's about watching Nature unleash her energy, putting us humans in perspective as *not* all powerful.

When I lived here as a researcher in this stark and magnificent land from the mid-1980s till the early '90s, hosted by semi-nomadic Ovahimba herding families, I devised a more complex interpretation of the results of rain – the dramatic flash floods and subsequent greening of a formerly dry and seemingly barren (but still beautiful) land. I was trying to understand local Himba worldviews by using Himba metaphors as a way of accessing the people's own conceptual model of their world. The term 'tanauka', meaning 'to turn round or turn over', is a well-used central concept applied to social, cultural and spiritual life here. It is also used (and perhaps derived from, I concluded) to describe what happens to the austere physical world in which the north-western Himba people live when it is transformed – turned around – by rain.

I think I was onto something with my search for metonyms, key cognitive oppositions and overlapping universes of meaning. But, for most of us from the so-called developed world including me, it is the sheer non-manmade power that flash flooding rivers let loose that is so compelling. For a few hours or days, in good rain years, the Kaokoveld's dry rivers become powerful, red-brown torrents, intent on re-sculpting the terrain, as if a long-suppressed energy has been freed. Big trees are swept away, terraces of bush disappear and river beds change course as rains in the large catchments of the main seasonal rivers converge to rush urgently towards the Atlantic Ocean.

Even though ours is a lesser river and the rain storm that birthed it was over in 30 minutes, we stay watching the surging water – mesmerised – till the sun dips below a rugged hill in the west. Already the water level is dropping; within an hour or less the flow will be spent and scattered pools will be all that remains of this spectacle.

Ellen, raindrops on her cheeks and hair, tells me above the now-muted roiling of the river that this is a perfect ending to a remarkable day. Earlier, she and her family had watched while the company hosting their safari paid out a cash dividend to groups of Himba people, members of Sanitatas Conservancy, one of the five Himba conservancies that together own the safari company.

'I won't ever forget this,' she says quietly. 'This, and the dignified gratitude of the Himba shareholders for the small amounts of money. I have been changed in ways I don't fully understand yet.'

Ellen has put into words her personal version of what we are all feeling. For the Conservancy Safaris Namibia team, of which I am a member, the cash dividend paid to households was one of those gestalt, inspirational experiences that made all our hard work trying to keep the little company afloat for the past few years seem worthwhile. Even though it was only just more than N$150 000 divided among 201 Himba households, over and above the half-a-million Namibian dollars in camp-site fees, daily allowances, salaries, bed-night fees, etc. that had been paid directly to the conservancies during the year.

The cash came at a time when the people most needed it, when milk – the local staple food – was in short supply with the families having lost most of their cattle in the four-year drought. Children – and adults – were going hungry.

The scattered February rain, some of it falling in cloud-bursts

3

like the one we had just experienced, would grow some grass but not end the drought. And, as a Himba elder said earlier in the day, 'Yes rain has now fallen in some places but where are the cattle?'

The fact that the money was coming as a dividend from Conservancy Safaris Namibia, the company they collectively owned themselves, was a deeply empowering aspect of this payout for a usually self-sufficient people whose resilience and confidence was being sorely tested by the devastating drought that had decimated Kunene's herds and crippled their livelihoods.

We had other reasons to feel proud of our efforts to keep CSN going: the company had hosted important conservation donor visits, influential community groups and decision-makers such as the new Minister of Environment and Tourism, his wife, the Governor of Kunene, and others – giving them a real, on-the-ground perspective of community-based conservation. Other tourism companies host such people, but usually in luxury lodges.

For me, the story of a Himba-owned safari company starts decades earlier in the late 1980s when a Himba woman called Vengape Tjiningire told me at her village in Puros: 'Not all tourists are the same. Some people greet you; they tell you their name and ask yours . . . such tourists are like visitors; there's time to see their faces and hear their voices...' But in the case of others, she said, even though they may give food and things, 'you don't see their eyes; only the eyes of their cameras'.

As a journalist-turned-archaeological researcher who then became deeply engaged in three decades of community-based conservation, I already knew during that long-ago discussion with Vengape that working in tourism was never going to be for me. I was too impatient, preferring animals to most people. But, as the Himba say, 'Life is like a kudu horn; you never know where it will take you.'

TWO

Lion at full moon

He who climbs a good tree always gets a push – Namibian proverb
about an idea whose time has come.

MY FIRST INKLING that something was wrong was the unmistakable
sound of sand particles falling onto the heavy-duty groundsheet
on which we lay under the full August moon. Before my brain
had time to process the meaning of this noise, my companion's
body jerked in his sleeping bag next to me and there was a blood-
chilling, guttural sound.

Later Garth said it must have been the lion growling as it 'tested'
– with its mouth – whether the lump under the blanket was edible.
But I still think it could have been Garth's instinctive primordial
snarl as the lion's teeth sunk into his foot. He denies he made any
noise, on the grounds that initially when he tried to shout, his voice
refused to cooperate.

My eyes shot open to see his tall figure jack-knifing up, with one
foot attached to a lion's head. Somehow, I found myself standing.
By now Garth had both feet on the ground and he was facing the
lion, which crouched three metres away, its pale mane fully erect,
its long muscular body distinctly visible in the bright moonlight. A
young adult male whose black-tipped tail flicking from side to side

clearly conveyed his mood. I'd seen my domestic cat do exactly the same just before she leapt on a mouse.

Garth found his voice finally, 'Voetsak! Bugger off!' gaining volume with each expletive. The lion responded with a deep snarl, flattening his ears. His tail kept flicking.

I tottered a step backwards and instantly the yellow eyes fixed on me. I knew he was going to attack, obviously deciding the shorter, fatter, quieter of the two creatures in front of him was the best bet for dinner. Later I recalled what I had seen and why I knew I was under imminent threat. My eyes had photographed those moonlit seconds: the tail stopped moving and under that smooth tawny fur, powerful muscles bunched.

Garth, too, read the body language and he stepped between the lion and me. He waved his arms aggressively and shouted. Now behind him, I was able to see his bloody mangled right foot. In the moonlight, the blood looked black and it seemed as if Garth was standing in a pool of blood. I thought I could see blood spurting from his heel.

But the lion wasn't going anywhere.

This totally true lion story, which happened under a full moon on a vast sand plain just above where the Mudorib River enters the Hoanib River valley, not far from the so-called President's Water Point subsequently built for elephant and other wildlife, has been told and retold many times. But there are two versions – Garth's and mine.

I had met Garth Owen-Smith only four times before we shared this lion experience in 1987. The first was in late 1982 when Blythe Loutit, who had just founded the Save the Rhino Trust, took me to his camp, Wereldsend. This former mining prospecting camp, about 140 kilometres west of Khorixas and 30 kilometres outside the Skeleton Coast Park's Springbokwasser gate, was a small oasis of 100-year-old green Euclea trees in a valley made up of red basalt rock and gravel. Some prefab buildings in the shade of mature trees was the remains of the miners' camp. A few hundred metres north where a smaller group of trees struggled to thrive, a caravan with a tin building doubling as a kitchen and office was Garth's home.

From here he was about to start his ground-breaking community game guard network – the first *practical* implementation of community-based conservation in southern Africa.

Both of us had partners at the time but our intellectual connection was immediate and deep.

I regarded myself as a staunch conservationist, having been among other things, environmental reporter for the *Cape Times*, a Cape Town morning newspaper, and I refused to believe that conservation was a 'white' luxury in Africa and/or synonymous with conservative right-wing politics. Our natural resources, including wildlife, were bound up with human survival and transcended politics. Yet, I had no response when a fiery ANC supporter, a young black man in Cape Town, said to me, 'Don't talk to me about wild animals when my people need land!'

From our first meaningful conversation, I realised Garth had some of the answers I was seeking: conservation could be and should be relevant to Africans. If wildlife was valuable to people they would look after it. Instead, they were alienated from it by colonial conservation laws which gave ownership of wildlife to the state.

Most African countries did not bother to change conservation legislation after independence and the low budgets and lack of interest developing African states afforded their conservation departments said it all. Conservation (back in the 1980s) was a white man's game, and wildlife, even though it was one of Africa's most valuable resources, was less important than people's domestic stock and crops.

'But this can be changed,' Garth insisted. 'Here we've taken the first step – directly involving local people and their leadership in practising conservation. If you want people to be accountable, they must have real responsibility. The leaders chose their community game guards – not us – and these men are answerable to their leadership. We raise the money to pay them and work closely with the leaders and the game guards. It's changing local people's attitudes.'

He told me about working – as a government nature conservator

– with white farmers in the south of Namibia who regarded wildlife as competition for their domestic stock and something to be poached, if you could get away with it. Most resented the fact you needed a permit to shoot game on your own property and few bothered to go through the cumbersome process of applying to government for permission to shoot a springbok or gemsbok. Then, in the 1970s, the law was changed. Commercial farmers who followed certain conditions – such as appropriate game fencing – were given conditional ownership of so-called huntable game such as springbok, kudu, gemsbok and warthog on their land. No more permits needed.

Within a few years attitudes changed and wildlife was being seen as valuable, to be managed and conserved. Groups of farmers were even taking down their internal fences and forming one joint conservancy so that game had more space to thrive. And thrive it did.

Garth's vision was for black farmers on the 40 per cent of Namibia which is communal land to get the same rights over their game – without fencing – but he was regarded as lunatic fringe by most white conservationists who were sure wildlife would be wiped out by meat-hungry communal area dwellers. They pointed to the widespread poaching of virtually all species, including black rhino and desert elephant, that was decimating the Kaokoveld's once-abundant wildlife right there and then in the early 1980s. White government officials and some individuals from the South African Defence Force (SADF) were involved but there was no doubt most of the illegal hunting was now being done by local men. It was obvious black people just saw wild animals as meat.

'That's just not my experience,' Garth told me. 'There are headmen and local people up north who care as much as I do about wild animals – they're sorry to see the game is being killed but didn't know how they could stop the killing. The game guard network has given them a role. And meant some small benefit to the headmen who can offer a few local jobs and to the men and their families who receive a small amount of cash and a more generous monthly food ration.' There were no shops yet so maize meal, sugar, tea and cooking oil delivered to your village was worth more than money.

We couldn't stop talking – into that first night round a camp fire and later when we travelled together in a vehicle for a few hours. It was heady stuff: how to nurture and grow a local vision of ownership of wildlife with joint action with communities every step of the way was at the core of what we were discussing. But importantly, I challenged Garth as to how one could generate tangible local benefits from wildlife, beyond a few jobs with a small salary and ration.

Neither of us had answers then and we had no idea that within a few years we would be jointly pioneering a small pilot project that would see benefits flowing to one small community. Nor did we dream that community-based conservation would grow into a national movement earning rural communities up to N$150 million a year, creating more than 5 300 new rural jobs and by 2018 contributing around N$1 billion annually to Namibia's net national income. Wildlife would be brought back from the brink in many of the 83 communal conservancies and one resident's trust inside a park – 20 per cent of the country – that would be formed across Namibia.

Elsewhere in Africa, people's local livelihood activities are encroaching on national parks and conservation lands; in Namibia people have embraced the idea of sharing their farmlands with wild animals and are benefitting from wildlife in various ways. As loss of habitat is the single greatest threat to Africa's wildlife, this increase in space for wild animals across Namibia is a remarkable achievement. It's not complicated why Namibia's community conservation programme works – at its heart is local ownership of wildlife, a fundamental concept developed right at the start in the early 1980s. Ground-breaking legislation passed by the independent Namibian government in 1998 subsequently entrenched legal ownership of wild animals to conservancies and their members: if you own something, you are motivated to look after it.

After an all-time high in about 2012, game numbers in the north-west were hit by a four-year drought, as were people's livestock. Some species – zebra, springbok and oryx – stopped producing young. But by 2018 with good rains in some places, game numbers were already rebounding. In the north-east of Namibia where rains have been adequate, wildlife continues to thrive after near-extinction in the 1980s.

In 1983, the year after I met Garth, I travelled again with my friend Blythe. She'd played a major role in recruiting Garth from his Etosha National Park job to run the anti-poaching project which he turned into a community-based effort with the early community game guards, aimed at *stopping* poaching as well as catching poachers. I helped raise some funding for this work from Cape Town.

Leaving her husband Rudi at his government conservation post at the Ugab Gate of the Skeleton Coast Park, Blythe and I drove north with bedrolls and enough food for about 10 days. Rudi reminded us that because of the liberation war in the north of the country we needed to choose western routes. He advised staying in the park, which runs all the way up the coast to the Kunene River, which we had no intention of doing as we wanted to meet up with some of the community game guards who lived outside the park, albeit in the north-west.

As a journalist, as well as an academic, I was probably a bit more politically aware than Blythe. Yet, it didn't worry me that we intended exploring territory that was on the edge of the war. If it crossed my mind that two women setting off into a very remote area with no satellite phone or two-way radio, and no way of contacting Rudi if we had a problem, might be somewhat reckless, my doubts were swept away by the wild beauty of the landscapes we explored each day.

I met my first Himba family at a small spring called Ochams in the far north-west. Kamasitu Tjipomba, one of a handful of community game guards, his wife Kavetjikoterua and their young son Kaororua had moved there with their small herd of goat – 16 animals – to take advantage of a little local rain which had greened the hill slopes. Soon they would need to move on. Tall, well-muscled and good-looking, Kamasitu was articulate and cheerful, in spite of the apparent harshness of the little family's current life. We talked, standing at the small salty waterhole, most of it covered by red algae. Although his English consisted of just a few words and neither Blythe nor I spoke Otjiherero, we seemed to cover a lot of ground.

The drought – as bad as the later one from 2014 to 2018 – had killed their few cattle. The family's situation was precarious and the game guard rations they received – maize meal, cooking oil, some soup packets, tea, sugar, matches and tobacco – were literally what was keeping them alive.

Kavetjikoterua, small and pretty, shyly accepted a packet of biscuits, apples and some droëwors (dried sausage) from us. I would have raided our food for more but Blythe sensibly pointed out we wouldn't see a shop for two weeks.

As we were leaving, Kamasitu indicated three gemsbok on a rise less than 200 metres from us. 'They're waiting to drink at the spring,' he told us, with his hands and a few words. 'They're thirsty; as soon as your car goes, they'll come.'

The gemsbok stood motionless, their black and white faces and tall black parallel horns like African masks pinned to the blue sky above the bare sand slope. I looked around, overwhelmed by the vastness of the vivid sky and the openness of this exacting land. A country wearing its skeleton on the outside. Words were inadequate to describe the sheer immensity of the landscape. It could not have been more different from the beautiful green and mountainous Cape Peninsula where I lived then at the southern edge of Africa. But, in that moment I knew that this severe, spectacular world, its people and its wildlife had changed my future.

Apart from the excitement of seeing a new way of conserving wildlife, an African way that directly involved local people and was not automatically in opposition to rural development, I could see a research route opening up for me. The semi-nomadic Himba people and the way they used their lands, built homes and utilised material goods could potentially answer some of the important research questions I was encountering as a mature archaeology student at the University of Cape Town. It could be ground-breaking research, and *not* because of the Himba people's apparently 'traditional' lifestyle. It was their semi-nomadism that excited me. Their mobility – in modern times – could surely contribute to a new understanding of how a group of people themselves recursively create meaning within particular social, economic, historic, symbolic and ideological contexts.

Over the next few days while traversing amazing lunar landscapes, I scribbled notes, on an intellectual high. A major academic preoccupation at that time was to move beyond an archaeology that was governed by general laws, aimed at scientific prediction, the so-called processual archaeology, which sought universal principles that could apply to all living systems including cultural systems. But new thinking was rejecting this empiricist, positivist, 'archaeology-as-science' paradigm.

The 1980s were an exhilarating time to be an archaeologist with pioneering thinkers like Ian Hodder of Cambridge University rewriting what archaeologists thought and did. The focus was on human agency – or the intentions of people in the past. To quote J.D. Lewis-Williams of Wits University in Johannesburg, we were seeking an archaeology that could construct an accessible past, populated by real men and women. We wanted the archaeological record to reveal issues that were intelligible as human concerns.

I could immediately see how the semi-nomadism of 'modern' Himba people living today could contribute immensely to the theory of this heady new approach. That Himba people rebuild their domestic space both physically and conceptually every few months, or even weeks, provided an amazing opportunity. This meant by working with and living with the same group of people, over time I could try to understand the relationship between their material culture and their social relations. What made it even more exciting were the social, economic, environmental and political changes taking place in Himba – and Herero – settlements in north-west Namibia. These had to have interesting implications for gender and age relationships.

I tried to explain all this to Blythe but she laughed at me and

changed the subject back to rhino as soon as she could stop my
flood of half-baked ideas. She did, however, make one very useful
suggestion. 'No one here knows the Himba people as well as Garth
Owen-Smith – if you want to work with the Himba, ask him to
help you get started.' Blythe also mentioned in passing that Garth
and his wife had separated.

So I contacted Garth, and in December the next year he guided
me, my then partner *Cape Times* editor Tony Heard and our good
friend and colleague, sub-editor and film critic Molly Green, on a
week-long trip to introduce me to some Himba lineages.

We met Matheus Uararavi, then headman of Puros, and five
of the seven families living there because of the drought and the
liberation war to the north. They agreed I could come back to work
there the next year. Most people laughed when I said I needed to
map their villages and ask them many questions. 'You can come,'
said the old man called Omukuu (Wild Fig).

Garth explained that these Himba people living on the pro-
Namib plains were on the edge of the main Himba population who
inhabited the highlands where the rainfall was higher. However,
because of the war, it was unsafe to go into those areas, which
were occupied by the SADF, and at times by South West African
People's Organisation (Swapo).

I came back to north-western Namibia in 1986 and spent six
weeks in and around the small settlement of Puros doing research
for an honours degree. A friend and fellow archaeology student
from Cape Town, Denny Smith, joined me for some of this magical
time. Once during that period Garth passed through Puros with
his two young sons, Tuareg and Kyle. They all overnighted at our
camp before going north.

Towards the end of that year, while I was giving my honours
thesis a final edit and working on my research proposal for a
Master's, Garth turned up on my doorstep – at the house I shared
with Tony in Hout Bay in the Cape Peninsula. He'd been visiting
another Tony – Tony Weaver, a journalist colleague of ours – and
had decided to take up our invitation to spend a few days with
us. Tony, my partner, was overseas on business and I'd taken the

opportunity to have our lounge suite re-covered, so apart from the fact there was nothing to sit on in our lounge, Garth was welcome.

I showed him our small spare room and made him a cup of tea. He was not a cheerful houseguest. He was jobless and broke after the South West African regime forced the Endangered Wildlife Trust of South Africa (EWT) to stop funding him and his small team – on the grounds that Garth was a subversive Swapo supporter and that having an NGO working in the area was 'confusing' the local people. It was also made plain to the EWT that they would not work in another park in South Africa or South West Africa if they continued to fund Garth.

He thus found himself without a salary, with alimony to pay for his two sons at school in Swakopmund. And to make matters worse, the team of game guards he and others had worked so hard to build up was nearly disbanded. Writing urgent letters and making long distance phone calls he could not afford, Garth had eventually managed to persuade the EWT to continue funding the game guards whose successes against poaching, including of rhino and elephant, had become manifest. More than 22 cold cases had been solved and led to convictions, thanks to community joint action with a few supportive members of the conservation authorities, notably the late Chris Eyre and his assistant Lucas Mbomboro. The poaching had been stopped. Even the South West African conservation department could not deny this. But the only way they were prepared to accept continued operation of these game guards was if they ran the network themselves.

Garth had no choice but to accept this – at least the men would still be working and would be paid. He had no idea what his future held and he was considering accepting a job offer from Kes Hillman in the Congo. But I could see his heart remained in the Kaokoveld – he just had no money at all and could not work.

While he was with me in Hout Bay, I helped him write a funding proposal that stressed the role rural African communities could play in protecting their wild animals. Later, I heard it was unsuccessful. The world wasn't ready for community-based conservation; it wanted white heroes to save Africa's endangered wildlife.

Garth and I kept in touch occasionally by post. Then in 1987 he wrote that he'd obtained a small grant from the New York Zoological Society to expand the rhino identification method that he'd initiated for the Save the Rhino Trust. He wondered if I wanted to travel with him further north than Puros to meet some of the other Himba lineages for my research in the next year. I jumped at the opportunity and this is why I found myself in the moonlight that August facing a snarling, tail-flicking lion. This is also where Garth and my versions of the story start to digress.

But as a journalist, the next morning I wrote down what happened so I reckon my story gives the facts. Garth, on the other hand, was injured and probably in shock – although he scoffs at this suggestion – so his memory may be less reliable.

Cowering behind Garth's tall figure, terror tasting metallic in my mouth, I saw the blood on the back of his seemingly mangled right foot where the lion had bitten him. At once, I was filled with righteous indignation and forgot thoughts of running away from this ferocious creature – who had damaged Garth so badly and possibly crippled him for life.

'Shoo! Scat!' I yelled loudly, stepping next to Garth, lifting up my arms to make myself big and powerful. In fact, I was strangely angry. I kept thinking: how could Garth survive if he could not walk? A man who only felt fully alive when he was out here, preferably on foot, and look what this damn lion had done to him! In between my furious 'shoo's!' I yelled for Duncan Gilchrist, Garth's colleague who was sleeping about 50 metres away in a dry river bed, next to his vehicle with his then wife Ruth and two relatives. I was hoping to wake Duncan before Garth collapsed from blood loss.

The lion was still going nowhere although he clearly recognised that he had lost the initiative. Two belligerent humans now confronted him.

Then suddenly, I became aware that Garth was no longer at my side. I was alone, facing the lion. My bravado faded. The lion instantly took back the advantage, reading *my* body language.

So this is how it ends, I thought.

A split second later, a shot blasted deafeningly into the night. Garth had stepped to the top of his bedroll, three metres behind us, to get the shotgun he'd fetched from his Land Rover and placed there earlier when he heard the lion roaring in the distance.

We had chosen not to sleep next to our vehicle, partly because Duncan and his group seemed set to party, somewhat noisily, and also as the ground where we had parked was uneven. Instead, we found a flat space on a sand plain above the dry Hoanib River where the bed of the Mudorib River enters it. After getting into my bedroll I had propped myself up on one elbow and looked across the plain that glowed pale and bare in the moonlight. Nothing grew on this surface and it was as though a huge tawny blanket had been rolled out towards the grey and indistinct hills a kilometre or two away. I remember thinking that we were quite safe lying there in the open; the moonlight was so intense that one could see for hundreds of metres. By contrast, down the slope where the others slept was full of shadows.

It was the first – and last – time I ever slept in the open away from the car.

'Listen to the wonderful echo of the lion roaring,' Garth had said softly as he returned to bed, carrying his firearm and his small metal camping trunk. He placed both at the head of our bedrolls. Sleepily, I asked him if we shouldn't move to the vehicle.

'Oh no,' said Garth, 'If a lion is roaring like that, chances are he's not hunting.'

Since then, we've noted all the definitive statements we are rash enough to make about the natural world, and we now know that just by making such a remark – The river never flows this early in the wet season; a young bull rhino won't charge; there are no cheetah in this area – we are ensuring that the river will come down in flood in early October, that a young rhino bull will scatter us before him and that we'll encounter a mother cheetah and three cubs.

Within the hour, the lion had crossed the plain and made his way to where we two strange creatures lay vulnerably in the open. Was he just curious? Did he see Garth get up to fetch the shotgun, and so he decided to investigate? Whatever his reasons, his persistence forced Garth to shoot. He could see the lion was not going to leave without some persuasion and he thought I could be trusted to hold my ground. So he grabbed the shotgun and swung round, saw that the lion was ready to attack me and fired quickly, from the hip, feeling he did not have time to lift the weapon to his shoulder.

Later, I would ask him why he fired above the lion's head if he thought the situation was so dangerous. 'Why kill an animal unnecessarily? It hadn't actually hurt you yet,' he said. After all, he had another shot in the second barrel and he was ready to use it if he had to. His tone of voice suggested anyone who thought otherwise was unreasonable: You don't shoot a lion simply because it is crouching a few metres away, snarling and preparing to leap onto you.

The noise was sufficient to cause the lion to retreat but he did so with the dignity of his species. By now Duncan had joined us and the three of us stood silently as the magnificent creature sauntered away. At about 20 metres, he paused to look at us over his shoulder and he snarled like a Harley Davidson motorbike, making the point that his departure was of his own choice, and not ours. Then he walked on and melted into the moonlight, and was gone.

The next hour was a high of post-terror relief: we drank Duncan's brandy and sweet tea; we quipped and joked and retold the story; I tried to emulate Garth and Duncan's nonchalance – as if lions were something I had frequently encountered in spite of my city life – but I fooled no one. Everyone agreed that I could not have had a more interesting introduction to my new life as a researcher in the Koakoveld. Ruth's Swiss relatives had little to say: probably they were in shock – in Switzerland you don't expect your sleep to be disturbed by snarling lions, shouts, shotgun blasts and having to attend to a man bleeding from a lion bite.

Garth was much teased about his courage in stepping between me and the lion.

'The man must have it bad,' Duncan mocked, 'must be true love!'

From my side, never having been so heroically rescued from the jaws of death before, I was starting to hope it was.

I bathed Garth's foot in hot water and Dettol. His wound was a lot less severe than it had looked in the moonlight. The lion had bitten him through his blankets and gouged a slice of flesh – like a segment of an orange – out of the back of his heel, missing any tendons or ligaments. Luckily, he'd been lying on his stomach, and even more luckily, the lion had made his investigatory bite at the bottom of our bedding and not from the top where our heads lay, thanks to the metal trommel Garth had fetched along with the shotgun earlier.

Duncan and I thought the wound needed stitches to close it but Garth laughed at us and dug out a battered half-tube of Germolene and a tatty roll of plaster from the decrepit little bag that contained all he needed for a few weeks in the field. At his request, I packed the wound with the ointment ('Apply for minor cuts and scrapes', said the faded instructions on the tube) and used the plaster to try to pull the wound closed.

We brought our bedding down from the rise and the Gilchrests made space for us. To tell the truth, we all huddled pretty close together between the two vehicles. It took a long time to fall asleep and dawn was already mother-of-pearling the eastern sky by the time I dropped off.

We were all keen to see where the lion had gone after he left us. His spoor was easy to follow in the crusty sand. To our extreme discomfort, we saw that after the shotgun blast, he had circled back and observed us from a rise not 30 metres away.

'Cheeky cat,' said Duncan.

I assumed we would head for the nearest doctor in the daylight. I assumed wrong: Garth was on contract to the New York Zoological Society to count and identify all the black rhino in the region and there were two more rhino ranges to cover. A lion bite was not going to interrupt his work and I watched him jam his swollen foot into his weather-beaten kudu-skin boot. As a concession to the painfully throbbing heel, he did allow me to drive his old Land Rover when we finally set off late in the morning.

The Gilchrest party headed east, back to Sesfontein; we continued up the Mudorib river bed making our way further west to where a small group of rhino survived. After this, we could combine Garth's work with my research, which involved mapping all Himba and Herero homesteads we encountered north of the Hoanib. Later, I would be able to find out from the people at Puros which lineages had used the various now empty camps and in what season.

The river bed narrows for a while after the Hoanib confluence – or it did in those days before massive flooding widened it – and we happened to be travelling behind a herd of elephant cows, with a very small calf, going the same way. Freshness of tracks and dung showed they were only a short distance ahead. Garth pointed out the saucer-sized spoor of the baby compared to the deeper hubcap-sized indentations made by the adults and guessed the calf to be no more than a few weeks old.

It was only a few years since the severe poaching had been stopped by the community game guard network and the Hoanib elephants were still panicked by any vehicle or sign of people.

Indeed, it is hard to imagine those early days. Today, you are able to drive right past a calm mother and calf who will continue feeding in the river bed metres from your vehicle or you may be privileged to have a dignified old bull or a cocky pair of teenagers come right into your camp to feed on acacia pods that have dropped from the tree which provides your shade. The bull could rise up on his back legs like a circus performer to stretch for a high cluster of pods still attached to the tree or put his forehead against the trunk, shaking the tree till pods rain down.

But then, less than 25 years ago, at the first sound of man or vehicles, the elephants would do one of two things: rush headlong into the thick Tamarisk brush on the river banks, screaming in anger and fear as they crashed away or they would use their bodies to make a security circle around their calves, adult elephants facing outwards. A car door slamming in the distance was enough for them to react. Security circles are heartbreaking. Adults stand in courageous formation, protecting their young who can barely be seen behind the massive grey backsides. But in reality, this age-old defence of calves against danger makes the herd horribly vulnerable. As the group stands belligerently in a circle, a poacher on a rocky outcrop above the river bed could chose his mark and take aim at his leisure.

The occasional human deaths in the last few years – always when a person is suddenly encountered on foot, giving the frightened elephant little choice but to attack – serves to remind one that the elephants have not forgotten the recent past when man's greed took this unique desert-adapted population close to extinction.

Knowledge of how to survive in the arid north-west, of where to dig for water in a drought and when to cross from one dry river bed to another, traversing the stark landscape between them on an ancient path that elephants may have been using for thousands of years, is passed on from generation to generation, from mother to calf, from old bulls and cows to younger animals. If the illegal hunting that reduced these elephants from several thousands to about 220 in the 1970s and early '80s – by South African military helicopter and from donkey-back, by cabinet ministers and barefoot subsistence farmers – had not been stopped in time, this special local geographical knowledge would have died with the last elephants of the desert.

Recent uses of the Hoanib River, by motor cycles and power-gliders, have disturbed the elephant and twice in the past few years we have again seen panic behaviour.

The very small calf within the cow herd we were inadvertently following the morning after our lion encounter was one of the few new offspring to be born into this till recently harassed population. Garth was not about to take any chances. If the herd became aware of us, it would be spooked into fleeing. A tiny calf could be accidentally injured or even killed by a running adult; just the stress of the panic when the herd bolted could result in its death.

So, for the elephants' sake, we stopped under a large Annaboom soon after we set off. As usual, Garth's first thought was to make a cup of tea, and he limped to the back of the vehicle to get his blackened and battered kettle. His boot was awash with blood and I prevailed on him to sit down and relax while I made the tea. Garth partially unrolled his bedroll to lean against. Fire-making was a relatively new skill of mine and the tea thus took longer than normal to produce. When I finally, triumphantly lifted a boiling kettle off my hard-won fire, I saw that Garth was fast asleep. Quietly, I put the kettle near the flames to keep warm.

He slept for two hours without moving, while I prowled around quietly and nervously. I couldn't very well get into the Land Rover and read a book in safety while Garth lay vulnerably in the open. How far had that lion gone last night? What if he was still around, hoping to finish what he'd started? What if there was a whole pride of the bloody creatures and they were busy stalking us at this very moment? I worked myself into a frenzy of fear, albeit a silent one. Senses straining in all directions I guarded the camp, jumping at every cracking twig and flutter of a bird's wing in the bushes, while I wrote notes in my field book about what had happened.

Eventually, Garth stretched and yawned. 'Must have dropped off for a moment there,' he said. 'Not quite enough sleep last night. Is the kettle boiling yet?'

When I arrived to start my anthropological research with Himba communities, basing at Puros in 1986, the government conservation authorities had taken over the game guards. I witnessed first-hand a white official turn up at Puros and drop a few bags of mealie meal and other rations on the ground near the game guard's hut. I saw him drive off without bothering to talk to the game guard to get his report. Usually rations were late, with two or even three months' worth delivered at once. Often the mealie meal was old and insect-infested. Inevitably, the game guards' motivation dropped as they realised that this particular official held them in contempt and was not interested in what they had to say. In other areas there were better officials engaging with other game guards but the man I saw on his occasional deliveries was running the game guard system into the ground.

'The EWT is wasting its money,' I told Dr John Ledger, new director of the EWT, late in 1986. I'd walked into his office in Johannesburg and invited him to lunch at the nearby zoo cafe to discuss the situation.

'The game guards in the far north-west – where I have been living and working this past year – are de-motivated and doing nothing. No one takes their reports anymore and even though there are some good people in government conservation, the official in my area is not interested.'

I didn't know then that this particular official was so contemptuous of local skills that he did some poaching in game guard Kamasitu Tjipomba's area, carelessly burying the bits of carcasses he didn't want in a shallow hole. However, Kamasitu, on seeing car lights in the far distance, went on donkey-back to investigate. He found clear evidence of the official's vehicle at the scene – matching the tyre tracks with those near his homestead where the official had dropped off rations. Kamasitu then did a round trip of more than 100 kilometres on donkey-back to report this case to another government nature conservator.

Amazingly, the official's wedding ring was recovered from the butchering site. It should have been an open-and-shut case. But the inexperienced conservation officials, investigating a case against a senior colleague, made some mistakes – including giving the official his lost wedding ring back before the case! To be fair, the official had written a confession when confronted by this ring and when neat packages of labelled game meat were found in his deepfreeze. The junior officials assumed the case would not be contested but after acquiring the services of lawyer Hennie Barnard, the accused's story changed.

The confession mysteriously disappeared from the docket, as did other key documents. In any case, the docket's chain of custody was shown to be questionable by the lawyer in the Windhoek court, where Kamasitu and I sat, listening incredulously. Within an hour, it was over. The magistrate could do nothing, he told the court, but find the defendant not guilty. He added that it pained him to reach this conclusion but legally he had no choice.

Later, we spotted the lawyer drinking coffee. I went up to him and asked him how he slept at night. Hennie Barnard was unfazed by my naive outrage. He was doing conservation a favour, he said, teaching the conservation officials not to present shoddy cases full of legal holes. Hopefully, some good lessons had been learnt today and next time they would be more worthy opponents.

There was nothing more to say. We tried to cheer up a baffled and crushed Kamasitu by telling him the lawyer would have cost the accused a lot of money – so he did end up paying a fine of sorts.

At the Johannesburg zoo's restaurant, John Ledger turned out to be a feisty character, iconoclastic with a fierce intellect and zero tolerance for bullshit. It took half an hour of talking to make up his mind. He would visit Namibia and look at the situation on the ground. As the new boy on the block at EWT, he wanted first-hand evidence before he took on his board who had made the decision not to continue funding Garth. 'I'll do the trip privately. See for myself and build a strong case.'

We met in Windhoek a few weeks later and I drove him north to meet Garth and others at Wereldsend. What John saw convinced him to make his strong case to resurrect support for Garth. Faced with his account, the EWT board agreed. Garth was to receive R1 800 a month – to cover vehicle running costs and to pay himself and his assistant Elias Hambo a salary. It wasn't much but at least they were back on the job and could start the process of rebuilding the game guard network to its former strength.

THREE

When Himba women turn their backs

In community-based conservation it's not just what you do; it's how you do it – Lessons from the Field: IRDNC's experience in Namibia, 2011

IDEALISTIC AND STUBBORN – but also in my case, naïve and, at our age, rather unrealistic, pretty much sums up our decision to keep the Himba-owned safari company – and a small remote lodge – going when the investor pulled out after three years. It was 2011, towards the end of our long and fulfilling careers in community-based conservation. Had we known that the national conservancy programme was about to face new and urgent challenges – including rhino poaching and a four-year drought in Kunene that caused rising human–wildlife conflict – we may have had second thoughts.

For decades we'd worked towards local people – those who live with and protect the wildlife that tourists come to see – benefitting from tourism beyond jobs and favours such as giving lifts (as one lodge owner listed under benefits to local communities). Although good progress had been made, with the concept of a fee to conservancies for every night a guest spends in a lodge –

so-called bed-night fees – legally entrenched through Namibia's national community-based conservation programme by the late 1990s, we still saw that what communities received from tourism was too little for the magnificent wild lands and protected wildlife they provided.

It wasn't just about money. Local people should be directly involved in tourism beyond running campsites. Local ownership had been the backbone of our successful community conservation work; people who feel ownership towards wildlife will also feel responsible for its management and protection. And so, by the same principle – a community-owned tourism company would strengthen the link between wildlife and benefits for the owner communities and it would also help change the pervasive idea in Namibia, and much of Africa, that tourism was a 'white-owned' industry.

We had picked the five most-remote north-western Himba communities to become owners of the company we jointly planned with the investor, a total of about 4000 people, far from the capital and not part of the elite pool of political party faithfuls or otherwise advantaged men and women who were finding their way onto the boards of some of the bigger tourism businesses.

The investor – a highly successful businessman – was keen to see this company compete on private sector terms so he rejected our proposal to obtain a donor grant to help fund the company start-up. This was to have major implications down the road.

Conservancies Safaris Namibia (CSN) was thus launched in 2009 with a soft loan and no written agreements, only idealism and excitement plus mutual trust and respect between the parties. After all, we'd known one another for years.

At no stage at the start did Garth and I have any intention of running the company ourselves, nor were we even on its board for the first few years as we were still more than fully engaged as co-directors of the non-government organisation called IRDNC (Integrated Rural Development and Nature Conservation) we'd founded.

We were happy to advise, involve ourselves in the community

liaison side of the business and Garth would do a little safari guiding as needed. He truly loves showing his beloved Kaokoveld to others, and to him such safaris are an important way to promote the concept of community-based conservation among influential international guests. I saw in CSN an opportunity to move away from voyeuristic Himba tourism to a more mutually dignified type of cultural exchange. We thus allowed our good names and reputations as community conservation pioneers to be used in marketing CSN. Others managed the little company with the investor closely involved in every important decision.

CSN's start-up business plan, drawn up by a consultant, was too extravagant and it predicted profits of several million within three years. Garth was the lone voice who criticised this plan as unrealistic but was not heeded by the rest of us.

The timing of CSN's launch – as the international money markets took their 2008/9 hit with tourism to Namibia crashing in 2010/11 – was deeply unfortunate. For its first three years of operation CSN, with its inflated overheads, lost money.

Although Russell Vinjevold, an experienced tourism guide and former nature conservator had been recruited as the first CEO of the company, the investor made all major financial decisions. And by early 2011, he had decided he'd put up enough money. He was persuaded by some of us, with Garth and I having joined the board after we stepped down from our leadership role of IRDNC in 2010, to give CSN the year to try to turn itself round. It came close, but by then relationships had broken down and the investor ceased his funding.

His intention was to amalgamate the Himba-owned company with a firm that owned a number of mid-market lodges in Namibia. Although Garth and my names – as international award-winning conservationists – had been used extensively in marketing, his rescue plan for CSN dropped us from our (unpaid) board of trustees positions. Our community conservation and development experience was apparently not relevant. Nor was there a role on this new board for Advocate Andrew Corbett, well-trusted chairman of CSN's board, with whom we had worked for many years.

We were outraged when this plan emerged. How could this precious joint concept – a social enterprise, as we saw it, dreamed up over many campfire discussions with the investor and others – be trusted to another company that had no track record in community empowerment, conservation or mobile safaris, and which from our perspective, existed just to make money? And above all, although CSN had been internationally marketed as Himba-owned, the new plan involved the investor taking back at least 80 per cent of the ownership. This violated the most important principle underlying CSN. Its community ownership was unassailable.

Even at that stage, it did not cross Garth's and my mind that we would end up running CSN.

After some fraught discussions with busy Andrew Corbett, well-known for his human rights record during the liberation struggle, we met with the five Himba elders who were also on the board of trustees. We put the investor's new plan to them. Unanimously, they rejected it. One of the elders put it this way: 'If you have a beautiful young cow, you don't send it away to another herd of cows where you will no longer be able to see it – you keep it in your own herd.'

All very well but keeping CSN meant someone had to put money in to keep it going. There were salaries, office rent and other costs to pay. And then there was the matter of the large start-up loan which the investor wanted paid back immediately, even though we'd been under the impression that at least part of this would be written off. The elders were adamant – they wanted to keep CSN. It was their finest cow. They urged us to find a way to raise money, and wondered how much they could raise if every family sold one ordinary cow. A not very practical idea in this remote area.

By then we'd got the opinion of a major British tourism agent, who described a plan to merge CSN with the lodge company as 'a disaster', warning us that the unique little company would disappear if this happened. The main reason he marketed CSN, he wrote, was because of its community ownership. If this changed, he was unlikely to prioritise selling CSN safaris – it would just be one company among many. And he observed that if CSN continued under a different type of ownership model, it would need to change its name which was now indelibly linked to its Himba ownership.

We did eventually find a way to keep the company going, which involved most of Garth's savings and a chunk of mine. We were indeed idealistic and stubborn (some would and did say rash) – and convinced we were right. The investor saw the situation differently and in spite of our decade of friendship, we found no common ground at that time. Eventually, a long-term 2 per cent interest repayment schedule for the start-up loan was agreed and signed. It was to prove a millstone round the little company's neck. Our decisions to put money into CSN to keep it going made little business sense, given that we have no personal wealth or savings to spare. But from a community conservation perspective, we felt keeping CSN going was a priority.

In hindsight, CSN has indeed made a major contribution to our conservation work. It has hosted donors in the field for IRDNC, Save the Rhino Trust and WWF. It has enabled flexibly priced expeditions such as hosting traditional leaders on a four-day mission to see where rhino poaching was occurring and taking influential community members into the area their conservancies wanted to set aside for the Ombonde People's Park – a new African version of a fully protected area, with conservancies as partners with government. These trips changed attitudes and facilitated positive action.

There were also donations: one group of guests contributed a considerable amount of money to build a school at Onyuva near Etaambura Camp to replace a shabby tent; other guests contributed to the emergency drought pay-out.

CSN moved out of its lavish warehouse space in Swakopmund to a home office, making drastic other cuts, halving overheads in a year. The following year, costs were cut even further. Russell went back to his passion – conservation, joining IRDNC as senior natural resource management facilitator, but working part-time as a CSN guide. For a while, our friend and former colleague Angela Howells took over, valiantly bending her human resource development and project management skills into running a tourism company. But costs were still too high for the amount of business CSN was attracting in a crowded market where every company claimed to be the most socially responsible and eco-friendly of all. After working without a salary for three months, Angela passed the ball and went back to earning a living.

And so as that saying goes, life took another kudu horn-like twist. CSN ended up being my and Garth's responsibility. It was not what we'd planned nor wanted for our remaining working years – both in our 60s, and few people could be less suited to working in tourism than me. For a start, you need patience, tact and a strong sense of humour. I have only the latter.

That's how I find myself – fortunately still with Angela on the team – at half past nine one cool 2014 August night on a dirt track near Onyuva village in the far north-west of Namibia trying to placate eight angry Italian tourists who have just become our responsibility. Before sunset, the group was meant to book into Etaambura Camp, a small lodge just up a high hill behind us. They are seriously late and volubly angry in that very Italian way. Why am I of all people here, I ask myself. The Italians pile out of the high, clumsy, 4x4 nine-seater truck and let me and Angela have it:

We want to fly out first thing in the morning!

You must get us a flight . . . this is unacceptable – we must all get refunded.

How can you expect us to spend 13 hours on this terrible road? It's inhumane!

Our guide is a lunatic! The company must send a plane.

They give us no chance to get a word in edgeways – to explain that we are just hosting them at the lodge. We had had nothing else to do with their trip, which was organised by someone in a prominent Namibian tour company who obviously did not know this remote rugged area.

When they start running out of steam, we suggest they get back into their vehicle and follow our 4x4 car to the lodge, where drinks and dinner await just a few kilometres away, and a satellite phone, which their guide can use to make contact with his company to sort out their vehicle problems, including, unforgivably, a puncture without the required tools to change the massive wheels on the truck.

The guide – let's call him Antonio – is short and dapper in leather boots and designer khaki and doing a good job at disguising the discomfort he must be feeling. He pounces on my mention of the satellite phone and shoots off a volley of fast Italian at his guests. I don't envy him being in the same car as this enraged group. Having worked in remote parts of Namibia for decades, I know how easily things can go wrong, so in spite of his carelessness in not checking he had what's needed to change a wheel on the road, he has my sympathy. But not for long.

We drive slowly up the narrow, steep, two kilometres of track cut into the side of the hill, using low range in the sharp corners. It's a pity it's too dark for the guest to see the dramatic view across the valley below. We hear Antonio's truck revving – he's taking the hill faster than us which annoys me as the road is fragile.

At the lodge while Kakuu Musaso, Etaambura's then trainee manager, greets the guests and presents them with tray of small, wet towels to wipe your faces and hands, I ask Antonio if his big truck was ok on the steep switchbacks up the hill.

'Huh, of course! Didn't even need four-wheel drive,' he shrugs. I turn away, irritated with his macho crap. Strike two against him.

As experienced a driver as I am out here, I would not go up an unknown, steep dirt track in the dark without engaging 4x4 gear, especially with eight other people on board in a high built-up vehicle. Decades ago when I started driving off-road into the Kaokoveld I was taught that it's easier on the car – and usually on the road itself – to use 4x4, low range or diff lock whenever in doubt. I recall my mentor's words: Don't think you're demonstrating your driving skills by not switching to 4x4 on bad roads. All you'd be doing is shortening your car's lifespan and quite likely damaging the track. And behaving like a macho idiot.

Right on Antonio!

Kakuu and the team have placed paraffin lanterns at the entrance to the spacious curving lounge and on the circular decks beyond. The soft lighting captures the warm ochre hues of the stones used to build the walls and the decks look spectacular. Dim solar lighting shows inviting leather couches, a large low coffee table and a few comfortable chairs in front of huge windows on the left. An elegant dinner table – places laid on white table cloth, with wine glasses and candles – awaits on the other side of the curved room.

Angela, who drove up from Swakopmund with me, is already offering drinks and making soothing small talk; she once ran a pub in the UK, truly likes people and is much more suited to this sort of thing. Soon people are relaxing, standing out on the decks and in the lounge, sipping from glasses.

Even though it's so late – well after ten now – some of the guests insist on seeing their rooms and washing before dinner, which is in pots, drying up on the edge of the fire since 8 pm. Kakuu and I quickly guide them along paths of fine ochre sand carved into the rocky marble hilltop to the spread out chalets.

'Let's just hope the showers work and are hot,' I mutter to Kakuu who rolls her eyes. Etaambura's plumbing has its challenges, as we both know too well.

As usual the chalets enchant the guests. Unassuming and unobtrusive from outside, each thatched room bonds organically into a rocky steep hillside. It's too dark to appreciate the colours and textures of the spectacular natural rock faces that have been incorporated into each individual chalet; this pleasure awaits the morning light. But Kakuu and I enjoy the appreciative gasps as we open doors and stand back, letting the guests see the wide, comfortable beds with white duvets and distinctive ochre-coloured blankets. Then the eye moves beyond, through roof-to-floor sliding glass doors onto a private wooden deck with a small table and two comfortable chairs. From there in all directions, stars decorate black velvet skies. Each bathroom is quirky and different, taking advantage of natural features and offering wonderful views from the shower or toilet.

The artist-builder who designed and constructed Etaambura is Trevor Nott, a volatile, one-of-a-kind, South African-born

Namibian who is based in Omaruru. Trevor is not an architect but a few of the big-name architects who are behind the multi-million-dollar luxury lodges in some of Namibia's iconic places could take a leaf out of his book. As the late Kerry MacNamara, one of the best architects I know, has remarked: A building has to refer to its environment, not impose on it. Trevor's creative use of space and deceptively simple but splendid buildings go beyond referring; his work showcases nature's own splendours. He is an artist indeed, distinctive within the tourism industry.

Over dinner we make plans for a late breakfast and then for a guided walk down the hill to where we hope some Himba people will be watering their cattle and goats mid-morning.

Although I'll be the guide, my role is really to facilitate the local knowledge of Uatjimbisa Tjambiru, a Himba sub-elder who works at the camp. He will show the guests different plants and discuss their uses as we meander along and then down the hill. Similarly, he will introduce guests to whoever is at the water below and remind the Himba people there that Orupembe Conservancy, their conservancy, owns 40 per cent of Etaambura Camp, and is a co-owner of CSN. So they are the hosts. As Uatjimbisa speaks no English, and my Herero is not adequate, we have with us a final-year tourism student, David Kasaona, to translate. I've been working with him for a few weeks and he's learnt that good translation requires using the Himba words as spoken, not paraphrasing them. Rich and mysterious imagery, worth discussing in itself, is often revealed by skilled translating.

After a large breakfast of eggs, grilled tomatoes, bacon and toast, washed down with good Italian coffee and orange juice, we set off. Antonio is deep in conversation on Etaambura's satellite phone trying to organise for a tyre – or a new nine-seater truck – to meet them en route to Opuwo, about six hours away. Chances are they will have to send a vehicle from Windhoek, a further eight-hour drive.

We've arranged that about two hours after we leave on our walk Antonio will drive down the hill, turn left into the 'main' track along which he drove last night and then left again up the first track he encounters after the first Himba homestead. This will take him close to the waterhole so that those who don't want to walk back up to the lodge can drive back. I've arranged for a cool-box of cold water and soft drinks to be put into his vehicle.

Etaambura Camp has worked its magic on the group and there's no talk of flying out this morning. Our ramble along the top of the hill past beautiful rock formations and unusual plants, many of them endemics, further lifts everyone's spirits.

We chose a route that takes us to strangely picturesque mining excavations where marble has been sliced out of the hillside, forming wide V-shaped marble chambers. People touch the marble walls around us and exclaim at the rock's silky coolness in spite of the sun on it. Most of the marble on the hill is brilliant white but one chamber's walls are a palely mottled rose-coloured hue. I tell the story of the marble mining – doomed because in spite of many excavations in the hills in this marble-rich area, no unblemished slab of the market-required proportions of one metre by one metre could be found. Thank goodness, says someone. Imagine if this beauty all around us had been turned into a mining quarry! We contemplate this, looking at the remarkable geology and botanical wonders around us.

'Being here, immersed in this wonderful piece of nature ... it is cleansing the anxiety and stress we endured yesterday,' one of the women tells me, beaming in the warm winter sunlight.

Uatjimbisa and David talk about plants and local customs as we stroll on. They point out the *commiphora wildii – omumbiri –* the so-called perfume plant. In the late 1980s when I was up here doing postgraduate research, I listed all the plants, what the Himba people called them and how they used them. I drew on an early ethno-botanical paper written by Johan Malan and Garth Owen-Smith for the then South West African Museum and published in 1974 in its journal, *Cimbabasia*.

Some of the commiphora species (the myrrh in the Bible) that the Himba women used as perfumes smelled so beautiful that I contacted Dr Tony Cunningham, a prominent ethno-botanist, then based in South Africa. He eventually visited the area and we collected resin from some of the plants and sent these samples to an ethical Swiss chemist for analysis. (Ethical meaning the firm would respect the Himba's indigenous property rights). The word came back that the resin contained valuable essential oils, definitely of high value for the international perfume and cosmetic industry. The resins were almost certainly also of medicinal value but further analysis and research would be needed for that.

For nearly two decades I sat on this information, keen as I was to start a project that would market this valuable resin and bring income to the Himba. I knew that letting the word out that these resins were marketable could start a free for all, with people from other areas coming in to harvest the gum, which exuded naturally after the rains each year. I could foresee plants being damaged and Himba women losing out. Eventually, however, the time was right.

After my research, I had helped pioneer what became known as community conservation (or community-based natural resource management) – which is a sustainable African, or in this case Namibian, way of doing conservation. It is based on a few key principles such as entrenching local ownership of a resource, adding value to it in a variety of ways and linking rights and benefits from such resources to responsible local management. The local legal structures through which community conservation is now practised and benefits realised are called communal conservancies in Namibia, with enabling legislation passed by the new independent government in 1998. Community forest legislation followed a few years later, and now we even have two community fish reserves.

The establishment of communal conservancies in the north-west, facilitated by IRDNC, the NGO we founded, coincided with the right person for the perfume resin project being in the right place. Karen Nott who has an MSc in the micro-biology of plants had joined our NGO in 2001. Karen worked her way through a variety of senior roles including grant management. Her grasp of project budgeting, precision and laser-like attention to important detail made her especially well suited to this job. But Karen is one of those people who knows what she wants in life and once her children were through basic schooling and away studying, she was determined to change her Windhoek-based role to one that involved being where her heart was – in the field. It took her a few years to establish an exemplary small business which is owned through a trust by five conservancies. A few years later a still – to render the resin into an essential oil – and a visitor's centre was built in Opuwo. Other high-value plants are also processed there. Essential oil and other cosmetics made from Himba myrrh are now on sale in Namibia, South Africa and in some European countries.

The Italian group, four medical doctors and their spouses who have previously holidayed together, are interested in everything they see on the hill and a pleasure to host in spite of the rocky start the night before.

We're lucky at the spring; cattle are coming in as we arrive and we watch the spectacle of the herd being controlled in spite of thirst, with groups of five or six of these large but nimble-footed beasts being allowed to drink at a time from a shallow trough carved from a commiphora tree trunk. Water is being lifted from a deep hole in the ground, bucket by bucket, and poured into the trough. One man stands in the hole, calf deep in water, and throws up the half-full bucket to a waiting woman part of the way up the pit who passes it to a youth at the top to pour into the trough. If the herd was not held back, there would be chaos with the trough being overturned and cattle falling or being pushed by others behind them into the deep water hole.

Himba women start sitting under what we call the hairdressing tree. Rocks and logs are stained with red ochre from the hundreds of times ochred haunches and goat-skin skirts have rested upon them. While some family members control and water the herds, young women use this opportunity to help one another undo and re-plait their ochred braids.

Hairstyles have changed over the years. When I first came to the Kaokoveld in the early 1980s, women with skimpy hair sometimes added some hair from a brother to their braids; cultural rules dictated that they could only 'borrow' hair from a member of their own matriclan, which is a sibling born of the same mother. Today, the braids are longer, well below shoulder length if possible, and each braid ends with a large teased up puff of black hair. For dramatic fashion statement, the bigger the hair-puff the better. And no longer are brothers required to donate hair to their sisters. Women buy hair extensions from the many Chinese shops in the region, which sell super-cheap super-synthetic Chinese goods, most items so cheap one has to wonder how the crowd of Chinese people who come with each shop are managing to make a living.

I tell the Italian group the hair-puffs are synthetic. I would have had a ball with this in the 1980s and early '90s when I was doing research into material culture's role in a changing Himba society. Namibia had not yet been neo-colonised by hundreds of thousands of Chinese people so Himba fashion tended to be more conservative, incorporating what was available then: zips, safety pins, drawing pins and buttons, and bullet casings. The latter, plus white plastic piping usually removed from military camp plumbing installations and fashioned into bracelets and belts, were dividends from the liberation war.

While most Himba women we meet and greet at the water holes are still ochred and more or less 'traditionally' clad, not a single man or youth, in their shabby Western clothes, could be distinguished from black men in most southern African townships.

I think back to the early '80s when men's only garment was an *erapi* of black or dark blue cotton material tucked into a leather hunger belt worn low on the hips. Married men had to keep their hair long, rolled along the top of the head into a distinctive shaped *ondumba*, which was covered by a soft, leather cloth tied low at the back of the neck, unless they were in mourning in which case their heads had to be bare, with their hair exposed. Only a decade earlier men wore calf-skin aprons, an *otuhira* at the back and an *ombuku* in front. But calf skins became rare in the great drought of the late '70s and early '80s, when an estimated 180 000 head of cattle died of starvation, so men started wearing cloth *erapi*. Men also gave up using ochre on their skin at this time because of the shortage of butter fat with which to mix it. The drought thus paved the way for modern clothing to be adopted by Himba men.

It remains to be seen, 35 years later, if the four-year drought that ended in 2018, with at least two-thirds of cattle dying of starvation, will be a tipping point for Himba women to stop using ochre and butter fat. By 2017 many women had started buying plastic pots of Vaseline to use in place of the now almost unobtainable butter fat with their ochre powder; others gave up using ochre at all.

Half an hour after Antonio is due to meet us I climb some rocks to look for his truck. He should be parked in the shade about 200 metres away and I assumed he would walk down to the spring and join us. No vehicle. A full hour later I am becoming anxious. It's noon and getting hot. People are thirsty and it's time for us to leave. By 12.30 pm I know Antonio has had a problem and we gather up the group, say our farewells to the people and start walking along the track Antonio should have driven.

No sign of him. Which means the party is going to have a long, hot walk home up to the lodge. There is not much shade; I can sense the good cheer dwindling. I hate to think what the mood will be like in an hour when we are faced with two kilometres of uphill walking! We could take a short cut and go up the hill now, a steep but shorter route, but I don't want to leave the track and miss Antonio. Where on earth is he?

Uatjimbisa's sharp eyes notice two young goatherds sitting on a high cliff above us and he shouts to them, asking them if they've seen our vehicle. They have – all this information is being exchanged at full shout over 100 plus metres – and they tell us they can see a big white truck in the river bed. This is about half a kilometre to our south, in totally the wrong place, but I decide to take a chance when the boys assure us that it is *wahenona* – very fat – a truck that can carry all of us, and them too. There can't be any other such vehicles out here; it has to be Antonio. So we change our direction and I lead us slightly back and down into the wide river bed. Some of the guests are muttering in Italian; most are too hot and thirsty to have much to say but I think I hear something about lunatics.

Just when I'm sure we've made a mistake and will have to retrace our steps – and face a riot in Italian – we spot the truck. Antonio is pacing around in the shade of the large Leadwood under which the vehicle is parked, smoking and looking hot and bothered.

'What took you so long? I have been here over two hours,' he hisses at me before turning to greet his guests in charming Italian. Showing great self-control, I ask David to fetch the cool-box and distribute cold drinks. Only then do I take on Antonio: he is in the wrong place – we asked him to take the track along the banks, not to drive in the river bed itself. I was very specific – take the first track left after turning out from Etaambura's road and passing one small Himba homestead. Antonio assures me I said no such thing. I can see that arguing with this man is a waste of breath. I find myself some cold water and ignore him. *Ek se maar niks maar die Here hoor my brom.* (I say nothing but the Lord above can hear my growl.)

The revived guests are keen to see a Himba village and although Onyuva is to me quite ugly with its tin shacks and car wrecks amidst dung and river sand-plastered Himba huts, we decide to call in there. Good for people from Europe to see how people here are living, real people in transition between different worlds, not exotic remnants of a Eurocentric vision of an old Africa. I tell Antonio that David is available to translate for his group – he ignores me.

Antonio parks next to a large pile of beer and wine bottles outside the shebeen. He is out of the car and leading his party to where five Himba women sit in the shade of a small tree. Having heard him talk at dinner last night about his great knowledge of Himba culture, so much so that he plans to write a book about the Himba, I hang back. Even though I have written and published a book about the Himba and did my anthropological-archaeological PhD research in this area. It's his show, his guests, after all.

But Antonio manages to annoy me yet again. He stands in front of the seated women and greets them all with a wave and loud Moro Moro's. The women respond cheerfully. The guests line up in an awkward semi-circle looking from the women to their guide. Now Antonio is talking rapidly in Italian, pointing out the finer aspects of Himba material culture – literally pointing at one woman's *erembe*, the orchred headdress she wears, then at the large cone shell round her neck and her bangles. His manicured finger almost touches her body as he talks. I am appalled at his rudeness and can see that the guests are not comfortable. Antonio is urging them to take pictures and a few do. I catch the eye of one of the Himba women and know that I am going to have to apologise later. I don't want to be associated with such bad cultural tourism and Antonio's just plain poor manners.

But the women have the situation under control. They speak languidly to Uatjimbisa, ignoring Antonio, and then all five turn their backs on him and his group. I laugh out loud. Good for them. Uatjimbisa drifts off.

David and I, under a small tree, talk about what we've just witnessed. It's a great opportunity to teach David – who plans to go into tourism as a career – how not to conduct a village visit.

Antonio did everything wrong, I point out.

For starters, he had no translator – having rejected our offer for him to use David. He did not introduce himself or his guests. He did not say where his party have come from. He did not ask the women how things are here. He did not ask permission for photographs to be taken – all common rudeness that some guides inflict on Himba people. And on top of it all, he was showing himself to be a really inadequate guide, giving his guests a third-rate, culturally impoverished experience and annoying the women to boot.

So what should he have done, asks David as we watch some of Antonio's guests take pictures of the ornate beaded decoration women wear on their backs. Antonio is looking pleased as if he engineered this back-view himself. I cannot believe he is oblivious to the snub the women have just dished out to him.

We talk about good cultural tourism. That the guide should simply be a facilitator between the people and the guests. There should be excellent translation so that real talking can happen. I remind him of how we always make sure that people speak directly to guests and vice versa. Lively conversations often start which are mutually enjoyable.

'But you know most of the people out here and they know you. Or at least who you are,' David says. 'It's not so easy for a stranger like Antonio.'

'Nonsense,' I say. 'It's a question of good manners in any society. Antonio would never behave like this in Italy – what gives him the idea he can do it here?'

'You don't know any of these women. David – your home is Sesfontein, 200 kilometres from here. Yet would you just walk up to people, say hello and then start speaking about them in English and taking pictures? What would you do as a well brought up Herero man?'

David nods, getting my point. Later, in the report, which he has to write on his five-month practical with Conservancy Safaris for his tourism diploma, he discusses good versus bad cultural tourism. Antonio had done him a favour by modelling bad manners and arrogance. David's ground-truthed report gets top marks.

I recall a day more than 25 years ago at Puros where I was living when a Botswana guide turned up with a party of Italian guests (I have nothing against Italians, just for the record – love the country, the food, the people and most Italian visitors to Namibia are a pleasure to meet). Just like Antonio, this guide led his group up to where two women were sitting and his people immediately started taking pictures. I hadn't yet been noticed, in the shade of a hut talking to someone. One of the Himba women – my friend Vengape Tjiningira – pulled her blanket over her head to hide from the intrusion.

A much younger me was so incensed by the rudeness of the group that I grabbed my camera and stalked over to the party. I pushed my camera into startled faces and snapped away. It didn't take long for the tourists to object and I angrily made my point. The Botswana guide was unimpressed and seemed to think that because he was black he had an inside lane for his guests into the

Himba village.

Vengape and I talked about the experience after they'd gone. It was the early 1990s and very little tourism was happening in the north-west in those days. Vengape's main issue, she said, was that she was only partially dressed – she had not applied fresh ochre yet that morning – and didn't want to be photographed thus.

'But didn't you feel insulted and annoyed with the rudeness of these people?' I asked. 'What right do they have to take pictures of you without asking permission?'

Vengape shrugged. Some people are a bit crazy, she said, especially white people. 'I haven't met many yet but I've learnt that you can't expect good manners from most of them. They don't know how to behave.'

'What about me?' I asked.

'We're teaching you well,' Vengape said, smiling.

Sadly, decades later it seems Vengape's views still hold true for some guides and tourists who visit the Kaokoveld, now called the Kunene region. They see the Himba as there to be photographed, and don't seem to realise that they are the custodians of the land and the reason there is still wildlife to be viewed in the north-west, at least in conservancies.

And as for me, I haven't forgotten what Vengape and 150 or so Himba and Herero people taught me while they put up with me as a researcher in the 1980s and 1990s. Working in community conservation since then, I kept on learning from the rural people my NGO supported in both the north-west and north-east of Namibia. Mentoring, building capacity and helping to run Conservancy Safaris and Etaambura lodge ensures my learning continues. But one of my very earliest lessons came from Kata, Vengape's older sister.

FOUR

Kata's lesson

Start your farming with people, not with cattle – Himba proverb

LIVING WITH A REMOTE community of semi-nomadic herders in north-western Namibia in the mid-1980s, hundreds of kilometres from a telephone or supermarket, could be expected to have some tough moments for a researcher from the city. There were – but often not what I expected.

Extended periods without city amenities didn't worry me as I had done some rough camping over the years. My mind, in those days, was on 'higher' academic concerns. Fieldwork tends to teach one as much about oneself and one's own biases – world 'filters' – as the subject one is studying. So for a Western, sedentary, city-dwelling, alienated capitalist, post-feminist, white-skinned, southern African woman there would be issues needing to be unpacked as I engaged with my Himba and Herero hosts who were among the most 'traditional' of southern African people.

For a start, the word 'traditional' was a minefield in the '80s: To the layman, even today, and to earlier schools of anthropology, the opposite of 'traditional' is 'modern'. As a brand new University of Cape Town honours graduate, I knew better. They are not opposites and you could be both at the same time, or different degrees of either at different times. The thrust of my study was to try to understand social relations – between age groups, between men and women, between people and the natural environment – as both reflected by and *produced* by the eclectic mix of traditional and modern (mass produced) material culture in use by a group of Himba households. And how these relations were changing.

The idea that the material items that facilitate our lives are active in changing our behaviour and our relationships was a fairly esoteric archaeological concern in those days. My approach stressed human agency – people's intent – but I also aimed to show just how powerful our material culture and technology is. Even today, you still hear people claiming that material goods are somehow neutral, merely tools to be used by people for either good or bad, as if mere access to them does not change our behaviour in radical and unplanned ways. Who could have imagined where mobile phones would take us? Unrelenting 24/7 connection, all pervasive social media, cyber bullying, fake news, election influencing, a new type of war, as well as much that is positive.

We are amazed by near sentient robots and discuss artificial intelligence as a research construct yet we are constantly steered into unintended new behaviour patterns by our smart technical goods. The ghost has always been in the machine.

It was there in the very first tool – no doubt a baby-carrying sling or a woven grass basket to carry veld food, made by a woman, obviously not preserved in the archaeological record. That ghost was also in the second tool – a multi-purpose stone Aucheulian hand axe made by *Homo Erectus* man to scavenge and break open marrow bones from a predator's kill – or to bash in a rival's head. The point being, he would have been a lot less belligerent without a big lump of specially shaped stone clutched in the hand behind his back.

Another hot potato was culture. Anthropological reading had equipped me with the concept of culture as a large cake, or round of cheese. Different peoples across the world merely used different parts of the cake/cheese, meaning the term 'culture' could never be plural. So there is no such thing as different cultures, just human culture: an Inuit takes his slice from one side; a Welshman or

Swedish or Himba person accesses the same cake from a different position and therefore cuts a different portion. Men and women, different age groups, all use and activate their pieces of this cultural confection slightly differently.

And to make it more complicated, culture is not static. It constantly changes, or rather is changed by its users – and by their access to changing technology, for their own socially strategic needs. So, the part of the cultural cheese you are using might have started out as cheddar, say, but over time it evolves into Stilton, or gouda or mozzarella cheese.

At least that's how I envisaged it in 1987, driving my second-hand Toyota 4x4 truck along the rutted 100-kilometre track between Sesfontein and Puros that took up to four hours to do back then. I'd tried to explain this cultural cheese concept to a Namibian radio interviewer, Sharon Montgomery, as I passed through Windhoek on my way to the north-west to start my PhD research. Eager to cram everything I wanted to say into the five-minute interview, I'd got a bit intense and I winced as I remembered the expression on Sharon's face when we got to the big cheese part.

The point about the old 'noble savage' syndrome had come across better – or so I thought. People such as the Himba, in their ochre and calf skins, are often seen *not* as real people but as symbols of whatever the outsider wishes them to be – usually, in the case of Westerners, as exotic, ancient (and very photogenic) people from an idealised old African or even stone age past.

Not having the sense to stop while I was ahead, I'd gone on to tell the bemused interviewer that doing research about people was a political and social act that impacts on how people view and assess their own and others' social status and worth. She'd stopped me there. Time up. Before I could explain that writing down oral histories and telling people's stories had consequences, that the image of the people constructed by the researcher could be used – or manipulated – by others, including politicians. So sadly, the latter pretentious (but true) pearl of second-hand academic knowledge was never conveyed to the Namibian radio-listening public, assuming they hadn't changed stations by then.

Around noon, we stopped to give my dog RDM (Rand Daily Mail) water. RDM, my young temporary translator teenage schoolboy John K Kasaona and I climbed a hill to a shallow cave that begged archaeological investigation. Dassie droppings and a single rusted Coke can. But the view was worth the exertion. Below, a half hemisphere of sapphire sky, low hills wore a sparse cover of tawny-lion-coloured grass. Beyond the hills, pale ochre plains unrolled towards the stark mauve mountain ranges of the Hoanib River canyon.

In the shade of the rock overhang, we ate cheese sandwiches (cheddar!), and I pondered the months ahead: Research could never be objective or neutral; it always reflected the researcher's own biases and particular social, economic and political theories.

The concept of 'participant observer', the term then frequently used by anthropological researchers to describe themselves in their studies, was a cop-out, I'd already decided. My research proposal threw down a gauntlet that envisaged full emotional and intellectual engagement with my host community. I would lay out my 'filters' (my piece of cultural cheese was Western, female, sedentary, capitalist-raised etc.) and let each reader of my thesis make of it what s/he will.

Work I'd already done in the north-west the year before for my Honours degree had convinced me that Himba and Herero knowledge systems, when allowed to stand on their own terms, were in some ways irreconcilable with Western academic imperatives. However, as my proposal had concluded pompously, this was no reason not to try to hear the Other or to allow academic epistemological jitters to stall attempts to affirm alternative interpretive logics. (I did actually write these words or something similar!)

Within hours we were at Puros, trying to put up my tent in a howling south-west wind under an Annaboom tree on the banks of the Hoarusib River's mostly dry bed. Everything including John, me and the dog were soon coated in powdery dust that swirled around in hot gusts of wind. John sensibly accepted an invitation to put his bedding in an empty hut in the nearby village.

The Hoarusib flows just a few days or, at most, a few weeks a year in the rainy season. But near Puros in a few places water rises continuously from linear oases, enabling people, domestic stock and wildlife to survive. Cattle and goats were not expected to remain at this permanent water source all year round; with the rains, stock was moved out, into the hills and plains, taking advantage of temporary or seasonal waters and grass.

Here was yet another popular myth, that the Himba and Herero people wandered round the north-west randomly seeking pasture and water, when in fact, their success as herders was the result of careful planning and the practice of collectively reserving pasture near permanent water for the late dry season when there were no other options. Grass, and not just water, was the key. After all, in a typical drought animals die not of thirst but of starvation.

By evening, I'd lost count of the number of mugs of tea or coffee that my camp kettle had produced. Kaupiti Tjipomba, also known as Maria, a smart young woman who had some Western schooling and spoke a little Afrikaans, reinstated herself as my second translator. I was relieved and delighted to see her as I knew there were issues that women would not talk about in front of men or even teenage boys. A stream of people who remembered me from the year before came to greet me. There was news to exchange. Another lineage had moved in because of the war to the north. People were planning to move out of Puros to temporary stock camps any day now so I had come back just in time. It had already rained to the north-east but not enough.

Maria's father, the old man called Wild Fig (Omukuyu) pointed at distant clouds in the east and said that maybe I'd brought the rain with me. And had my family acquired any cattle yet? Not even goats or sheep? He shook his head sadly.

Tukupoli, his wife and Maria's mother, who always wore a Herero big dress, wide full-length skirts brushing the ground, even though Omukuyu dressed as a Himba, reminded me I'd promised to bring her some material. Had I remembered? I had but hadn't unpacked it yet. She said she'd come back tomorrow. Tukopoli's everyday dress was made from different pieces of materials, their patterns and colours artfully combined. But what she yearned for was a dress made from the same material and this was what I'd brought her: 12 metres of a bold royal blue print that she would wear for special occasions for many years to come.

Nowadays, the big Herero dress is only seen on older women or only on ceremonial occasions such as funerals or celebrations. But in the '80s and '90s in Puros the Herero dress was the daily attire for all women from the Herero lineages living there. Their colourful full-length and full-skirted dresses, gathered under the breasts, are an adaptation of dresses worn by missionaries' wives in South West Africa at the turn of the century. An extract from one of my field books:

> Komiho and Kwatherendu are hard at work picking mealies in the furrow irrigated gardens in the bed of the Hoarusib River. The women talk and laugh – friends and neighbours, the two widows are omuhoko (matrilineally related), having been born into the same eanda (matriclan). The bold red and blue full-length floral dress worn by Komiho makes an eye-catching contrast with the lush, green, chest-high mealie plants. Her graceful Mother Hubbard-style Herero dress is made from up to 12 metres of material. Under its wide skirt, despite the heat, she wears five gathered petticoats. Her Himba companion Kwatherendu presents a colourful contrast of a different kind: her bare upper body, arms, face and hair gleam red from the powered ochre, mixed with butter fat and aromatic herbs which she smeared onto herself that morning. Her short, pleated calfskin front apron is also ochre-red while the more elaborate back skirt is of soft black calfskin.

On that first evening back John barely left my side. As soon as one group left, another arrived and he was needed to enable us to communicate. Today John is Executive Director of IRDNC. I like to think that his several stints with me in the Kaokoveld contributed to the values-driven route he chose for his life.

Eventually I fell into my bedroll, dusty and exhausted but happy, having just said goodnight to the 12 Himba men and women who'd shared our dinner of rice and tinned stew. There were no car fridges yet so you carried tins and packets. My mind teemed with information and ideas. I kept sitting up, switching on my torch to make notes in my field book, afraid I'd forget by the morning.

The next morning Puros was transformed. The hot, gritty wind had emptied its lungs in the night leaving the air still and clear. Slanted rays of morning sun painted the sand plains in shades of apricot. The Hoarusib river bed green-snaked through the middle of the vast hill-fringed bowl that is Puros valley. We walked the 100 metres to the nearest homestead. Sitting on a stone on the sand, outside the cattle-dung plastered dwelling, I started picking up where I'd left off the year before. It was wonderful: everything was interesting to me and people were welcoming. A researcher, especially a woman, was still a rarity so I was as interesting to them.

The days flew by, full and rich. I filled up one notebook, then another. Most people were intrigued by what I was doing and liked the idea that their ways and ideas were being recorded. Very few Himba children went to school in those days. The nearest school was more than 100 kilometres from Puros and children would therefore have to stay in the overcrowded hostel during term time. This meant the family lost youthful labour which was simply essential for a subsistence herding economy.

But many parents believed that their younger children, or at least their children's children, would and should learn how to read and write, and that therefore they would be able to know their grandparents through my work, a pleasing idea to most.

'Tjanga, write that down,' I was frequently reminded if I was slow to make notes during a conversation.

As fast as the days passed, so my food supply dwindled. I had come supplied, I thought, for about two months. Then I planned to drive the 700 kilometres to Swakopmund to stock up and sort out my preliminary data. On a tight research grant, I didn't have money to spare. Naturally, I'd brought several emergency bags of maize meal, some powdered soups, an extra 10 kg of sugar, plenty of tea and a large box containing 24 packets of biscuits. After two weeks with all my visitors, even my extra sugar and tea was fast running out. My main food supply – tins, rice, pasta and various dried foods – was also uncomfortably low by then. I had not expected to be cooking dinner every night for anything up to 10 or 12 people.

My academic reading was no help in the situation: I felt like a frantic suburban housewife trying to cater for a large number of unexpected guests. I stopped enjoying the social evenings and started feeling anxious and even resentful when people strolled into my camp just before my dinner time, and sat down at my fire. I tried delaying dinner, hoping people would leave but my own hunger usually forced me to prepare a meal eventually. Or John, also hungry, would put on the water for the pap or rice. In this part of the world it was the height of bad manners to eat in front of people without sharing so share I did, cutting down on the generous portions I had first served.

I expressed my concerns about our food shortages to John but got a noncommittal, typical teenage shrug. It seemed I would have to do something about the situation myself. I felt petty and mean to begrudge my informants a plate of food – after all I was going to obtain a doctorate from what I was learning here. Nevertheless, as fears of hunger or cutting short my research trip loomed, I steeled myself to speak about this to the people who assembled in my camp each evening.

After a skimpy dinner for 10 – maize meal, bully beef and my last onion – I cleared my throat and, with John translating, explained that my food was nearly finished and that we would therefore not be able to have dinner guests any more. My statement didn't seem to elicit much interest and the general conversation – we were talking about the different colours of cattle various patriclans were required to keep – quickly resumed. I doubted we'd made our point adequately.

Early the next morning, I was woken by the sound of a bleating goat. I stuck my head out of my tent and saw that someone had tied the creature to a tree at the edge of my camp. Then Vengape, who I had particularly befriended, arrived with a large sack. She emptied it into the back of my truck – a pile of fresh green mealies for roasting on the fire. Before I had finished thanking her, a man who had been at dinner the night before walked into camp carrying a large shoulder of goat for me, with a smaller piece of meat, which was, he said, for my dog. He hung both in a tree near the living goat and drifted off. Then Kata, Vengape's sister, appeared with a large watermelon in her arms. She laid it next to the mealies and told me through John, who had now got up, that one of the children would be bringing me some honey but that she needed a container to put it in. I went to get a jar, and grabbed my last packet of biscuits to give to Kata as I knew she loved them.

She took the packet but gave me a long look.

'What?' I asked, not needing to be translated.

Kata heaved a sigh, and motioned me to join her at my fire on which John had placed the kettle for our first tea of the day.

'Why,' she asked me, 'do you always make yourself *high*?'

I struggled to understand although she, John and Vengape, who was still with us, seemed clear about what was being said.

Eventually the penny started dropping.

What Kata meant was that by giving her a present back each time she 'gifted' me, I was keeping myself in a superior position and never allowing her to be the dominant gift-giver.

Himba women lubricate their social relations by giving gifts to one another. The aim is to try to be the last one to gift someone and therefore to whom a gift is *owed*. So when something comes along that you really want – such as a new supply of the red ochre in daily use by women – you are in a strong position to ask for some. If you're always in other people's debt, you risk others asking for things you'd rather not give them but which local etiquette requires you to hand over. This concept of reciprocal gifting is well entrenched in many societies. Those who have the skill to keep others in their debt are admired. But to be in the game, you have to play it, which means *taking* as well as giving. I was effectively excluding myself from this community by always being the last giver.

Kata had been observing me for two weeks and was becoming tired of my gauche manners. The packet of biscuits was the last straw.

As we talked that morning, possibly one of the most insightful sessions I'd had in spite of my copious notes to date, I realised that for all my academic pretensions about laying out one's world view as the filter through which one does research, the most pernicious biases are the ones you don't know you have.

I carried an unexamined Eurocentric assumption that relatively speaking I was wealthier than the people here. After all, I had a 4x4 vehicle, a share in a house back in Cape Town, some money and many modern material goods. The people, however, who had learnt that my family had no cattle, goats or sheep, saw me as relatively poor by their terms. The goat brought to my camp was to be the start of a small herd I would accumulate during my years in the north-west. My guests were not eating my food because they needed to – but because they were enjoying the social occasion, the novelty of the different foods I served and they thought I needed the company.

As soon as I mentioned that my food was running out, people automatically started sharing some of theirs with me. They were glad to have an opportunity to do so, which meant a more balanced relationship between us.

Some years after my research ended, my thesis was produced and like most other PhDs, its main use was to fill space in a few academic libraries. But I stayed on in Namibia, wanting to give back some of what I'd gained. Community-based conservation work in the north-west and later the north-east of Namibia, aimed at linking development, democracy and conservation kept me in touch, from time to time, with the Himba families I lived with.

More than a decade after Kata's lesson about taking as well as giving, she and her husband Wapenga appeared at the door of our NGO's Windhoek office. Mostly, I worked in the field so it was just luck that I happened to be in town. Over tea and after an exchange of news, Kata explained the serious health reason that had caused the couple to hike to the capital, 1 200 kilometres from Onyuva where she lived. She needed help and it didn't cross her mind that she wouldn't get it from me.

That afternoon I took her to a doctor and the next morning she was admitted to hospital for a serious operation. She recovered well and after a month in town, she and Wapenga returned to the north-west. Before she left she took both my hands in hers and looked into my eyes. 'No biscuits to give me?' I asked. We both laughed: no more words were necessary. This time it had been my turn to give, paying for their stay in the capital, and Kata's turn to take. But, we both knew, the gifting wheel would turn and at some time in the future when I was up north, in her area, she would be the giver. A sheep or goat would be slaughtered, and there would be some serious meat feasting.

FIVE

Other ways of being

I am discussing the use of domestic space inside a dung-plastered hut with its occupants. I note that their left and right are from the perspective of standing inside the hut, looking out. Yet much of the literature about the domestic architecture of similar pre-literate societies that I had brought with me used the opposite view. In these academic papers left and right were from the perspective of the researcher outside the hut, looking in. From field notes: 1987.

SOCIO-ECONOMIC NETWORKING was just one of many things Himba people taught me, and what I learnt often challenged my frame of reference.

Gaining an insight into another's point of view – standing, if only momentarily, in Kata's or Vengape's or someone else's car-tyre sandals – is surely the most exciting part of social research. And surely too, it is why many millions of people travel to distant places each year. There are those of us who want our frames of references shaken up – such as the intrepid groups who travel with a Himba-owned safari company. Then again, incomprehensible to some of us, there are others who want to take their own world with them – hence the bland, universally familiar fast food chains across the world, in the place of local cuisine.

One hot, humid morning in a temporary post-rain stock camp when the *onganda* seemed particularly full of people and flies swarmed around us, (something that only happens in the rainy season), I was sitting watching Kata repair a split gourd with a leather cord. Grumpily, but tactfully I thought, I remarked that an aspect of Kaoko life that was very different from what I was used to in Cape Town was that here I was rarely alone or out of earshot of other people. With her usual sensitivity, Kata picked up my sub-text and she drew out of me what I was really thinking. That I was sick of never being alone, that I found the flies – landing in the milk, in our eyes and mouths in between visiting dung droppings, particularly disgusting that day. I hated that my back, like everyone else's, was a shifting black thicket of flies. I longed for a can of Doom, and wanted to feel clean and cool instead of hot, sticky and dusty.

Kata was philosophical about the flies – they came with the rain and would disappear in the dry season. The layer of ochre, butter fat and aromatic herbs she wore on the exposed parts of her body (just about everything from the waist up and mid-thighs down), kept out the dirt and her near nakedness ensured she was cooler than me, covered up in baggy knee length shorts and a T-shirt. But she was interested in my first point.

We discussed my perception of privacy which included being able to be alone when one wished in the sense of closing a door (to one's house, bedroom or office) on other people. Kata grasped the concept, even though neither she nor my by now well-trained and almost-verbatim translator Shorty Kasaona could think of a Himba/Herero word for privacy. A word they come up with was *omukarapeke* which means recluse, not the same as privacy at all. What she was unclear about was why one needed to be physically separated from people – by a door or other structure – to be alone.

Now it was my turn to struggle to understand. Eventually, she got up to illustrate. Instructing me to watch, she sauntered around the homestead, past the score or so of men, women and children in sight, ending up back with Shorty and me.

'*Momunu? Mbari erike nao?*' 'Did you see?' she asked, beaming.

'I was alone.'

'No you weren't; there were people all around you.'

Kata insisted that she was alone for herself.

What did you do, I wanted to know. 'Did you block out the other people?'

It was the opposite, as she explained it: 'I made myself open (*munina*) so that people could see through me. That's the way you can be alone.'

Later I found a translation for *munina* – translucent or transparent, a word people may use to describe very clear water that one can see through. Kata's concept of privacy, so different from mine, was posited on an opening up, somehow making one transparent, rather than on the erection of barriers. I had been shown another way of being.

This story and one about counting goats that follows were both recounted in my PhD thesis, successfully submitted to Cape Town University in 1995. Years later at a yoga retreat in the Daintree Rain Forest in Australia, with the aim of learning to meditate, I was reading Eckhart Tolle's *Practising the Power of Now*. He writes about 'a realm of deep stillness and peace, but also joy and intense aliveness' which exists within all of us when we are able to switch off our minds and just be present in the now. He uses the phrase *becoming transparent* which happens when you are able to achieve an all-encompassing sense of beingness, no longer identifying with your mind and its thoughts, and how, in this meditation exercise, the inner body is felt to be without a boundary. The distinction between inner and outer dissolves.

It is not my intention to present Himba people as the proverbial 'noble savages' or as more spiritually evolved than the rest of us (although the latter is sometimes tempting when one thinks about the morals of some bankers, politicians and corporate leaders).

Most economically secure small-scale societies, who live in communities small enough for members to know one another personally or at least by sight, share the same characteristics: A sort of honesty and basic integrity where a set of common values are known by all and upheld by the majority. You can't easily get away with crime without the anonymity of our big societies. Just a little more than 100 kilometres from where we were, criminal activity by a minority of residents was already present in larger settlements such as Sesfontein, home to a few thousand Damara, Herero, Topnaar and a family or two of Himba people. As the settlement size grew, so did crime.

Even lying was regarded as wrong by my host community. And when women heard that a youth they knew (a son of someone they all knew who'd drifted away from his community and gone to live in a town) had knifed someone in a fight, they were genuinely shocked and distressed. 'How can this son of ours behave in such a bad way?' someone asked. Note the collective 'ownership' of the offence and offender, a member of their community even though he was not a blood relative to most of those present. Taking responsibility for our own actions, or those of our communities, is not a strong point of most so-called modern or developed world people.

Only once was anything stolen from me in five years of living with rural Himba and Herero communities, as materially laden and tempting as my camp was. A boy of about 12 or 13 took a packet of biscuits from my table. Shorty, with whom I discussed this minor issue was upset and quickly found the culprit; he'd scoffed the sugary biscuits and guilelessly left the empty packaging in his sleeping hut, shared by others. Again, several of the adults, not just the boy's mother, were ashamed and took responsibility for the petty theft.

In yet another example, a Himba father turned in his own son who had illegally shot a gemsbok after this community had agreed to engage in an early form of community-based conservation. The father offered to pay a fine of cattle to keep his son out of prison.

Of course, the community was full of the same gossip and intrigue (usually around who is sleeping illicitly with whom) that happens when any group of people live together. People were quite tolerant about sexual matters – but only within cultural limits. If a child was born out of wedlock, it was not a disaster although marriage before children was preferred. The baby was usually taken into the lineage and patriclan of the girl's father, and more importantly, the matriclan of her maternal grandmother and mother. All children are members of their mother's matriclan for life whereas a girl's patriclan will change after marriage to that of her husband. So there are rules and mores.

A note in my field diary observed that as X was cheating on her husband and Y was sleeping with someone else's wife, and everyone seemed to know about it; it felt as if I was living in any city suburb. One man whom I nicknamed Kamasutra pushed his philandering tendencies too far, however. When it was discovered that he was sleeping with both a mother *and* her daughter (although neither knew this initially) people were scandalised. By popular opinion, he was asked to leave the area, taking his stock and not-very-happy wife with him. The problem was not that the daughter was too young to be having sex – she was late teens and of marriageable age, I was told – but because his actions risked causing a rift between mother and daughter.

An area of difference where I struggled to adjust my frame of reference was about dogs. As a dog lover, I was distressed by the skinny local canines. But then, walking down a street in Windhoek or Cape Town, I would see or just hear scores of well-fed dogs whose barking displayed their boredom and frustration. Confined behind high walls, many of these creatures may never get to leave their own yards or meet other dogs. Watching groups of Himba dogs interact, establish hierarchies and have a canine social life, I was forced to question my perspective.

Unintentionally I signed the death warrant of a local dog that I befriended and fed each day. People called him Diesel because he could run as fast as my truck. It was a thoughtless act on my part; teach a dog to eat from a plate on the ground and it is inevitable he will start taking food from people who live without furniture such as tables and who place their own plates of food on the ground. I went away for a few weeks, and needless to say Diesel was gone when I returned, killed by someone for repeatedly stealing food from people's plates.

Why don't you feed your dogs, I asked? How can I feed my dog when my children are still hungry? Vengape replied. So I learnt to gauge the level of prosperity in an *ozonganda* by the condition of the dogs. These became sleek when food was plentiful, which was after good rains when the cattle were producing a lot of milk, or when there was plenty of mealie meal and goat meat to spare.

Later, when I brought my own dogs with me – first RDM, a collie-ridgeback, and then over the years a succession of Staffordshire terriers – people were amazed how obedient they were. So could your dogs be if you trained them, I said. But people weren't convinced. They did find my dogs entertaining, especially when my staffie Tjaba wore his red-striped jersey on very cold nights. People came from far to see this dog that wore clothes, shaking their heads and laughing at this weird sight which shook their frame of reference.

I don't believe I am being romantic or cloaking my Himba friends and informants in mysticism when I talk about catching glimpses of spirituality, a way of being beyond thoughts that is illusive to me as a Westerner. Eckhart Tolle tells us that we are all more than our minds and that we should not identify with our thoughts but try to be a witness of them, thus entering a realm of being in the now. I have little doubt that most of the Kaoko people I got to know in those years already knew, perhaps without knowing they knew, how to be fully present in the now. For all my books about meditation and in spite of hours of practice, I still have problems turning off my thoughts for more than a few minutes at a time . . . for Kata, with whom I discussed this deeply on several occasions, it seemed to be a skill that she took for granted.

At another camp in another place a different way of knowing and seeing was revealed by Kata's father, elder Venomeho. We were sitting together at the end of the day as the goat herds streamed back towards the *ozonganda* for the night. The section of Venomeho's family herd present at that time numbered about 140 animals. We watched the goats casually as we talked. As the last of the animals straggled past us, mothers bleating their greetings to the youngest kid-goats who'd spent their day in a kraal, Venomeho rose. A pregnant ewe was missing.

The 10-year-old boy who'd accompanied the herd last remembered seeing the animal at the spring which was a kilometre or so from the homestead. Venomeho, the youth and I set off at once to find her before dark. She was not far, in the process of giving birth. Had we not found her, her kid would certainly have been killed and eaten by the ever-near jackals. If hyena or leopard were around, the ewe would also have lost her life.

When Venomeho had finished talking to the young goatherd about the need to keep a special watch over pregnant animals, I asked him how he'd noticed one brown and white pregnant animal was missing among a dozen or more brown and white pregnant goats, and scores more of the same colour. He and others had told me previously that goats were not counted, nor named as cattle often were.

We struggled to reach common ground, just as Kata and I had over concepts of privacy. This is what I eventually understood. Venomeho, who'd grown up long before any kind of formal schooling was available in Kaoko, did not count his goats in the 1-2-3 method of enumeration familiar to schoolgoers everywhere. What he did was carry in his mind a sort of picture of what the herd looked like collectively. This was based on a group of pictures or perhaps patterns, constructed on age, gender, colouration and condition. Thus he could easily see that one animal was missing from his composite mental image. The mental picture was not simple or static as the patterns required regular re-negotiation to keep up with changing situations, as herds were split up for various reasons, animals were traded, slaughtered or given away and newly born young joined the group.

Women as well as men shared this method of seeing stock, although some were better at it – or better motivated, it was suggested – than others. Vengape said good management of goats depended on 'knowing' all the animals, even though neither she nor most of the adults could count, in the sense of knowing the words for figures beyond about 20. The school-going children were learning to count in the white man's way, I was told. But as she and others agreed, much more was involved in the local way of knowing and seeing the herds than simply giving them a number.

Can the children who go to school still count in the Himba way, I asked?

A mother who had two children at school in WarmQuelle, more than 100 kilometres away replied: 'We only see them a few times in the year now, when the school is closed. So these things that they learnt from their parents and the elders are losing their strength.'

My question whether this was a bad thing or not evoked a lot of discussion. Parents were concerned that their children were becoming strangers and they wondered how these children would live in the future if they lost the skills needed to thrive as herders in the arid Kunene Region. But most also believed that literacy and being able to speak some English were new skills that, as one woman said, their children needed or the future would pass them. Shorty was not being poetic as he translated this particular mother's sentence; he was using her exact words. The people I lived with did indeed see the future as behind you and yet to pass you. The past is ahead – where you can see it.

People were bemused at my very different concept of time – that in my world the past is behind you with the future ahead, still to come. This literally didn't make sense and I was asked: How can you put your past behind you? It's in front of you; you can see it and not forget it. The future hasn't arrived yet so it must still be behind you.

Another key concept in the Himba worldview was that there was no hierarchy of higher and lower species. The significance of this resonated deeply for me as a conservationist, as did the words of a Himba community game guard that we called Langman. He was remembering some white men who in the '70s had shot many springbok. A whole herd, it sounded like. The men took some choice cuts of meat from a few carcasses, and left the rest to rot in the sun. Years later, Langman still displayed anger and distress at this 'wasting'.

Waste of meat? I asked. No, of springbok, he clarified.

Clearly, older men and women did not see nature as existing only to be of use to people. It was fine to eat meat when you needed to but the rest of those springbok had the right to live.

Cow dung was a substance I noticed at first as something to avoid standing in. And it was only when a hut was built for me by some of the women that the subject came up. Interestingly, as much as my dome tent was admired for the speed with which I could put it up, the women worried that even in the tent I was sleeping 'outside', and they had offered to build me a hut so that I could sleep safely inside.

The saplings that were bent and tied together to make my conical hut were rather draughty when the wind blew and the women said I needed to acquire some cattle dung. They would mix this with river sand and plaster my hut for me, at least on the inside, including the floor. The cattle herds were away from Puros so I needed to drive to the nearest stock camp.

When I was about to do this, Vengape offered to help me collect the dung. I pointed out that Shorty would be coming so he and I could fill two or three black plastic rubbish bags with dung quite easily. Vengape looked at me in a strange way. I assumed she needed to go to the stock camp for some reason and wanted a lift, and said she could come if she wanted, but that Shorty and I could handle the dung. I think I wanted to show that even though I'd been a spectator, taking photographs, while my hut was built, I was also prepared to get my hands dirty. Vengape shrugged and left us to it.

Although I could sense her disquiet, I was anxious to get a move on and we drove to the stock camp. A few women I did not know well were at the camp and after we greeted everyone and explained what we wanted, Shorty and I started collecting the plentiful nice big cowpats on the ground.

An angry altercation stopped us. Three hostile women were arguing with Shorty; the dung was the issue. I asked Shorty to explain that lineage head Venomeho had said we could collect dung from his herd. But this was not the problem.

Shorty filled me in: Only women were allowed to handle dung.

I laughed. Typical. As usual women get the dirty work while the men sit around and talk – I gestured at two older men sitting in the sun.

I could not have got it more wrong.

When I started listening and stopped using my own Western gender ideology to interpret another world, I learnt that cattle dung was regarded as a very valuable substance and Himba women jealously guarded their special gender-based right to it. Thus the three women were appalled when Shorty started picking up dung. Slowly, as we talked, Shorty and the women unpacked a rich cultural practice that my own assumptions had hidden from me.

Far from relegating the menial work to women, cattle dung *added* to women's power and increased men's dependence on women. Because men could not collect dung they could not have a 'proper' dwelling – with plastered walls and floor – unless a woman, wife, mother or perhaps a sister, was available to complete the hut. In fact, as women built the dwellings, these were regarded as belonging to women. But it was culturally unacceptable for a senior man to live in an incomplete un-plastered hut, particularly at his main late dry season *onganda* where a lineage usually returned each year. If he could not find a woman prepared to plaster the hut, the man would be regarded as a bit of a laughing stock.

Why didn't you tell me this, I asked Shorty. Like Vengape he shrugged. You didn't ask, he said. And you were *hakahona* (in a hurry). He was too polite to add, 'as usual'.

In the end, the women decided that even though Shorty had been raised as a Himba, he was being paid by me to do this work. So he could go ahead and pick up dung today. The involvement of money somehow temporarily exempted him from his normal gender role.

I recalled how Venomeho had been brusque with me the night before when I thanked him for letting us use the dung. He'd abruptly changed the subject. Senior men do not like to even discuss dung – an ambiguous substance that could be dangerous till it is transformed by women.

But there's more to understand. One of the larger lineages living near Puros was Herero. The men wore ordinary Western clothes and the women wore the typical 'big' dresses. Each woman usually had at least two dresses: one of them for everyday wear, made from multiple pieces of material neatly stitched together; the other 'best' dress from material of one colour or pattern, preferably with a shiny satin-type finish. Their dwellings were square or oblong rather than round. Elderly members of this family recalled living in round huts when they were young. Herero women told me they liked their 'modern' bigger houses, with their wooden doors and tin roofs, and seemed proud of them.

However, things were not as they seemed. Changing to such a 'modern' dwelling shifted gender and power relations. Himba women actually felt sorry for some of their Herero neighbours because the new houses took away a woman's independence. None of this was articulated till I opened the subject and probed.

The new shaped huts cost money – and needed men to cut and transport the required heavy poles as well as erect the house. Its tin roof and door, often with a lock, had to be bought and brought in by vehicle from a town. Women 'helped' the men and were still responsible for plastering the walls. But the male input was seen as the greater contribution and the house tended to become known as his house, rather than his wife's house.

On the surface, it seemed that Herero women had gained in that they had less heavy work to do than Himba women, and this was a new and modern perspective articulated by some of the younger Herero women. They had also started associating status and leisure time. Somehow women in this lineage had seen pictures of the British monarch, Queen Elizabeth, in a ball gown. They knew she was the traditional leader of a big and rich country, and they were sure that as she wore such beautiful big dresses, she did not have to work like ordinary women. Or like me who wore baggy shorts and slacks because I had to drive a car and work for money because my family had no stock.

Yet normal physical exertion was not regarded as a hardship. I once berated some youths for lounging around while a grandmother staggered past with a heavy burden of firewood balanced on her head. The older woman, exasperated by my intervention, asked: 'Am I too weak and old to fetch wood?'

There are different ways of perceiving male involvement in house building: the division of labour among Himba families meant that a Himba woman can build a house herself from local resources, without needing money or a vehicle. It is her husband who is dependent on her for a culturally acceptable dwelling. On the other hand, a Herero woman is dependent on her husband for her house, even though her labour is still required for extensive plastering. These nuanced shifts in roles and responsibilities linked to built space and material culture thus have practical implications, not simply reflecting social relations, but also creating new social and gender relations.

Widows requiring square housing are also dependent on assistance from male relatives. Kwazerendu was one such widow from a mixed Himba-Herero lineage. She made the decision to change to a square modern house and found herself trapped between two worlds. While she had built conventional dome-shaped huts all her life, she now wanted a square room as a more permanent base at Puros. She said this was because she was growing too old to move or build houses. Another reason was that a favourite granddaughter had recently 'turned round', switching from Himba garb to Herero dress. The girl often lived with Kwazerendu and with her new clothes, she needed more space.

But over several years, the old woman never managed to get her male relatives to help her erect a Herero house and she occupied a series of temporary wood, plastic and cardboard shelters. She did not like living thus and frequently complained. But even though she or her granddaughter could have built a Himba hut in a few days, they never did as they were now 'Herero' and preferred to wait for male help to build a house.

Some of my most useful data and insights about my host society came about without intent on my part. Weeks of just being in a homestead, listening rather than asking questions and thereby not steering a discussion in a direction of my choice, engaging in ordinary conversations, with my ever-present notebook closed and temporarily forgotten, revealed aspects of Himba life which no one ever articulated.

Boundaries and oppositions inherent in my city life faded as the people around me moved seamlessly between secular and ceremonial activities. It's one thing reading about these things in anthropology 101; it's another to have your assumptions undermined by people going about their daily lives.

My understanding of public and private, culture and nature, temporary and permanent, work and leisure, far and near, individual and community, modern and traditional shifted. I discovered the reality of the Himba not being homogenous: men and women, different individuals and different age groups used different strategies to cope with modern challenges and situations.

I started grasping how one's assumptions enslave one and why it's so difficult to communicate across these constructs with someone who does not share them. The well-meaning Namibian government officials who have exhorted the Himba to 'upgrade' themselves from what they perceive to be a 'squalid and primitive' state are no different from the tour operator who describes the Himba as survivors from an ancient Africa. All of them – tour operators and politicians – fall into the trap of thinking that the opposite of modern is traditional. And on the subject of traps, practising and respecting your cultural traditions does not trap you in the past even though those customs may seem bizarre to outsiders.

One of the most modern families I know, Swedish people living in Britain, celebrate the ancient summer solstice festival each June with a feast of raw fish, called gravure lux, and other traditional dishes. For Himba who refuse to eat any meat that does not have four legs, this would be seen as an amazing – and horrifying – custom. I've met 'traditional' Sami reindeer herders in northern Norway who use snowmobiles and have under-floor heating at home. In New Zealand men who work in banks and offices strip off their clothes and become Maori warriors once a year on Waitangi Day. San or Bushmen community game guards in West Caprivi can use a GPS for their wildlife monitoring work but still have a partially 'traditional' diet of plant food gathered by their wives and daughters. Most of us combine the traditional and modern without thinking but apply labels to others. These are not academic issues to be relegated to universities. As I failed to explain in my radio interview all those years ago, these labels and misinterpretations of concepts such as culture and tradition directly affect people's lives and how decision-makers and others treat them.

Just as the Himba people easily fitted into the former apartheid and homeland vision – a stereotype of what was then called 'an ethnic group clearly differing from other groups by virtue of objective cultural differences' – so, too, they make uneasy bedfellows in a modern developing African state. For many decades, the Himba people generally resisted the penetration of outside values and institutions from the former South West African and later the Namibian socio-economy. The form this resistance took was, and to some extent still is, adhering to 'traditional' values and socio-economic activities, including the use of 'traditional' technology and material culture. They were able to do this because of their cattle wealth.

But their strategy of negotiating 'change through continuity' or using 'active conservatism' has counted against them in modern Namibia. In spite of their relative cattle wealth compared to other subsistence farming groups in the country, their 'traditional culture' – as signified by bare red-ochred bodies, calf skin garments, wood and shell adornments, dung-plastered single-room dwellings and nomadism – is seen as an obstacle to development and progressiveness. Because they are thus seen as 'backward' in the scheme of the Namibian nation state, it is also assumed they have little to teach us. That assumption is quite wrong.

The last 25 years on the Himba highlands has seen an increasing loss of perennial grasses, accompanied by the related topsoil losses and soil erosion. Elders will tell you that the customary rules of good grazing – the *ozonduninyo yo maryo* – have broken down.

Now every man has his own plan and just does as he wishes.

Like the great drought of the late 1980s, the recent drought that only ended in 2018 drastically reduced cattle numbers. After the '80s drought, cattle rebounded to an all-time high. But restocking to that level is not an option for modern Himba. Human numbers have increased and without strong local descent-based authority structures to collectively manage pasture and other natural resources, degradation of grasslands will continue. Coupled with the divisiveness of party politics, the future is uncertain for those people who call themselves Himba. One hopes they are able to take their rightful place as full citizens of Namibia, while being empowered to steer their own development, not have this done for them or to them.

The communal conservancy programme has a role to play in this future. At its best it gives remote rural people development options, and links wildlife conservation to job creation, income and socio-cultural benefits. Communal conservancy legislation was deliberately non-prescriptive so that different societies in culturally diverse Namibia could use it and adapt it to suit their own social systems. But community-based conservation is no panacea and can merely diversify local rural socio-economies, not replace all other ways of making a living. Many researchers seem to have missed this point.

Most Himba conservancies have done better at managing their collective money than many other more 'educated' conservancies. Generally, these conservancies also display a lack of selfishness and a strong sense of communality.

When Conservancy Safaris paid a cash dividend to its owner conservancies at the height of the drought in 2016/17, Marienfluss Conservancy made the altruistic decision not to take a share of this as the conservancy had earned enough by itself from its tourism fees to make a drought relief payment to its members. So they told CSN to share the dividend among the four conservancies who earned less than Marienfluss. And then there was the unselfishness of a majority of members in the other four conservancies who responded to a survey question about how the money should be divided among them. More than 80 per cent of those who did the survey thought that those conservancies who had earned the least should get the largest share of the dividend. Should we be surprised that those who disagreed were the 'modern' young men and women who had been to school?

Community conservation work has convinced me that we have much to learn – or re-learn – from people who do not put the individual before community, who do not see themselves as at nature's apex instead of just one of its parts and who do not celebrate excessive greed and self-centred consumerism. This stance is not anti-technology or against a modern way of life. Once we acknowledge the real cost of most of our technology – including and especially how it contributes to our lethal sense of separation from our natural world – we may be able to adjust how we use it. Or is this really the era of *Homo stupidicus*? Frighteningly, green energy and green technology is no solution: the devastating effects of mining the so-called rare earths essential for solar and all pervasive digital technology speak for themselves.

Old-fashioned Himba values and customs, and those of people like them, are a valuable resource, for themselves as well as for the rest of us who are so alienated from nature. But first we need to start seeing them not as quaint and exotic, or as an embarrassment to a modern African state, but as having stuff to teach us about our own impoverished values today and in the future.

For those sceptical about the value of indigenous knowledge in a modern world, here's just one small example. A paper I gave in Cairns, Australia, in 2012 about community conservation as a tool for climate change adaptation, led to an understanding of how indigenous practices can contribute to actual *mitigation* of global warming. My two talks at this conference included a few pictures of Khoe San hunter-gathers from our community conservation work in Bwabwata National Park in north-east Namibia. I mentioned in passing the fire monitoring we'd done in Zambezi (formerly Caprivi) Region, and the 'traditional' early season burning regime we'd help re-instate. We already knew that this indigenous burning pattern could stop the destructive late-season hot fires that were becoming increasingly common in the area as a result of a massive fuel load build-up, caused by a government ban on veld burning.

Australian fire ecologist Dr Jeremy Russell-Smith approached me at the conference. He was keen to learn more about the traditional savanna fire practices IRDNC was facilitating and told me about Australia's pioneering work, combining indigenous knowledge and practice with modern science, in northern Australia. His story took what we were doing in Zambezi Region to a new level.

Savannas, as the most fire-prone vegetation type on earth, are a significant source of greenhouse gas emissions. Over a decade, Jeremy and team had developed savanna-burning projects in northern Australia combining customary indigenous (Aboriginal) approaches to landscape-scale burning with development of scientifically robust emissions accounting methodologies. Formal acceptance by the Australian government – and the United Nations Climate Change Committee – of that methodology and its inclusion in Australia's developing emissions trading scheme, paved the way for Aboriginal people to commercially benefit from modern savanna-burning projects.

We were facilitating indigenous early burning in Zambezi but Australia had developed the science and the math to prove that in northern Australia similar types of burning actually contributed – counterintuitively – to climate change *mitigation.*

The next year both Garth and I were invited to Darwin to contribute to a proposal to expand the northern Australian customary burning projects to other savanna sites in the world where indigenous people still remembered their fire history. We were treated to an incredible field trip by light aircraft, helicopter and 4x4 vehicle into Australia's northern territory – Arnemland – where we met Aboriginal communities who had returned to their lands and who were living with pride and dignity as its managers. We watched local fire-managers set alight vast swathes of land. The people we met here could not have been more different from those we met outside liquor stores or sleeping it off in parks in Darwin.

All of this is very well, but as in the conservancy movement in Namibia, the question is what happens when the next generations, all school-goers, take over? Will they respect – and connect with – nature, culture and community as do a majority of their parents and grandparents? How do we make this happen before it's too late?

Our visit to Australia led to 10 fire ecologists, including Jeremy and two Aboriginal fire specialists, coming to Namibia. Neither of the Aboriginal men had formal university qualifications but there was no doubt, as they connected with local Namibians, that from a practical and cultural perspective, they were fire experts. Conservancy Safaris made life easy for us all by taking care of the logistics for this trip that started in Zambezi Region, crossed the huge Etosha Park savanna and ended in Swakopmund. Here we held a three-day workshop, with delegates from seven African countries and the visiting fire ecologists. The eventual outcome was a pilot project in Botswana – excellent news in a country that had long banned local burning.

So things aren't always what they seem . . . modern scientists, on their own, no more hold the answers than do modern economists, IT specialists and politicians. We need to be humble enough to seek wisdom from sources many of us currently pigeon-hole as too 'primitive' to have anything to offer a modern world.

SIX

Missionaries, beer and popcorn

I can hear a green branch squeaking – words used by an elder to
put a young man in his place.

DON'T TOURISTS DISRUPT Himba life? is a question frequently asked
by visitors to the north-west. Of course they do. But then so do
government officials, schools, shops, researchers, NGOs – you
can't build a wall around the Himba. And no one has the right
to try to keep what is useful from the modern world from them.
Some interventions are good, others not so much. The key, I'd
add if anyone was still listening, is that people are empowered – as
far as is possible - to take charge of the change happening around
them. Local empowerment is the foundation of community-based
conservation and of the kind of cultural tourism that we try to do
with a company that is owned by the people themselves. Helping
people to steer their own lives.

And then there are the missionaries.

Missionaries have done both good and bad in Africa. I have a
nephew who is a missionary, an admirable, values-driven human
being whom I am proud to call family. But it was hard to find much
good in an encounter in Puros with a group of black and white
theology students from South Africa in the late '80s. These young

Christian men, travelling with a minister and his wife, had come to Namibia to 'practise' their skills on the small Himba and Herero community in the area. I thought it was rather unethical to use real people as guinea pigs, not that there's an alternative, I suppose. So I cannot claim to be an unbiased witness to this mass blitz to spread Christianity in a few days.

Hearing there was a white woman living in Puros, the Afrikaans-speaking minister (an SADF chaplain, if my memory serves me) and his wife visited my little camp. I gave them coffee and asked about their visit. Then it was their turn to ask me about my research. Pleasantries over, the wife asked if I felt safe all alone out here. I explained that as many as 80 people lived at Puros, depending on the season, so I was not alone. She narrowed her blue eye-shadowed eyes at me.

'Yes, but it's not the same', she said.

They left soon afterwards, both shaking my hand and wishing me well. The wife had one last piece of advice: Be careful of getting too friendly with the 'locals', especially the men. Anything could happen. Give these people an inch and they could take a mile, she warned. I didn't think there was much point in telling her that I felt safer in Puros than in any city street and that everyone treated me with respect, courtesy and warmth. She saw sinful lusting heathens; I saw people I knew. I wondered what she would have made of a discussion I'd recently had with Rutako, husband of Vengape. I struggled to establish common ground with cattle-obsessed Rutako but eventually we found one another and could spend a pleasant hour or so talking now and then.

On one such visit to my camp, after he'd updated me at length about his cattle, over a second cup of sweet tea Rutako revealed that when he first saw me he thought I was very ugly. I looked to him like a creature who'd been born too soon. My colouring – white skin, pale green-brown eyes and reddish hair – had turned his stomach (*ondjijaukisa*), he said. But now that he had got to know me he was no longer bothered by my strange looks; now when he looked at me, he just saw me – a good and friendly person.

A day after the student missionaries arrived, old Omukuyu

called Shorty and me to his *onganda*. The frail Himba elder was sitting in the sun on his battered, much-repaired folding chair. He wanted to talk to us, he said, because something he'd heard would not leave him alone, even when he tried to sleep. The missionaries had told him that if he continued to use his sacred fire to talk to his ancestors, and did not convert to '*Christus*' (Christ and Christianity) when he died he would burn forever in a big fire.

What did I think? Who was this *Christus* who wanted people to abandon and disrespect their ancestors? Could this be true? Or were these young men just green branches squeaking?

Omukuyu was a kind, dignified old man who did not lie, steal, injure or cheat anyone. He had once told me that the worst thing a person could have was a deceitful heart – you should not think one thing and say another. He was one of the most decent people I knew. How dare a group of arrogant young upstarts mess with his head without finding out anything about Omukuyu's spiritual beliefs and values.

Omukuyu was in real distress and I did the first thing that occurred to me. It was quite inspired, even if I say so myself. I picked up a stick and drew a circle in the sand: 'This is the creator, as you call him; God to the young South African men who are here.' Then I drew a line going to the circle: 'This is the Himba's road to your divine creator, Njambe Karunga: you talk to your ancestors who live and walk with you and who talk to the creator on your behalf.' I drew another line. 'And this is the route people called Jews take.' Another line was a Buddhist road. I drew lots of lines, all going to the circle in the middle. 'Different people all over the world walk different roads to their God.'

And finally, I drew the South African student missionaries' line.

I tapped it with my stick: 'You know that when people are lonely and afraid they try to convince other people to walk with them on their road. This could be why these young men are telling you about what they call hell. They're scared to walk alone and they want you with them. Because you are a wise elder who has experienced a long and good life'.

Omukuyu heaved a sigh of relief. He studied my diagram in the sand. 'I thought it could be something like that,' he said.

The middle of the next day when the temperature was above 38 degrees and heat hazed the horizon, a visiting friend and I strolled to the Hoarusib River. Here, a series of linear oases rise to the surface in this mostly dry river bed and blissfully cool ankle or even calf-deep water can be found. We walked down the river, well clear of where people collected their drinking water. It was one of my favourite times of day when I could bathe and relax in the water in the river canyon, as long as one did not mind occasionally sharing one's stretch of river bed with a donkey or a few cows. They were after the lush green sedge grasses and herbs that thrived in the crystal clear shallow water. Groves of tamarisk trees grew on the pale sands of the river banks, providing shade where one could lie down and read when one had had enough of the water. With community-based conservation just starting to take effect, elephants had not yet come back to this river, and there was almost no other wildlife. Soon, one would not be so relaxed under the tamarisks as elephant and lion could also be enjoying the shade, the latter hoping to surprise a gemsbok who may have been lured into the canyon by the green vegetation.

Denny, my companion, was a fellow student, visiting from Cape Town for a few weeks to assist me with my research. We talked as we strolled along, looking for the place we usually used, deep enough for us to have a good wash. We'd put down our bucket, shampoo and towels and were about to strip off when I spotted a movement on the rocky cliff above us. Not a bird: I was sure I'd caught a glimpse of someone's head and shoulders. In my months at Puros I'd never once been bothered by anyone during my daily ablutions; parents had told children to give me privacy and no adult would be rude enough to intrude. So this was new.

I told Denny to hang on and sauntered casually under some tamarisks so that I could not be seen from the cliff. Then I quickly took a back route to the spot where a young man, one of the student missionaries, crouched on the cliff. He was too busy leaning forward, watching Denny, to notice me till I was close. He started, full of the guilt of a peeping Tom. Sliding the bible he clutched in one hand into his lap, he looked up at me and tried to recover himself.

Amazingly, the first thing he said was: 'Sister, have you been saved?'

Having made the totally unproven but circumstantially based assumption that he was intending to spy on Denny and me while we bathed, I did not turn the other cheek. I laughed out loud and told him to bugger off back to South Africa to practise being a better Christian. Or words to that effect. He scrambled away, red-faced, which I took as evidence that he was ashamed at being caught. Of course, in retrospect, it is entirely possible that the young man was simply sitting on the cliff, coincidentally at exactly the same spot where Denny and I bathed each day. He could have been innocently reading his bible or just enjoying nature. If so I hope he wasn't too traumatised by my rudeness.

The group left a few days later having made little overt impact in the community.

Missionaries who live in an area and try to assist people to improve their lives somehow seem more acceptable. At least they are in it for the long haul and presumably get to know people and often try to do something useful locally. At one stage, a missionary and his family lived in Sesfontein. Their house was virtually next door to the small army base where I had to present my South African-issued research permit every time I drove into Kaoko in last years of the 1980s.

I visited the missionary family and was invited to stay for lunch. We enjoyed robust discussions about a range of issues. The young wife, pregnant with their fourth child, mostly listened. She looked tired and drawn which was not surprising as the other three children, all under five, were a handful. When I next passed I took her some fresh fruit to thank her for the meal. Her husband was not at home and over a cup of tea at her kitchen table she told me about her life. She felt guilty about complaining, she said – after all, compared to the people in Sesfontein, she had so much. But it was hard to be raising three lively small children in this isolated place. There was no phone or contact with her family or the outside world and the nearest hospital was in Khorixas a day's drive away on dirt tracks. She was worried about the new baby due in four months and just did not see how she could cope.

I fell into the habit of visiting the family each time I passed, every two months or so, enjoying their company as well as hoping that a bit of female camaraderie from a similar cultural background would cheer up this young mother. Soon after their fourth baby was born, I turned up on their doorstep quite late in the afternoon. A puncture and various chores along the way had delayed me and I knew I'd not make Puros that day. The young mother was alone – her husband off doing some good works somewhere else. Obviously pleased to see me, she invited me to stay overnight. The children fell on my dog RDM and we sat outside drinking tea, watching the dog good-naturedly play with them.

It wasn't long before the new baby started crying and his mother rushed inside. She came out holding the squalling infant and burst into tears. It was her milk, she said. She'd had no trouble breast-feeding the other three but this time her milk did not want to flow properly. She was beside herself with worry: the baby was not gaining enough weight and he cried endlessly and she was exhausted all the time.

I did my best to comfort her. I thought of my brother's first wife Christine who also had four children and how she'd coped. I seemed to remember something about beer helping breastfeeding. And I just happened to have a six-pack of Tafel lager in my truck.

It took a bit of persuasion to get this missionary wife to drink a beer – they were strictly teetotal – but as it was for medicinal purposes and I assured her it had helped my sister-in-law with an identical problem, she agreed. One beer led to another – the older children were happily engaged in a ball game with the dog, the second youngest child fell asleep, having insisted on climbing onto his mother's lap and the baby eventually quietened in a carrycot next to her. As the day's heat and light faded we talked, laughed and sipped our lager. I watched the exhausted young woman's face relax and reckoned the beer was doing a good job even if it didn't help the breast feeding. But it did that too or maybe it was the relaxing and having company. Before we'd finished our second beers, the baby stirred and whimpered. Without thinking, she passed me the sleeping toddler from her lap, picked up the infant and put him to her breast. It was a few seconds before she registered: 'My milk – it's coming!' The baby suckled lustily while his slightly tipsy mother and I smiled from ear to ear.

On my next visit to Sesfontein I was accosted by the missionary. He was unhappy, he said, that I'd given his wife alcohol. But it had only been to solve her breastmilk problem, I said. Hadn't it done that? Wasn't she feeding their son easily now? Yes, but I'd crossed a line, it seemed. Beer, even though it had solved a distressing problem for his wife and their child, was a bridge too far. Lecture over, he stalked away.

The next time I found myself in Sesfontein needing to overnight, I went to the army base and asked if I could pitch my tent in their parking area. I wasn't sure of the reception I'd get at the missionary house. The group of 24 or so South African conscripts were fighting for a cause I did not believe in, but they were not the enemy. Aged 18 or 19, with a few older officers, they were mostly just youngsters missing home and counting the days till their enforced time in the army was over. Someone's sons and brothers.

I was treated like visiting royalty and as usual, my dog was a great hit. Several of the young men told me about their dogs back home. They were bored and I was a welcome distraction. I was invited to dinner and enjoyed the evening.

The huge shiny stainless steel pots in which cooking was done at the base intrigued me – I'd never seen such big pots before. The pots, coupled with what some of the men told me, that they were tired of the army food and longed for something less bland than the generic stews and rice they were mostly fed, gave me an idea. I always travelled with popcorn and often made it on my campfire. The offer of salted popcorn went down well.

We put the smallest of the pots – one with a 20-litre capacity – on the stove and added some cooking oil. One packet usually lasted four or five servings but this time I poured in a whole packet. It didn't look very much – barely covering the bottom of the pot.

So I added another packet. When the corn started popping, it sounded like a war. We all rushed back to the stove. I caught sight of my reflection in pot's steel wall, surrounded by young soldiers, all of us waiting for our popcorn to be ready to eat. A bizarre and incongruous moment in an army camp during the border·war.

I had one more encounter with the Sesfontein missionary before the family moved on. The news of my night at the army base had reached him. He told me he did not think it was 'appropriate' for me – a woman on her own – to be sleeping at the army base.

Speechless for a moment, I blurted the first thing that came into my mind: 'Evil is in the eye of the beholder.'

While he was digesting this, I smiled and patted him on the arm. 'Tell you what,' I said, 'next time I'm there come over with your family and have some popcorn.'

This time I stalked away, no doubt leaving him mystified.

SEVEN

On grass, water and tobacco

Let me tell you about the Ovahimba before the white man made us stupid – elder Venomeho Tjipomba

SHOWERING EVERY DAY is taken for granted by most of the people who do holiday safaris. Or at least they start out like that. On Conservancy Safaris trips, a mobile shower is provided most nights but sometimes camps are dry. The team ventures off tourism routes whenever possible or changes the plan because something interesting is happening locally, which then might mean that water, all of which has to be carried in the vehicles, is just enough for cooking and drinking.

The canvas wash basin in front of your tent gets filled morning and evening – it's enough to wash hands and face and other essentials; it won't kill you to go without a shower for a night. Or two.

Think how much you'll enjoy a good hot shower when you get it.

Learning not to take water for granted is good for people from the developed world.

And by the way, dust is not dirt.

All of above has been said to guests by CSN guides. As mentioned before, we all work in conservation and some of us may be a little deficient in hospitality skills. Not that CSN has had many complaints and returnees are common.

I once went 17 days without a proper wash and a canvas wash basin would have been an unthinkably selfish luxury. It was the beginning of May 1988 in Kaokoland – searingly hot and dry. Temperatures rose into the 40s well before midday and stayed high into the evenings. The modest rain clouds that gathered every afternoon in the far north-east remained tantalisingly distant, as they had for most of this rain season in the west. Some evenings lightning taunted us but always from afar, and one could almost sense its power waning. The wet season, inadequate as it had been, was over, bar a bit of rumbling, flashing and spitting.

The cattle plodded out mournfully each morning, raising dust clouds as their hoofs broke the dry ground. Soon they would start losing condition, having to walk further and further each day for scarce grazing, and then return in the evenings for water at Tomakus windmill, or Okotjitenda, as the area is called locally.

There were discussions and consultations among the men of the two Himba lineages with whom Shorty and I were living, as well as with a third lineage, a Herero family, originally from Sesfontein, who also used Tomakus. It was time to move away from permanent water so as to preserve what little grazing was left for later in the year. This meant finding water where there was grass. The Himba lineages were worried. With more than six months to go before the next rain season, the younger members of the Herero clan wanted to stay put. I could hear the disapproval in the older men's voices as they discussed the matter at the sacred fire where the ancestors are believed to be present to advise the living and bear witness to important decisions.

Ancestors aside, certainly this custom of debating anything of consequence ensured a high level of cooperation within the group and promoted sound decisions, with all options thoroughly examined. I was starting to understand why the Himba people are renowned herders – their planning process, taking into account local environmental, economic and social factors, and drawing on the knowledge and experience of the elders was as good as any group of farmers anywhere. The Herero neighbours regarded themselves as 'modern' and had discarded traditional customs such as sacred fires. But they had not replaced it with any other forum for good planning and it seemed that every household did as it wished.

Venomeho, the most senior elder of the two Himba lineages and at whose sacred fire planning therefore took place, was grumbling about young people with their radios and beds, and other heavy possessions that made moving difficult; they didn't think about the future. What were the cattle supposed to eat in November if all the grass up to a full day's walk from the windmill was used up? What use would these new things be? There was a brief silence as we all thought about the goods in question: Metal bedsteads with foam mattresses bought in a shop and transported here in an old truck, wooden tables and chairs, boxes and boxes of goods.

Then, sub-elder Rutaka spat in disgust: 'You could lie on the bed and watch your cattle starve to death,' he suggested.

Thus the men's meeting ended in subdued laughter.

But a decision had been taken. For one last time some of the elders would talk to the Uararavi's lineage about the foolhardiness of wasting the grass near this permanent water; in any case, the two Himba lineages would leave. Even though they knew that the others might stay and use up grass that would have kept all three lineages' stock alive in the critical dry months before rains came again at the end of the year. Some of the younger Himba people had suggested staying too and thereby at least getting a share of this grass. But older wisdom had prevailed; the two lineages would do what they knew was right.

Our group would split up. Five men, seven women and four children, plus the cattle and some of the goats, would trek deep into the hills to the north of Okotjitenda. Water would be found by digging a pit in a sandy wash. Two boys of about 12 or 13 and an older sister would take most of the goats to another camp further west where there was temporary water, also from a pit, in a dry river bed for a few weeks. Rutaka had walked to both places in the past week to confirm this plan was viable.

A few days later, Shorty warned me that departure was imminent and that I should pack up. This time I would have to leave my Toyota truck behind as there were no roads into the hills. Shorty assured me that Otjiviyo was not far and that we would walk to the place easily in a day. Then he looked at my huge pile of camping essentials, which I had pared down to a minimum, and shook his head. Maybe he and I would take longer, carrying all that. He went off to find a donkey we could use.

I tackled the pile again, packing my cooking pot back into my truck and keeping only my kettle. Morning tea was not negotiable. Then it occurred to me that I could boil water in the pot as well as cook in it so I swapped it for the kettle. I pulled all my clothes out of my rucksack and discarded most of them. Five of the ten books at the bottom of my bag went back in the car, then I repacked three of them. By the time Shorty returned with the good news that we had a donkey, my heap of goods looked a little more manageable. Even so, I was taking about as much as would a large Himba household.

A day or two later, we set off. As usual, I was taken by surprise because I could see no obvious signs of packing up. I should have noticed that the stock had gone out early with two of the men and the older children. Everyone else rose in the morning with the sun as normal, gathered up some goods and started walking. Shorty fetched my donkey, a sturdy, self-reliant creature, and tied my goods onto his broad back. By the time we were ready, the others were out of sight.

Our grey donkey ambled ahead, bearing his load with apparent ease. He seemed to understand Shorty's occasional command and twisted his long ears back to listen for us if we fell too far behind him. The rugged hills soon had us sweating. We crossed a ridge and dropped into a valley where we stopped for a drink and a rest. I found my hat and applied sunscreen. Only about 10 am and already the sun was scorching.

As we followed a narrow route up into another range of hills, higher than those we had already traversed, I began noticing green fuzz on the slopes around us. Enough rain had fallen two weeks ago to raise a light stand of annual grasses and because no one had used the area for a few years, there were sufficient perennial grasses, from previous rains, to provide weeks of fodder for the stock.

Our destination Otjiviyo was a dry sandy gulley where deep pits could be dug for water. It was here, many years earlier, that a cow broke the leg of a male relative, Venomeho told me the night we arrived. People laughed when I assumed Otjiviyo was the name of the man. It was the cow's name, of course, as I should have known after more than a year living with these herders.

I set up my little tent under a scrawny mopane tree, near the main camp – a semi-circle of shelters, which the women expertly erected within the first two days, using saplings and mopane foliage.

The next two-and-a half weeks were probably the hottest of my life. Noon till about 4 pm was spent lying in the deepest shade I could find, trying to read, but in reality sliding in and out of a sweaty, restless stupor. In between these uncomfortable siestas I asked questions, recorded information and joined in the time-consuming task of watering the stock. The pit that the men and youths started digging as soon as they arrived was more than three metres deep. At the bottom lay a small pool, half a metre of tepid, clear water. We drained it every day, but overnight water would have seeped back, returning the pool to its former level.

By now, I had come to realise that water was not the key resource – grass was. There was enough water in the west to ensure nothing died of thirst but without grass, any spring was of little use. The stock would survive the walk back to Tomakus windmill and they could go two or even three days without water. Without food, for the same period, they would weaken; another few days and increasingly, they would be unable to walk to seek food. Death from starvation would follow.

Talking around the fire at night, men recalled desperate days of drought, from the late '70s up till 1982, when they used branches to try to lift cattle that had given up and collapsed back onto their feet. Some of them had taken their herds down river beds into the Skeleton Coast Park where there was still some fodder. Nature conservation officials had told them their cows would be shot if they took them into the park but what else could they do?

The Otjiviyo pit, containing the only water in these scorched hills, acted as a magnet for most people, and everyone who was not engaged in another task found their way to this water. Starting from about 4 pm, cattle were allowed to drink from of a long wooden trough. Someone had found the right species of commiphora tree and carved the trough the day the cattle arrived. An old one, last used many years before, lay nearby, broken and split.

It took a team of people – men, women and the older children – deep into the evening to complete the job, which was deliberately done in the afternoon instead of the morning, to allow the pool to re-fill overnight, and ensuring thirst brought the cattle back each evening, avoiding predators in this remote area. As at the water hole below Etaambura Camp, one person on the floor of this hole scooped water into a bucket and hoisted it above his head to another person, lodged part-way up. And so on till the person at the top emptied it into the trough. A second bucket was already on its way up, passing the empty one on its way down. It was heavy work. At least four people were needed to manage the mass of frantic animals bunching up nearby. They could see and smell water, and there was always the risk of the trough being overturned or broken, and the danger of an animal being pushed into the hole.

Controlling thirsty cattle required skill – and experience, as we saw when some youngsters took on the job and nearly muffed it. An older man quickly stepped in to avert the near chaos that ensued when cattle mobbed the water trough. The boys weren't working as a team, Shorty explained. Each was doing his own thing. Having tried it I can confirm it takes teamwork to allow a group of beasts forward to drink briefly, while keeping the rest back till it was their turn. I also tried being a bucket-filler at the bottom but only lasted about ten minutes before my arms and shoulders gave in. I kept going until my muscles burnt, simply to continue savouring the coolness in the hole. Standing knee-deep in water was wonderful but I did better at wielding a long stick and making sure that the smaller animals and my donkey also got a drink.

Our water came from the same pit and I climbed down the rough steps made from branches to fill my two plastic bottles twice every day, very conscious that the five litres I was using most days was more than double what everyone else used. There was no question of bathing and as hot as it was, I reduced my toiletry to a small mug of washing water morning and night. I alternated what I wore each day and instead of washing the garments, I 'aired' them overnight. By the second week I noticed that my unwashed skin and hair felt quite comfortable.

The camp ran out of mealie meal on day 16. The diet now comprised milk and meat. Milk was adequate but not plentiful because the cattle were under some stress. A goat was slaughtered every two or three days and shared among 18 of us. I had been doing okay on two handfuls of muesli and two cups of tea each morning, a tin of sardines every other day and some dried fruit or nuts most days, supplemented by a chunk of goat meat and pap in the evening, but my stocks were down to tea bags and a packet of raisins. The raisins were my last ditch fare, not to be opened till starvation threatened. I had to hide the packet (from myself) because the sight of them, juicy and sweet, in the bottom of my empty food box was too tempting to bear.

After a day on just milk and meat, I broached the subject of my food trunk in the back of my truck. I had spent more than a few minutes the night before thinking longingly of its contents. Imagining biting into a Provita biscuit spread with peanut butter and honey made my mouth water as did the tins of pickled fish and chutney I knew was there.

Shorty and I, both a few kilograms lighter than when we had left Tomakus, discussed what was in my truck. There was a 25kg bag of mealie meal, tea and several kilos of sugar, which I was happy to contribute to the camp, as well as sufficient dried food, biscuits and tinned fish to keep me going for another two weeks or so. Shorty estimated that the grazing would only last another few weeks, and my *oruhere* and sugar would improve life in the camp.

85

He wandered off to tell Venomeho and some of the others that we wanted to hike back to the truck to fetch a donkey-load of food.

Our grey donkey was found and kept tied to a tree overnight. Four of us – Old Venomeho, his son-in-law Rutako (who unusually lived with him because Venomeho had only daughters), Shorty and I – set off early the next day. The two herders wanted to see if the Uararavi people were still at the Tomakus windmill, as well as check on the youngsters and the goats.

I rode the donkey for some of the way and the trip took us just four hours. We intended overnighting at Tomakus and returning the next day, without Rutako who would follow us in a day or two after a visit to the goat camp. I drank several times on the way, but all three men refused water. Rutako said that he'd rather have a pipe of tobacco. Sadly, Shorty's tobacco supply had finished in the first week.

My Provita and peanut butter feast later that day evoked no enthusiasm among my companions. I knew better than to offer them sardines or pickled fish. Real food had four legs and fur. Eventually the men settled on sharing two tins of bully beef mixed into a pot with baked beans. After eating, and drinking some water, the men's thoughts again turned to tobacco. But we were at least two hours hard driving from Sesfontien where a strong, pungent tobacco was grown. In any case, I told my companions, smoking was unhealthy.

A doze in the shade next to my vehicle was interrupted by the sound of an approaching car. Traffic on the Tomakus-Puros road was unusual in 1988 and as expected, the car stopped when my vehicle was spotted. The truck pulled under a nearby tree and two white men emerged. We exchanged the usual information: Where have you come from? Where are you going? You working in the area? Everything okay here? And so on. I wished I had not postponed my bucket wash at the Tomakus windmill till later as I was suddenly aware of how dirty I must be after nearly three weeks without showering.

Speaking in Afrikaans the men told me they were prospectors, seeking and trading in semi-precious stones. By now Shorty and the others had joined us. I introduced them; Shorty was in Western clothes, while Rutako and Venomeho were bare-chested and traditionally dressed in black cloth skirts kept up with a leather hunger belt. Affable nods were exchanged.

Then one of the newcomers, the one with the large belly, took a packet of cigarettes from his shirt pocket. I sensed the quickened interest of my companions. I was offered a cigarette and automatically shook my head. Apparently his mate did not smoke either for the man pulled out one for himself and lit it with a cheap plastic lighter. He did not look at the three adult men standing alongside me; it was as if they did not exist on this particular social plane.

In an instant I was outraged, ashamed of my fellow whitey. I opened my mouth to tell the man how rude and racist he was, but a tiny movement from Rutako caught my eye; he was looking hard at me, and I received his telepathic message loud and clear. I bit back the flow of angry, self-indulgent words and took a deep breath.

'Um ... I've changed my mind; could I have a cigarette please?'

'*Ja, natuurlik. Vat maar. Ek is nie kort nie.*' Yes, of course, help yourself. I'm not short.

I took the packet and shook one, then two more, out of it. 'For ... later,' I said. Then I offered the packet to my companions, irritated with myself for feeling like a defiant schoolgirl.

The man was not as insensitive as he looked, or perhaps he just felt outnumbered. Red-faced, he lit Shorty, Rutako and Venomeho's cigarettes with his lighter, then refused the half full packet I tried to hand back to him.

'*Hou dit, ek het nog in die kar.*' Keep it; I have more in the car.

Dankie, said Shorty. Thank you. His tone leaving no doubt about the depth of his gratitude.

After the men drove on, Shorty divided up the cigarettes we'd scored. None of the three had finished smoking their first cigarette. Each carefully stubbed it out after a few puffs, keeping the rest for later or perhaps for someone else. Tobacco was a precious commodity. Like grass and water.

I couldn't let the white man's initial rudeness go without comment and we discussed it briefly. But it was obviously a bigger deal in my head than for the others. Whites weren't known for their good manners out here, as I already knew.

Venomeho shrugged philosophically: 'If you're hungry you don't refuse meat just because the owner of the beast is a fool,' he said before going to find men from the other lineage, most of whom were still, disastrously for everyone else, at Tomakus with their stock. He was too polite to say it, but I realised that he had much more important things to talk about than rude white men.

We each make our own reality, I reflected. The white man did not see three black men standing alongside me when he offered me a cigarette; the Uararavi lineage could not see a few months beyond today when their failure to move and preserve some fodder round this reliable water point would quite possibly mean the cattle would starve to death.

EIGHT

Just another Van der Merwe story

NOW AND THEN I WAS able to take a break from my research
and explore the Kunene Region with Garth and friends. Easter
weekend 1988 was one such occasion. But the jaunt did not turn
out as expected and demonstrated how easily one could die in this
land which does not forgive errors in judgement.

'Something's wrong,' Garth said suddenly. He stopped the
Land Rover to examine the spoor along the track that he'd been
watching for the past few kilometres.

'There shouldn't be a man in European-style boots walking
alone here,' he told me and Shorty.

The latter nodded. 'It's not a local man,' he said. 'It's a white
man or maybe Swapo.'

By now, the second vehicle in our party had caught up with us
and Namibian botanist Pat Craven and her husband Dan Craven
joined us on the dirt road. We were probably the only two vehicles
for 200 kilometres or more, and an eagle's eye high above would see
us as a few specks in a vast desert landscape, on a pencil-thin track
along the floor of a huge sandy valley. There was little vegetation:
clumps of low dusty scrub and the occasional stunted mopane tree.
To the east the valley was contained by a rugged mountain range;

in the west substantial hills, stark and stony, separated the valley from a maze of dune fields – many kilometres wide - that blocked easy access to the icy Atlantic Ocean.

It was 4 pm in April. We were about 50 km from the Kunene River via the Hartman's Valley, the western-most route, apart from the beach, to the river which is Namibia's northern boundary with Angola. After years of war between Swapo and the South African Defence Force, few vehicles used this rough track across what is probably one of the remotest parts of southern Africa. Even today, with a booming tourism industry, this route is one of the lesser travelled, and guests to the two Hartman's Valley lodges on the Kunene River are usually flown in.

Our reason for being there – at the edge of the war – was to assist Pat to do a botanical survey. The plan was to camp in the dunes above the river for two nights helping Pat collect plants. Given that the area was uninhabited, we could see no reason for any military activity so far west.

'There's definitely a problem here. This man is walking out, away from the river. His tracks are fresh, maybe yesterday's. He's hours from any water,' Garth observed, lighting his pipe, the sign that he needed to make a decision.

It didn't take him long to propose that Pat and Dan should continue to the river, in case there was a broken down vehicle ahead, with people in trouble. We would turn back and follow the footprints.

A very disappointed Pat Craven pointed out that our time was short: this delay could abort the whole trip. She'd waited a long time to have Garth guide her into this inaccessible north-western corner of the country. He knew this vast dry region and its desert-adapted plants well, having first worked there in the 1960s, doing a lot of walking with Himba men. It had taken the Cravens two-and-a-half days' driving, much of it 4x4, from their home, then in Swakopmund, to get to this point, about an hour from the Kunene River; understandably Pat was reluctant to see her guide turn round to follow some boot tracks in the sand.

I kept silent, although like Pat I too wondered if Garth wasn't being a little melodramatic. Probably, the tracks belonged to a Himba who had somehow acquired some boots. But Garth was implacable and Dan backed him. I always thought of Dan, son of South African rugby's Danie Craven, as Deep-Throat because of his courageous role in the '70s, tipping off the media about serious illegal hunting in north-west Namibia being undertaken by senior South African politicians and military officials.

We watched the dust from the Cravens' truck disappear. Even though the sun was no longer high it was still very hot – mid-30s at least. The Himba youth, Kaororua, son of community game guard Kamasitu, who had hitched a lift with us, was discussing the tracks with Shorty. We turned round and drove slowly back the way we'd come. The man's footsteps were clearly visible now that Garth had pointed them out to me, and you could see that he was using a walking stick, its tip indenting the sand at regular intervals, to the left of his boot prints. Sometimes when the side of the road was firm and flat he walked there; at other times he walked in the road and our tyres had obliterated all signs of him. But then his tracks would show up again.

Strong evidence that he was not a local man was not long in coming: After about 10 kilometres Shorty banged on the truck's roof to stop us and pointed out the remains of a small campfire near the road. An empty tin of beans and vienna sausages lay next to the ashes of a little fire. This was no Himba traveller. The ashes were cold but Shorty and Kaororua were certain the fire had burnt no more than two nights ago.

Soon we reached the section of the road that does a sharp loop to the south-west. There, we found a deep arrow, gouged into the side of the track, with the man's stick. Its message was clear: the walker was taking a shortcut through the desert, heading south-east, directly towards what is today called the Bluedrum junction. This way he would cut out about 15 kilometres, which suggested he knew the area.

Garth and Shorty wondered if he was heading for the small spring in the hills below Omatjinguma Mountain, in the bed of the otherwise-dry upper Munutum River. But this was at least 40 kilometres ahead of him so we hoped he was carrying adequate water.

We were now even more worried because tracking a man in the hard gravel plains would take much more time and effort, and it was already late in the day. Should we not forget about this and follow the Cravens back to the Kunene River? Probably the man had walked out safely by now. But Garth and Shorty were not prepared to let it go. There could be a man dying of thirst out here.

Then Kaororua spoke up, and irrevocably changed the events of the next few hours. He had seen, he said, another arrow drawn in the sand at the junction about 25 km southwards, which we had passed earlier in the afternoon. So, we decided to abandon the man's tracks and drive straight to the arrow, hoping to pick up his prints there as it seemed he had made it that far. We sped off, arriving shortly after sunset.

Kaororua was right: there was an arrow but it did nothing to clear up the mystery. This arrow had been made by the heel of a boot, not a stick, dragged through the sand, and was quite obviously older – maybe a week or more – than the previous arrow. It should have been even fresher than the first one if the man had reached here and drawn it.

After a few minutes we concluded that it might have nothing at all to do with the first one. A strange coincidence that two people could have each drawn arrows alongside this remote road as markers; or perhaps the man's group had marked the route thus on the way in? We scoured the area for tracks but found nothing.

By now it was dark and we drove around, widening our search, without success. At about 8 pm, we reluctantly gave up, and made camp in a wash of the dry Enjo River just before the junction. At first light we'd resume the search. We cooked supper and prepared to retire for the night, a sombre group, mindful that somewhere out in the desert a man might be in a terrible trouble. As a former city dweller, who'd only lived in the north-west of Namibia for a few years, I found it hard to believe that someone really was lost and that we were needed to rescue him. It all seemed too much like a movie. I was sure there would be a logical explanation for the tracks and remembered Shorty's earlier suggestion that the man could be part of a Swapo group on its way in from Angola. The end of the long border war was in sight and we all knew it was just a matter of time before Swapo took over South West Africa. But the South African Army was still in occupation.

What if a group of Swapo insurgents, of whom the lone walker was one, saw our fire and decided to investigate? Wouldn't we, two white people, be seen as a target? Garth dismissed my nervousness. There would be no point in Swapo coming into this western valley; there was nothing here, no people, no infrastructure of any kind. And in any case an insurgent would not walk openly along a road, leaving tracks.

But still I looked out into the dark uneasily. We were pro-Swapo but how would insurgents, no doubt armed with AK47s, know that?

Shorty's imagination had been captured by the situation and he insisted on gathering huge amounts of wood for a massive two-metre-high blaze. He vowed to wake up at regular intervals to keep his inferno going to give anyone lost out there the chance to be guided to our camp by the huge fire. We laughed at his earnest determination and left him to it. From my bedroll next to the vehicle, I watched leaping orange flames shoot sparks high into the black sky and wondered what the next morning would bring. But we didn't have to wait that long.

Minutes after we had settled down, our two dogs started barking. They sounded ferocious and we knew our bush-wise Staffordshire terriers were seriously worried. Then we all heard a dragging sound in the dark. My hair was standing up on the back of my neck.

Garth and Shorty were already on their feet and had to step out of the way of the stumbling man who lurched into camp. He was near blind, the lenses of his eyes having buckled from dehydration, and he could only see Shorty's fire, not the two men in his path.

The man was wizened; in dire straits. Although it was dark, a sweat-stained leather hat was jammed on his head, and attached to his belt was a tin mug. He wore shorts, a shirt and good walking boots with the laces undone and carried nothing. Garth caught hold of his arm to stop him staggering into the fire. He swung towards Garth, and stood there, swaying.

'Water, oh God, please, water,' he whispered in Afrikaans. I ran to get some. I started pouring him a cupful but he grabbed hold of the 1-litre canvas bag and fell to his knees, swigging desperately.

'Slow down, don't drink so fast,' I said. 'If you're very dehydrated, you could make yourself sick.'

His head turned towards my voice, momentarily lifting his mouth from the water. 'Are you short of water? Please just a little more,' he pleaded in a creaking rasp. As we all watched, he flattened a litre then begged for more.

This time I gave him a large mug, quickly adding some re-hydration powder – basically just salt and sugar – that I kept in my medical aid kit for Himba babies with diarrhoea. He quaffed it, and sunk to the ground, obviously exhausted.

I mixed him another mug of water and powder and we all gathered round him.

'Are you injured in any way,' I asked. No reply. He stared blankly at the fire, muttering incomprehensibly. A few minutes later he asked for more water and we passed him another mug.

'Thank you very much', he said politely in Afrikaans.

He seemed to be reviving, and so I asked him his name. Immediately he stuck out his hand: 'Van der Merwe,' he said, like the punch line of the South African joke. Garth and I couldn't help ourselves. We burst out laughing, eliciting a puzzled glance from Shorty and Kaororua.

In the next hour, Van der Merwe's strength started returning. We made him a comfortable place to lie, and, at his request, put water nearby. He drank a cup of tea with lots of sugar. His mind still wandered and in the middle of telling us his harrowing tale, he suddenly started talking about ostriches. The following day, when Dan Craven, a medical doctor, examined Van down at the river, he reckoned that the man was a few hours from death due to dehydration when he staggered into our camp and that he was as strong as an ox to have recovered so fast.

Van's story came in fits and starts. He was a prospector, aged 50, living in Opuwo, and a descendant of one of the Thirstland Trekkers who had trudged into Namibia in 1875 from the Western Transvaal in South Africa. This group of hardy Afrikaans farming families, travelling by oxen-drawn wagons, had endured massive hardship and high mortalities – starvation, thirst and malaria – before finding a place that suited them, and would accept them, in Angola. But after a few decades there, the pious descendants of the trekkers returned to South West Africa, professing themselves unable to continue living in the Portuguese colony where the official religion was Roman Catholicism. Our Van der Merwe obviously shared the toughness and wanderlust of his forefathers.

Nearly a month earlier his nephew, a policeman based in Opuwo, had dropped him at the Orupembe windmill. He was to spend four weeks in the Hartman's Mountains, making his way towards the river, seeking semi-precious stones. Then he planned to return and meet his nephew back at Orupembe. All had gone according to plan until he fell and injured his knee, just before he was due to walk back to his rendezvous spot. The knee swelled and was very painful. So he decided to walk along the road because he knew he would not make the rough mountainous route, even though there was water in the latter but none in the flat valley traversed by the road. He estimated that he could cover 50 kilometres a day and that he could therefore walk the 140 kilometres to Orupembe windmill in three days. His plan was to eke out the two litres of water he could carry, for day one and two, and then walk the last 40 kilometres waterless, but knowing he would reach water by the evening. He decided to walk in the daytime, in spite of the intense heat, just in case a vehicle came along. He knew that at best there were two or three vehicles on this road in a month but he couldn't bring himself to risk being asleep and missing a passing car.

Disaster struck early on day one when one of his battered water bottles sprang a leak, and he lost some of his water. Even so, he had sorely miscalculated the distance a fit man could walk in the searing temperatures of the Hartman's Valley and found, with his sore knee, that he only made about 30 kilometres on the first day.

He'd also underestimated how much water he would need.

His water ran out early on day two and that night, already badly dehydrated, he ate his last tin of food – viennas and beans. Having found the remains of this camp, we could calculate that he had thus walked about 60 kilometres so far. The small amount of salty liquid in the tin – a sort of tomato sauce – did little to quench his by-now raging thirst and he spent a bad night, sleeping little and plagued by thoughts of water. He wished he had waited for help at the Kunene River and considered turning back. But he thought he had covered more ground than, in fact, he had and believed, incorrectly, that Orupembe was closer than the river.

He managed to walk on for another day, without anything at all to drink. It was not a day he wished to repeat. He sucked a pebble continuously and at first this helped. He'd slept for several hours in the heat of the day, near the road, and woke up dizzy, with an excruciating headache. He walked on, his mouth now too dry to tolerate a stone.

After another very bad night he set off at dawn. Each step was an effort and his head pounded; his tongue felt hugely swollen and he could not bear the sun's rays on his body. He searched for shade and on this his second full day without water, he started becoming confused, no longer sure of his way. He lost his rucksack – presumably taking it off his back when he stopped to rest and forgetting to pick it up when he moved on – and could not remember much except the unbearable heat of the sun, and his obsessive search for cool shade.

'My body felt as if it was burning up; it was terrible,' he said in his scratchy voice, in between tearing at two leftover lamb chops. Near dead from thirst he may have been, but he had not lost his old-fashioned courtesy and every offer of food or drink was politely acknowledged.

When Van encountered us, he had been at least two full days without water, although it could have been three. He wasn't sure. That afternoon, he said, he had given up and just wanted to find some shade in which to die. All sense of direction was lost. He crept into a little rocky overhang, said his goodbyes to his children who lived in South Africa with his ex-wife and fell into a stupor. But bees woke him up, buzzing around his head, no doubt in search of liquid, and he crawled away to lie under a bush. He took the boots off his swollen, hot feet. Not long afterwards, he heard the sound of something that he had been praying for – a vehicle engine. He had staggered up but was unable to move fast on his bare feet. He stood watching 200 metres from the road – which he had not known was so close – as our Land Rover passed.

If he had been able to cry he would have, he said, but there were no tears left in his dehydrated system. He'd collapsed back on the ground when the unbelievable happened and a second car passed – the Cravens. This was the final blow. Now he knew he was destined to die in the desert.

Nevertheless, so that someone would eventually find his body and let his children know his fate, he crawled towards the road and hung his boots on a sturdy stick which he dug into the ridge of sand in the middle of the track. Then he lay down to die. We would have found the boots and his body in two days when we returned from the river.

He lay there, alongside the road, for some hours, too weak to move and drifting in and out of consciousness. After dark a cold breeze blew from the west, cooling his burning hot body and slightly clearing his head. Then he heard something, or rather felt the vibrations of the noise, through the ground. It was undoubtedly the engine of our vehicle. It seemed we had been within a few kilometres of Van, when we drove around, trying to find his tracks after discounting the second arrow. Amazingly, the sound of the old Series 3 Land Rover engine had reached him. Somehow, Van got his boots back on his feet. He staggered around blindly, till hours later, having walked two or three kilometres, we estimated, he had spotted a distant light: Shorty's huge fire.

Eventually we all settled down for the night, leaving half a 25-litre container of water next to Van. Early the next morning, with a Van who had visibly grown in size as his tissues re-hydrated, we set off for the river and found the Cravens not far from their vehicle. Dan examined Van and prescribed liquids and soft foods.

All we had in that line was some canned fruit and we left Van resting in the shade of one of the vehicles, with two large tins of canned peaches, while we did some plant collecting.

To be honest, Garth and I were relieved to have a bit of a break from the man because as his strength returned, so did his voice. He barely stopped talking and we wondered, after several hours of this onslaught, whether he was always like this or if his volubility was just a reaction to his near-death experience. He spent the next day-and-a-half recovering – and talking. He seemed a small man on that first night: I remember noticing that his knees were the widest part of his legs. In fact, Van was sturdy and muscular and his body quickly regained its solid robustness. We rigged up a shade shelter because he still couldn't endure sun on his skin. Garth was his hero and he must have told us a hundred times that he would be dead if it were not for Garth spotting his tracks and insisting we search for him. True, but we grew tired of hearing it.

Garth tried to share the burden of the man's gratitude, pointing out that Kaororua had seen the second arrow and even though it had nothing to do with Van, it had drawn us straight to the area where he was. If it had not been spotted by the Himba youth, we would have spent at least a day painstakingly tracking Van's spoor across the gravel plains and may have found him too late. And it was Shorty's huge fire that Van had seen. Yes, this was so, Van agreed, but it was Garth who turned his vehicle back to search for him.

On our way back we took Van to the Orupembe windmill, and equipped him with some blankets and food. We did not have enough fuel to take him to Opuwo but we promised to contact his nephew as soon as we got to a telephone. Shorty spoke to some Himba people who were living nearby and asked them to make sure Van was okay till his nephew came to fetch him. Then we left him, a wiry, tanned figure, waving goodbye from the shade of a mopane tree.

A month or so later, a letter arrived from Van. He was very keen to see us to discuss something of the utmost importance. The next time we were in Opuwo, we tracked him down. He was living alone on the high hill above the town, in a makeshift tented shelter. Chickens pecked busily around us as we sat and watched Van make us tea on a gas stove. He had a tape deck attached to a car battery, which played us his favourite music, an Afrikaans woman singer with a bent for the sentimental. Delighted to see us again, over tea and biscuits he once again formally thanked us for saving his life. Then he produced a large tan-coloured blanket with a picture of a springbok on it – a gift in return for the bedding we'd given him. We kept this handsome rug for decades – till it was destroyed in a fire at Wereldsend in late 2017 which burnt down Garth's office, my office and our spare room.

On the Opuwo hill, we caught up on Van's health. Then Van presented his business proposition. He was keen to go into partnership with us, he said, talking mysteriously about some valuable find in the mountains. Our lack of interest disappointed him but he accepted that our work in community-based natural resource management was as much and more than we could handle. We couldn't contemplate going into the semi-precious stone business as well. We parted amicably and never again saw Van, although news of his exploits periodically found their way to us, still exploring the mountains in the Namibia's arid north-west, going on foot where few people, black or white, had ever ventured.

Then we heard he was missing in the Otjihipa Mountains along the Kunene River. We fully expected to hear that he had once again had a miraculous escape and that his long-suffering nephew had received a message to fetch him somewhere. But this time, it seemed, his number was up, and as far as we know Van never came out of the rugged mountain range. His family contacted us from South Africa after a few years to check whether we had any idea what had happened to him. His body has not been found and probably never will be. By now the ferocious desert sun, which so traumatised him in 1988, will have desiccated his remains. No doubt his bleached bones lie somewhere, scattered by vultures or wild animals on some inaccessible slope or in a deep valley.

In 2017 we hosted three MacIntyres – brothers Richmond and Chris and their cousin Garth – plus a friend who is a Scottish mountain climbing guide. The Mad Macs, as we took to calling them all, are New Zealand born but the two brothers have made southern Africa their home.

Richmond, an engineer living in Hermanus in the Cape, South Africa, is an avid adventurer sportsman/explorer, climbing, sailing, mountain-biking and extreme hiking – preferably where others fear to tread. He holds the distinction of being the first and only Hermanus resident to have climbed Everest, and what makes this feat more impressive is that he did not go as part of a team. One Sherpa guide accompanied him and for various reasons, part of another story being recounted in a book his wife Avis is writing, he did the last pitches solo, very nearly losing his life in the process. Brother Chris MacIntyre, as exceptional in his own way as his older brother, is one of the three original founders of the now multi-country Wilderness Safaris. He and their cousin Garth, who's into salvage diving, are not as fanatical as Richmond about physical and mental challenge but they join him on some of his trips and seem to have no trouble keeping up, while engaged in non-stop verbal jousting and robust banter.

The Mad Macs planned to climb the highest peak on the Kunene River and do the most extreme part of a walk inside the Kunene Gorge from Epupa Falls to the Marienfluss that my Garth did as a young man, in 1969. This was a remarkable feat, given that Garth had no backup and was heading off into unknown territory. He wrote up his hike eventually in a 1970 edition of the South African Wildlife Society's journal, then called *African Wildlife*. Richmond had long wanted to do this expedition, as discussed when we occasionally visited Hermanus or when he and Avis, a lifelong friend of mine, visited us.

We agreed that Conservancy Safaris could do backup for the expedition and arranged that Kaororua – now a man in his early 40s – would be their guide in this punishing landscape. As our friend Koos Verwy, Epupa Falls restaurant and camp owner and himself an extreme hiker and explorer, says: There's no one better to have at one's side than Kaororua in these mountains.

Our part of the backup involved, among other things, meeting and restocking with food the party of five men at a little-known third route down to the Kunene River – Otjimborombongo. Only problem was that for the last 12 years no vehicle had been on this precipitous track – not since massive rains had washed parts of the road away. And the last known vehicle to attempt that route failed, needing many Himba men to get the Land Cruiser out. For Garth, of course, this was merely a throwing down of the gauntlet, not a problem. Then 73, he'd declared himself not fit enough to accompany the hikers but he was pleased to take on this challenge.

The Mad Macs later agreed that the four-day hike, sticking to Garth's original route close to the river, instead of using an easier more popular track that goes out the gorge when it becomes too steep, had been one of their toughest to date.

But we in the backup team – Garth, Sonia Hambo, Eddison Kaisuma and me – were convinced we'd had the hardest role. While the five walkers ambled along at their own pace, admittedly having to climb up and down some steep slopes, we were the ones who had rebuilt an overgrown, washed away and eroded track that zigzags dramatically through mountains and valleys en route to the Kunene so that we could get two Land Rovers down to Otjimborombongo. Under a blazing sun, we averaged four kilometres an hour, and all of us had moved many rocks, with bruised hands to prove it, and had our hearts in our mouths many times as the vehicles laboured upwards and down in low-range diff-lock.

Down at the river we attracted a lot of Himba attention and were welcomed. There were children around who had never seen a vehicle in their lives, and possibly not white people either. We set up camp under shade trees on the river bank, and apart from keeping an eye on our three dogs so they did not get taken by crocodiles, we enjoyed three pleasant days in this wonderfully unspoilt part of the Kaokoveld. Of course, the news of two vehicles making it down – and out again – has already spread and there will be others who take on this challenge.

The Mad Macs came in two days after we dropped them upriver, all except Kaororua looking a bit worse for wear. After one of chef Sonia's splendid fire-cooked dinners – plus much beer and wine – the group had a comfortable night in CSN's good bedrolls, inside tents pitched on soft flat sand. They refilled their rucksacks with food and left at first light for the last two days of walking. We would meet them in the Marienfluss, having to drive round and doing 500 kilometres to their 50-kilometre walk.

When we drank a toast to the men for successfully completing the expedition, all raised their glasses to Garth who did the hike alone decades ago. The word Richmond used about their four-day experience was 'unrelenting', which, with his record, means it was a worthy test of the team's mettle.

Kaororua proved every bit as valuable as we hoped. The fact that the Mad Macs spoke no Himba/Herero and Kaororua spoke almost no English hardly hindered communication. Praise from Richmond was that Kaororua had an unerring eye for the safest route on every slope – and he never lost his cool.

The non-stop repartee of Chris and Garth MacIntyre, and their prank-playing, amazed Kaororua, even though he understood virtually nothing they said. He'd never known, he told us, grown men who joked and played the fool so much. In spite of this, his verdict after their week together was that they were all good men. The worst part for him was the food. Freeze-dried hiking fare in plastic packets needing to be reconstituted in water in a pot was not his idea of sustenance. Several times, when the others were lying exhausted in their sleeping bags at night, he'd hiked an extra few hours to the nearest Himba village – and back before morning – to get some real food: milk and meat.

As the group crossed the terrain our Van der Merwe would almost certainly have explored, we hoped that they would find some sign of his remains. A bleached bone or two, or a pair of old walking boots, cracked by the sun, still hanging on or near a sturdy stick, planted in the sand. But they saw nothing that gave any clue as to what happened to this other intrepid explorer of the Kaokoveld whose name was Van der Merwe.

NINE

Palm trees and the private lives of cattle

. . . the earth will heal
eventually
magnificently
when our species
is gone the way
of the last Redwood . . .
– Armand Garnet Ruffo's 'The Reckoning'

VISITORS TO THE KAOKOVELD often assume the cattle there have a hard life compared to those on farms with higher rainfall. They couldn't be more wrong.

Most Himba cattle have good lives, real lives, compared to what happens to hundreds of millions of animals raised for the beef we eat, with hormones and feedlots before that final cramming into death trucks destined for the abattoir. People who proclaim themselves anti-hunting who eat domestic meat need to visit their nearest abattoir and think deeply about the logic of their convictions. Large-scale livestock farming is a major driver of greenhouse gasses, requires 20 times more land per gramme of edible protein than high protein crops, consumes a tenth of the world's fresh water and causes large-scale deforestation, according to the US-based World Resources Institute. It is also just simply cruel. Spending time around Himba cattle, goats and sheep that live more or less naturally changes one's attitude towards so called domestic stock.

Older Himba men have such interest in and respect for their cattle that many are given names and some men even sing songs about their beloved cows, oxen and bulls. Given half a chance, men in the lineages I was living with were keen to talk about cattle for hours and I often longed to change the subject. I was finding the men boring!

Interestingly, a number of male researchers working with similar societies have complained about not getting much sense out of women whereas men, they claimed, made excellent informants. Anthropologist Paul Spencer's pioneering work, *The Samburu*, with the Samburu people in Kenya in the 1960s wrote famously about finding women 'quite ignorant of many aspects of the total society and usually unhelpful as informants'. He talked about women being less inquisitive than the men and slower to grasp situations. They found it 'harder to comprehend my remarks and questions . . . their demeanor was sometimes listless and frequently sour. They often lacked the general conviviality and warmth that typified the adult males...'

My experience was usually the opposite, as this 1987 quote from my field book shows: 'Now that I know Vengape and she knows me, I find her and the other women much more articulate than the men. Vengape is interested in everything; Rutako only talks about cattle.'

As I pointed out in my thesis, these two field views expose the bias in the researchers, one male and one female. Had I been a man, Rutako may have talked to me about other subjects, assuming there was anything else, apart from cattle, on his mind. It's not that Himba women weren't interested in and involved in the lives of the cattle; we, as women, just had many other things to talk about.

It's a Eurocentric misperception to associate only men with herding as in *he's a herder; she's just a housewife*. Himba men and women have different roles, both of which are critical to the herd's well-being and its survival at times. Men's work tends to be outside the homestead; women's mainly inside the *onganda* (homestead). And even in our post-feminist society, there is still a tendency to value work outside the home as more important than work done in a domestic context. Just ask any stay-at-home mother.

Apart from doing the milking, Himba women have allocative rights to milk and play a central role in the day-to-day management of the family herds, cattle as well as small stock. What this means, as in probably the majority of homes in the world, is that the wife or mother is in charge of food and broadly decides who gets to eat what.

A Himba woman milks into a wooden commiphora milk pail, which is identified with her husband or father – and till recently, used to be made by one of these male relatives. But she then transfers that milk into a tightly woven tall basket. These beautiful containers made by women from palm fronds are waterproof, with ochre and butter fat rubbed onto the outside. From the moment the milk is in her basket, it's hers. She would most likely not refuse her husband's visitors milk, but, as I was often told, her husband would have to ask her for it to be served.

The palm baskets served as an entry point for a lot of learning on different levels, including conservation, rural development, milk distribution and gender relations. They also showed me as an academic and later as a development worker/conservationist how easy it was to make assumptions that led in the wrong direction. Anyone trying to facilitate any kind of community action – in a city or village – could learn from our early mistakes in and around the small settlement of Puros.

I was one of the earliest people to promote Himba basket-making for sale. This started from 1986 onwards because women I became friendly with often asked me to bring them a blanket or some other item they needed from town. As a researcher on a small study grant I simply couldn't afford to buy too many such gifts, even though I was mindful that I owed my host community a lot – not least the material for my doctorate.

One day, widow Kwazerendu asked me to bring her a yellow plastic bucket, just like the one I used.

'Why', I asked, 'do you want an ugly plastic container when you own and can make beautiful woven baskets that are waterproof? Not only that, your baskets can be repaired whereas my cheap plastic bucket will break easily and need to be thrown away.'

Kwazerendu was truly surprised that I thought the palm-frond baskets were beautiful and more valuable than my bucket. We got into a lively discussion that morning with others joining in. I tried to explain that to me, and many people like me, something made by hand was more special than a mass-produced item. This meant I had to explain mass production – a place, a big building, where tens of thousands of plastic buckets are produced each month and sent to different shops all over the country to sell. No doubt a machine did most of the work, not people – that's why the buckets were all the same, cheap and from my perspective, ugly. We talked about how each basket in the homesteads was slightly different, according to the style a particular woman used in her weaving and how she chose to decorate it – some with a pattern in the weave itself; others with a few wire beards on a leather thong. Surely, I suggested, this means a basket is more valuable and more beautiful than what a machine makes – because it contains something of the person who wove it? The women got that – most of them derived pleasure from making baskets and agreed you could usually tell who had woven which basket because of its distinctive style.

But I could see some of the younger listeners, in particular Katondoihe, Vengape and Rutako's teenage son, didn't agree. He would find a factory where machines made buckets much more interesting, he said.

Here was a youth with a fascination for machinery of any kind and once he saw the engine of my vehicle, he was hooked. Often he asked me if he could open its bonnet and he spent literally hours examining what was in there. Once, after studying my car's innards, he looked up, eyes shining, and said with absolute reverence: 'One day, I hope I can just look at, just see with my own eyes, the man who made this car's engine.'

Well, it was a bit late to meet the inventors of the internal combustion engine but he did eventually learn to drive, and even got a driver's license. No mean feat when the entire learner's license manual needed to be memorised, and he had never seen most of the traffic signs that were in the book, nor been in a town bigger than Khorixas where he took his test. At one stage while working as a field officer for IRDNC, Katondoihe had a 4x4 vehicle assigned to him. He kept the car spotless and treated it with great respect – unlike some of the other young men who drove IRDNC cars over the years. Eventually Katondoihe returned to cattle herding, and regretfully handed back his vehicle to the NGO.

The basket vs bucket discussion led to the beginning of a small local craft industry in the Puros area among the seven lineages who were hosting me. It was Kata, who has a very good business sense, who challenged me to put my money where was mouth was: 'If these baskets are so valuable, take them with you to your town and see if you can get people there to give you the things we need that we cannot make.'

And so it began – women started weaving baskets specially for sale. Cash was not in widespread circulation yet so in the women's minds it was bartering. 'This basket is for sugar and tea, and this one is for a cooking pot.' There were no shops yet at Puros and the nearest little store at Sesfontein, 100 kilometres away, was more often closed and out of all stock than operating. As a good anthropologist, I refused to take people's own possessions – items that had not been made for the market. Over the next few years I recorded more than 500 sales to a Windhoek craft shop. I would then buy whatever had been ordered. It became quite time-consuming and there were times when I regretted what a comment about a yellow bucket had started. When the word went out that I was due to go to 'town' people would drop off a basket or two and ask very specifically for an item. Often food, but also household needs and goods intended for body decoration.

Himba women may not have been used to handling cash yet but they knew all about quality. 'This basket is for a blanket, a thick, warm one, not the thin kind that some shops sell in Opuwo,'

I was reminded after I made the mistake of bringing back a skimpy blanket. Once I bought a large packet of plastic beads, having been unable to get the glass beads that had been requested in return for a fine basket. I handed over the packet and watched the recipient, an older woman called Maipangwa, pour some of the beads into her hand. She put one between her teeth and bit it. Naturally, it broke. She spat it out. Wordlessly, she handed the packet back to me. The disdain on her face said it all. Not good enough; not what I ordered. Try again. It took a while, and required her to wait for me to go to Cape Town to my university for some or other reason, but I did eventually find her good-quality glass beads.

Inevitably, as the basket making increased, it crossed Garth and my minds, as Western conservationists, that we should check whether or not the palm tree resource was being sustainably used. Young pliable fronds were used for weaving and we'd noticed several of the palm trees close to Puros has died due to too many new fronds being broken off. By then I was wearing two hats – both a researcher and starting to do some community-based conservation work.

We were pretty sure we knew how to handle this problem and head it off before it became serious. We called a community meeting at Puros and explained the problem. People were defensive at first about their rights being taken away by 'nature conservation'. But soon the then headman Mateus Uararavi solved the problem by pointing out that in the old days people knew to use the palms sustainably, only taking a few young fronds per tree. And all that was needed was for the women to walk a bit further so as not to over-use nearer trees. No problem, he said, he would monitor the situation and ensure women did not kill the palms.

Problem solved we thought – and wasn't it great that a traditional way of sustainable utilisation had been revived. But trees continued to be killed.

We went back to the headman who called the women stupid and lazy. He blamed them for not listening to him and even deliberately killing some palms by taking all the fronds they could. So I found some of the older woman and asked what was going on – why were they not sticking to what had been agreed at the community meeting some months earlier? No one was very forthcoming but eventually I understood.

Our superficial solution – the headman would monitor palm use – had, in fact, altered this community's relationship with one of their natural resources and disrupted gender relations. The women felt their right to control and use cow milk – marked by the transfer of milk from the 'male' wooden pail to the 'female' palm basket – was under threat. If Mateus now controlled the palms, which traditionally had always been seen as the women's resource, next thing the men could be controlling the milk, taking away women's right to use and allocate milk as they wished. So the women had been challenging Mateus by deliberately over-using the trees.

The solution was simple once we understood how clumsily we'd blundered: We asked Mateus to back off and leave the palms to the women. We asked the women how they thought the palms could best be monitored. They agreed to take responsibility for this themselves, and thousands of baskets later, palm trees still thrive in the Hoarusib River.

The Himba saying that a lazy wife can ruin a rich family goes beyond women's essential tasks of producing and maintaining storage vessels for milk, fat and water. Apart from doing the milking, making the butterfat and allocating milk in the family, women are also in charge of the daily milking strategy: they decide which animals to milk and how much milk to take. A careless woman who takes too much or milks an animal too often can directly affect the condition and growth of calves. Women make such decisions based on input about quality of available grazing and its distance from water. These decisions draw on women's knowledge and experience in the same way that the more visible male task of selecting grazing areas draws on men's knowledge and experience. A woman has to balance the nutritional needs of her household with the needs of the calves – most take this in their stride, and still find time to talk about subjects beyond cattle.

However, as the months went by in various Himba camps, in spite of my bias that there's only so much to be said about cows,

I found myself noticing these creatures more. Not that I learnt all their names or sang songs to them, but I started admiring the beautiful sheen of a red and white cow's coat as she strolled past me. Or I might find myself examining – and really seeing – the intricate patterns of different coloured spots on an oxen's shoulders, as if someone had flicked wet paintbrushes over him. I especially liked those cattle with wide long horns and started listening to the noises a young group made as they played or mock fought or just jockeyed for a better position at water.

I'll confess that the odd cow or two even wandered through my dreams, meaning that these animals were starting to sink deep into my subconscious life. I was becoming interested in cattle's *umwelt*. This word, used by ethologists, means the animal's point of view – how an animal experiences its own subjective world – and was first used by German biologist Jakop von Uexkull in the early 1900s. And of course, once you glimpse another's point of view, it's much easier to understand and respect the Other.

One hot November day the peace of the *ozonganda* (homestead) at Puros was disrupted by the news that lions had killed a cow downriver. The cattle had been allowed to go out without a herder, as was becoming common these days. They'd wandered seven or eight kilometres down the Hoarusib River, staying in the river bed with its plentiful green sedges and herbs and shallow sweet spring water.

A group of men immediately set off with the youngster who'd found lions on a carcass, with the rest of the cattle scattered into the hills. He'd been sent to find the herd when they stayed out overnight. The men never saw the two lions who had been lying in the shade, having eaten their fill for the moment. No doubt they'd been lazily ignoring the jackals, vultures and crows that had honed in on their kill but they heard the men coming and slipped away into the rugged hills. It was left to the men to chase off the birds and the jackals. They retrieved what meat they could and hung the cow's head in a tree. In a few weeks it would be picked dry and only the skull and horns would remain to mark where she died.

The rest of the cattle were rounded up by the end of that day and moved to another grazing area, this time with some youths in attendance. Community game guards were asked to track where the lions went so that the herders could avoid losing more stock.

More than a month later, when it was certain that the lions had moved well away, cattle were allowed back into the Hoarusib River bed. I went with the young man and two youths who accompanied them. The only sign of the cow's demise was the nearly clean skull and horns still high in a tree on the river bank. The pieces of carcass that had not been taken away by the men had disappeared, cleaned up by scavengers. If one looked for it you could see a faint patch in the sand where blood and other fluids had seeped from the cow's carcass. But five weeks' worth of the prevailing south-west wind had erased all other tracks and traces of the kill.

The bull of the herd was the first to react. He went straight to the patch, sniffed it and pawed the sand with his front legs. Then he bellowed. Again and again his mournful call echoed in the river canyon. Was he remembering what had happened to one of his cows, something he might have seen, in reaction to traces of her smell in the sand, assuming such traces could last that long? What did his bellowing mean? We'll never know his *umwelt*, but it didn't seem too much of a stretch, standing in a remote dry river bed with a herd of cattle, to believe that the bull was mourning. At any rate, he was marking the event by his reaction.

But it wasn't over. He moved on, and one cow after another, not every animal but every second or third, did the same as the bull. They pawed the ground and then mooed loudly. With the echo in the canyon it sounded as if there was a response from a ghostly cow . . .

I was stunned. I'd heard about elephants being aware of the death of one of their number. But cattle? These slow, dim, bovine creatures? The youngsters displayed a certain playfulness but once adult, let's face it, cattle did not seem to have much going between their horns. Or so I had thought, as much as I was growing to like them.

The behaviour we witnessed fulfilled at least two parts of episodic memory – the what and the where, if not the when.

Episodic memory was long held as exclusively human until quite recently when experimentation in animal cognition, coupled with field observations of non-captive members of a species, levelled the playing field to suit the animal's *umwelt* and physiology. Not surprisingly to many ordinary people who live closely with dogs, cats, horses and other non-human animals, the work of renowned primatologist Frans de Waal and scores of other animal cognition researchers has shown how much we have underestimated the extent of animal intelligence. And not just with non-human primates; many species – including rats and birds – have eroded humanity's pedestal.

I asked the others if they'd ever seen such a display before. They'd heard of this happening from their elders and unlike me, they were not surprised at the display we'd just seen.

Living with cattle and the behaviour of that herd in the Hoarusib River changed my views. While I have been known to eat beef occasionally since then, you won't find me *buying* beef unless it is clearly free-range. Travelling a lot and working in the field means one does not always have a choice in terms of food, and must eat what's available – or go hungry. But wherever possible I'll choose wild game knowing that it is highly likely the animal lived naturally and then died quickly with a bullet in the brain.

Having seen cattle have an overt response to the death of one of them, the thought of for example, keeping cattle crammed in feedlots to fatten them before they are sold for meat, is unacceptable, to mention just one aspect of the mass meat industry. So too I hate travelling behind a cattle truck, seeing terrified animals jammed into too little space and hurtling along a road to the abattoir. What happens once they are there clearly reveals how far humans have strayed from decency and respect for other creatures. If our humanity was ever to be measured by the way we treat other species and those weaker than ourselves, we surely deserve re-classifying as inhumanity.

Some young Himba people are by no means exempt from this lack of compassion for another species, of course. Nowadays domestic stock is yelled at, hit with sticks and stones are thrown at them. The old language of clicking, stamping, hissing, calling and snapping fingers with which the past herders communicated with their herds has all but died out with the elders who practised it. Shorty once played a joke on a herder we came across fast asleep under a tree while his cattle ranged around, grazing. Shorty whistled and stamped – as I recall it – and within seconds had the herd paying attention. Then, using hand, body and voice signals, he sent them on their way back to the homestead where they overnighted, a few kilometres away. When all were out of sight, he casually woke the sleeping man who was startled – and rather worried – to see that not a single one of his cows was in sight.

I've seen modern Himba youth botching the traditional ceremony of wrestling an ox to the ground and quickly suffocating it to death. Excited and laughing, they turn what should be a short, dignified display into a gross and cruel parody of an old custom, with the frightened animal being chased around and allowed to struggle to its feet again and again after being thrown onto its back and half suffocated. These school-going boys lack both the skill and strength of their elders.

But it's more than that. On one such occasion at Onyuva, an older man intervened. He stalked over and deftly put his knee, and full body weight, on the struggling, upturned animal's wind pipe, instructing the boys to hold its horns. In a minute it was over. He berated the youths for their ineptness, but most of all, for their lack of respect.

Not long ago, I behaved badly outside Maerua Mall in Windhoek where a cattle truck had remained parked in the sun for some hours. One of the animals was twisted and crushed under others at the back, calling out in distress from time to time. After a reasonable discussion with the driver failed, I threatened him with the police. When he shut his window in my face, I lost my temper and banged on it with my fist, attracting a small audience, but for the wrong reasons. Most people probably thought I was on an illegal substance.

I wish I'd been more effective. The cattle crammed into the back of the large truck continued to stand in the boiling summer sun for the rest of the morning; the injured animal eventually fell silent. As their destination was the abattoir, the men in the truck – and most of those who had watched my temper tantrum – could not understand what my problem was.

As the Himba elder said, it's our lack of respect.

TEN

A story to dine out on

SHORTLY AFTER INDEPENDENCE in 1990, the first British high commissioner to Namibia, Sir Francis Richards (although he had not yet been knighted) decided to give Garth and me a new Land Rover for our community-based conservation work. It was our project's first new vehicle and sorely needed. My Toyota Hilux truck was aging and Garth's ancient Series 3 Land Rover had been round the clock a few times. The new vehicle was also where the name of our nascent NGO came from.

Francis pointed out the British government could hardly give a vehicle to Garth and Margie, as much as he admired our work. So he needed something a bit more ... formal. Thinking on my feet, and horrified at the thought there could be a hitch, I described what we did – integrating rural development with nature conservation – hoping that we could develop a clever name from there. But the high commissioner was a busy man. 'Right, we'll call it Integrated Rural Development and Nature Conservation,' he said, scribbling something down in a book.

And so in passing, the uncharismatic name was born. IRDNC for short. Or, as some Namibians who find the name too cumbersome to remember, call it, IR what and what.

Garth and I had joined forces by 1987, four years after he'd

pioneered community-based conservation with the community
game guard network which by then had already brought illegal
hunting under control, and two years after my Himba study
had started. I was still trying to complete my research but the
conservation work was fast becoming my priority – which
probably explains why I took eight years to complete my PhD
thesis. Directly involving local people in conservation as practised
on the land they communally farmed and finding ways for them
to benefit from living with wildlife made such sense. If thriving
wildlife could be linked to improved quality of human life, we were
making sure that conservation would become sustainable in this
young African country. We had resisted becoming an organisation
– our focus was the work in the field, not running an institution.
Being a project and then a nameless non-government entity was
enough for both Garth and me who are hippies at heart whose
values were honed in the '60s. But there comes a time when getting
the work done requires more than passion and commitment, and
more than four people, the two of us and our two local assistants,
as we were in those earliest days.

We couldn't cope with the workload and we were missing
opportunities to increase community conservation's impact. This
meant raising more funds and employing more people. It also
meant more structure than Garth and me working out game guard
salaries on the kitchen table at our camp Wereldsend, with Garth
recalling a loan or salary advance he'd given someone as I put
money in an envelope.

'We need to write this stuff down,' I'd say, 'What if you got
flattened by a rhino?' Garth would grin, and recall another loan.

I hated being the one calling for bureaucracy but we'd reached
the stage where there was no choice if we were to have real influence
on changing the colonial way conservation was still being practised.

We'd already got a small environmental awareness project
going with local schools run for its first years by a young South
African man Charles Cadman, with Endangered Wildlife Trust and
Rossing Foundation support. But there was much else to do.

There have been moments at strategic planning events over the years when we discussed changing IRDNC's name to something more memorable – but in the end we and those who work for the NGO have stuck with our tongue-twister. The name's non-slickness has itself become a symbol of IRDNC's down to earth, field-based culture. And as clumsy as the name is, IRDNC and its staff went on to break paradigms and do cutting edge work. By 2019, the organisation, its staff and some of the communities we work with had been recognised internationally and locally with more than 20 conservation awards.

Back in 1990, gratefully we accepted the shiny new Land Rover at a ceremony hosted by Swapo's first Minister of Environment and Tourism, Mr Nico Bessinger. Nico was a visionary in his own way. An architect who had studied, among other countries, in the USA, he chose to remain in Namibia during the struggle years, as a member of Swapo's internal wing. As such he was a target for the South West African security police.

He and his family were harassed, his phones were tapped and several times he was detained – without charges or a trial. One such detention was particularly harrowing, amounting to torture. He was held for days in a small tin shed at some unknown place a few hours' drive from Windhoek. It was summer and temperatures were in the upper 30s. Inside the shed with its tin roof and tin walls temperatures rose into the 40s. Nico was denied water and left alone. He shouted and banged on the walls to no avail. He eventually passed out, he told me, not knowing if he had been abandoned to die. On the second day, a tin mug of water and a plate of food was pushed into the shed. On day three his interrogation began. Nico attributed some of his subsequent ill health to that week of severe dehydration as well as physical and psychological stress.

One of his earliest actions after his appointment to the Environment portfolio was to send his deputy minister Ben Ulenga, who had spent several years on Robben Island after being captured in the north of Namibia, to do some research into how nature conservation was being practised in communal areas. We had three projects – the re-started community game guard network which involved ration and pay deliveries each month and collection of reports; and after 1987 the Puros project; and the small environmental awareness project. The Puros project was the first time a Namibian community had earned a direct income from tourism. Garth had been taking Endangered Wildlife Trust members on safari a few times a year; they overnighted in Puros and we then paid a small levy per guest to Puros – for use of their land and for conserving their wildlife. The amount was small but it made a difference. It also added a bit of mutual dignity to the interaction between tourists and community members – all lineages received their share of the levy whether they met the guests or not. With tourism slowly starting after independence we hoped other operators would follow our lead. Most did not at that stage.

We got a message that the new deputy minister was to call in at Wereldsend. He arrived mid-afternoon and stayed a few hours. We drank tea and talked about politics and conservation. Our enthusiasm for community-based conservation poured out that afternoon and it seemed that the idealism of early Swapo resonated with this approach. Ben left us promising to brief his minister.

Life continued as normal for some months; nothing changed on the ground because the same people were running nature conservation. Then we received a radio call at Wereldsend. Minister Bessinger wanted to see us in Windhoek. A time and date was set. Garth and I looked at one another – we were used to being in conflict with conservation officials and other authorities by now. A senior white official based in Opuwo had tried to stop the Puros project, for example. When I challenged him, pointing out there were no legal grounds to stop a voluntary payment to a community, he backed down. But he complained that we were corrupting the Himba: 'You used to be able to buy a basket or some jewellery from them for a packet of biscuits. Now they want money! You're spoiling these people with this money story.'

Decades later, community conservation in Namibia was to face similar challenges from certain members of a black elite who wanted to be the beneficiaries of tourism concessions – the fruits of community conservation – rather than the rural Namibians who managed the increasing wildlife through their conservancies. And every misstep in using conservancy funds – and naturally there have been plenty as these rural institutions learn how to run what are in effect communally owned businesses – was pounced on by a few as evidence that conservancies were not cutting it. The irony seems to have been missed – that such officials often came from government ministries that were mis-managing their own budgets – taxpayer's money. But those challenges lay ahead...

So in 1990 we wondered, when we were summonsed to the minister's office, whether we were not already in trouble with the new conservation authorities. In fact, what Nico wanted was to talk to us about community-based natural resource management. It made perfect sense to him, and he told us that Namibian conservation legislation would be changed to support and accommodate this approach. He wanted to tell us he knew we'd had problems with the previous regime, but that from now on, he wanted us to work together – with him and his team. Community-based conservation would be mainstreamed on communal land, learning from our modest projects that were undoubtedly the most democratic, African and sustainable way to do conservation.

We left his office floating on air. Here was an opportunity of a lifetime to grow a small local success story to scale and have a real impact across Namibia, and hopefully further.

Of course, realistically it was to be years – 1998 in fact – before new legislation was passed. That same year the first four communal area conservancies were registered. There were many steps along the way, some of which we were involved in, such as the remarkable consultative process with communal area dwellers who still lived with wildlife. We did the social components of socio-ecological surveys in West Caprivi, East Bushmanland, Damaraland, East Caprivi and the Kuiseb River area with MET's Brian Jones.

An early event was a Windhoek workshop called by the new minister for his staff. He required representatives of every section – from labourers to senior wardens and directors. To our surprise, he also invited Garth and me to attend this several-day-long externally facilitated meeting. We turned up on the first morning to discover that we were the only delegates who were not government staff. When the minister greeted us, I asked him how he intended to introduce us. He smiled and said don't worry, it'll all work out. He left us to endure many puzzled – and not a few hostile – glances as people drank tea and coffee before the meeting started. Over the years we'd been called communists and Swapo supporters by some of the white conservation officials – presumably because we saw black communities as part of the solution to conservation in Africa, not as the problem.

To my discomfort the minister said nothing at all about us at the meeting and people were left to speculate. He told the 80 or so people there – who'd come in from their stations all over the country – that the plan was simply to make a start on rebuilding the various directorates of conservation into a better and stronger conservation ministry.

For the next two days, he said, there was no rank and people should speak their minds. He wanted and expected everyone to make a contribution. White nature conservators, many of them men who'd expected to be hearing that they were to lose their jobs to black people, looked at one another. The fear in the hall may have eased slightly but the suspicion and insecurity were tangible.

The workshop began with skilled South African facilitators taking us through a strengths and weaknesses, opportunities and threats process – the well-known SWOT process. For most, it was new and refreshing to be asked to look inwards at what they thought was right and wrong with their directorates; they were more used to an authoritarian, hierarchical style of leadership where junior staff did not question their bosses.

This way of running a government department reflected the way most of the staff had been educated at schools in South Africa and Namibia called Christian National Education, which did not promote free thinking, although there were always notable exceptions. How much has changed in post-colonial Namibia where party loyalty is often put above productivity or qualifications to do the job? Hopefully, we are close to a new era when our born-frees will insist – with their votes – on leadership that puts people and the country, and not parties, first.

In Windhoek, because of the size of the group of conservation staff the SWOT process was cumbersome. Late on the first morning, Dr Chris Brown, the government ornithologist, stood up. He was a leading member of the group we called the Young Turks because of their progressive, non-racist thinking. Frustration was etched on his face. Alongside him sat another prominent Young Turk, Brian Jones, a journalist of great integrity, who had joined conservation's information service.

We knew Brian understood and supported community-based conservation; I was less sure of Chris – an impatient, articulate and fiercely intelligent man who believed he knew best – and annoyingly, he was often right! Later these two were to become what we and others called the dream team – because of their advanced conservation thinking. The name didn't do them justice as they were extremely capable of turning many of their dreams into reality. Few conservation officials had more of an impact in the early years than Chris and Brian.

But this was before they started and ran the Directorate of Environmental Affairs, a new planning section within the government conservation ministry. On that morning in Windhoek, Chris became a spokesman for the progressive group who wanted to move the meeting on – to where real planning for the future of conservation in Namibia could start.

'Mr Minister,' he said. 'Some of us have put our jobs on the line because we have challenged some of our seniors' backward thinking.' He went on to say that it was obvious to some in the room, including the minister, where the new ministry should be aiming. Was this laborious, time-consuming process really necessary? Shouldn't energy go into planning for the future rather than navel-gazing? As I understood it, a subtext was to question whether some of the extreme right wingers – real racists – in the room deserved to have their views taken into account. I could relate to that.

Nico stood up. 'Very well,' he said. 'I will step back into my leadership role to reply to Dr Brown. But if the majority here disagree with what I am to say, we go with the majority.'

Nico went on to make one of the most powerful reconciliation speeches I have ever heard. He quietly reminded the audience that he was a black man in Namibia who could not settle with apartheid. Accordingly, he chose to join Swapo but remained inside the country during the struggle. As such he and his family were hounded by the establishment. Many times over the years he was detained without trial. His wife and children and his employers did not know where he was. He was held in solitary confinement, intimidated and threatened. He chose not to go into details but left us in no doubt he and his family had suffered.

Now, he said, we are a free Namibia and we are busy writing a new constitution. We have embraced reconciliation as a national policy.

'I walk down the street and pass the man who was one of those who interrogated me; I sit in a room contributing to the new constitution and some of those who ordered my arrests, who persecuted me and my family, are there at the table.'

Nico paused and let this sink in.

'There are two choices. We could punish these people and do to them what they did to us. Or we can work towards writing the best damned constitution in Africa so that what happened to me and other black Namibians could never happen again in Namibia.'

If the Young Turks in this room wanted blood on the walls, they should go ahead and throw out this SWOT process, he continued. 'Or everyone here could go on working together today to transform what exists now into the best damned conservation and tourism ministry in Africa!'

He sat down. There was a long silence. I think it was Chris and Brian who started the clapping. But within seconds the entire hall was on its feet and giving Nico Bessinger thunderous applause. In that moment a new Ministry of Environment and Tourism was born.

As this is not a fairy tale, it would take many years for real transformation to happen. Apartheid policies had ensured that black people had been kept out of the professional conservator ranks so when black empowerment policies started being applied, very inexperienced staff took over. The standard of much of the work dropped accordingly, but a flame that was fanned at independence and which steadily strengthens each year is community-based conservation. Namibia has received many accolades for its innovative policies in this regard – for much of this we have the late Nico Bessinger to thank. Community-based conservation – like the Ministry of Environment and Tourism – is still a work in progress but it remains ahead of most of the rest of Africa.

The day after the car handing-over ceremony, Garth and I set off from Windhoek for our base camp in the north-west. Travelling with us was a British couple, Tim and Rosie Holmes. They had applied to lead our environmental awareness project, after our first EA officer, Charles Cadman finished his year at Wereldsend. We'd invited the Holmes to spend a week with us, looking at the job and the conditions, before a mutual decision about whether or not they joined our team.

Apart from the remoteness of the area, and our particular approach to environmental awareness (that we were not 'educating' anyone, that the local people had as much to teach us about their environment as we had to teach them), the living conditions were quite basic. They'd have to live in a tent until they could build themselves a simple reed and Hessian house and working area.

Then, as now, Garth believes people should build their own home if they want to live and work in the field. This combination of designing a living and working space, building it with a team of local workers, and having to handle the logistics of making it all happen (buying reeds locally, collecting stones, acquiring all you need in terms of poles, Hessian, cement, nails etc. from town, hundreds of kilometres away) is a good introductory test, he says. You have to be creative, practical, able to motivate and work well with people. And have a good plan in advance which you will need to change and adapt several times before the house is complete. All these are useful attributes for a field worker.

It was April and the height of the late rainy season. Although hot and relatively humid, the sun was shining brightly in a cloudless sky as we turned west onto our usual shortcut 40 kilometres before Khorixas, taking the Twyfelfontein Road to our camp. Just two hours to go. As we sped along in our new truck, Rosie, Garth and me in the cab, Tim on the back amidst our luggage and field supplies, we had no idea that the Holmes' mettle would be tested sooner than we thought.

Seven kilometres along the shortcut, the track crosses the wide bed of the Guantagab River. It is a tricky crossing when wet and the Holmes were surprised, given the clear skies, to see that this river was running sluggishly with muddy brown water. We explained that this is a characteristic of the north-west; rivers are dry for all but a few hours or at most days in a year. Some have such big catchment areas that it's easy not to know it has rained a hundred or more kilometres upriver. So you can be taken by surprise when a river suddenly comes down in flood.

We stopped on the bank and Garth waded into the water to check its depth and the condition of the track underfoot. There was some hard ground and he chose his route accordingly.

'It's fine – let's go,' he said.

Just then another vehicle joined us – a German-speaking supermarket owner from Swakopmund and his elderly father with a truckload of supplies for Palmwag Lodge. The driver was nervous of the water and we promised to wait till he was safely across.

'Lock the wheels in 4x4 and just follow the same route we take,' we told him as we all climbed into our Land Rover and safely crossed the water. We stopped on the other bank and watched the other vehicle, also a Land Rover, slowly enter the river bed. To our consternation, the driver did not follow our route but chose his own. In seconds he was stuck in deep mud.

We all waded to the truck which was well and truly mired up to its sump. Our only option was for us to reverse back into the water and attempt to tow it out. But our tow rope was too short to reach without putting our vehicle in serious danger of getting stuck as well. Garth and I knew that there was a chance of the river coming down again, and that what we had driven though was yesterday's flood. So getting the vehicle out was a priority.

Some local people joined us and suggested using some fencing wire from a nearby fence, which was a relic of the pre-Odendaal Commission days when Damaraland was briefly farmed by white Second World War veterans. A long length of wire was cut and a triple strand used to attach the two vehicles. Garth climbed back into his vehicle, which was standing in ankle deep water and mud, and started the engine.

Then a cry went up from the people on the bank: the river was coming down again. A calf-high foaming brown wall of water moved inexorably towards the vehicles. Behind it was more water. Garth's vehicle strained forward and the wire pulled taut. Again and again he tried to pull the other Land Rover but it was too late. Already the water was at the bottom of his door and rising. Garth switched off his engine and climbed out – I assumed he was going to disconnect the wire so he could get his vehicle out of the river. But he waded quickly through the rising water to the other Land Rover, which was already submerged to mid-door level.

Of course – the old man! The rest of us, including the man's son, had forgotten about him still sitting in the stuck vehicle. Garth struggled around the car to open the door that was downstream. He helped the old man out. The volume of water now gushing down the river was such that he had to drag him along.

Tall Garth had been knee deep when he went to the vehicle; on his return, a minute later, he was thigh deep, and the river was still rising. Tim waded in to help half-carry, half-drag the old man to safety. Then we set about cutting the tow wire and trying to get some of our valuables out of our truck before it was too late. It was already too late for the other vehicle whose bonnet was under water. Tim, Rosie, Garth and I formed a crocodile and passed items from person to person: my laptop, the Holmes luggage, Garth's cameras, our food trunk, some shopping and our bags made it to the bank before the water rose too high to continue. We struggled to the bank in water now nearly waist deep, abandoning what was left in the truck to the flood. I suddenly realised Garth was not with us: there he sat on the bonnet.

'Come to the bank; it's no good,' I yelled. I doubt he heard me over the tumult of a desert river in full flood but my body language said it all. He shook his head. Garth was staying with his new Land Rover.

The sun had already set and as the light faded we saw Garth move from the submerged bonnet onto the roof of the truck. I was terrified the river would overturn the vehicle: he could get washed away and drown. Huge branches of trees and other debris in the fast-flowing water would make it virtually impossible to swim. I found a flashlight in my luggage and focused the beam on our vehicle just 60 metres away. It still stood on all four wheels and I could make out a lanky, hunched figure on the roof. As we watched, a match flared and I realised, with a sob of laughter, he had lit his pipe.

I stayed on the bank pointing the torch across the water, feeling that the sight of a light would keep his spirits up. Of course, it did no such thing. Being a practical man, he wondered why I was wasting the batteries.

My spirits were kept up by Tim and Rosie: Their under-stated British humour made me laugh often in the tense hour it took for the ferocious flood to smash its way past us on that dark night. They passed their first test with flying colours – grace and humour under pressure.

As soon as the water started dropping, Tim and I waded to Garth who was already knee deep in water, inspecting the inside of the vehicle. Wordlessly, in torchlight, we looked at the mud and debris which filled the cab – literally – to the dashboard. Garth opened the bonnet: mud covered everything; most of the engine was no longer visible.

'Hope there's a good car valet service in the neighbourhood,' quipped Rosie who'd joined us. We laughed but felt sick as we looked over the once shiny new vehicle.

'At least it stayed on its wheels,' said Garth, who had opened the windows deliberately so that water could flow through and not turn the truck over. The other Land Rover had not fared so well; half submerged in mud, it lay on its side where it had been washed 100 metres downriver.

I peered into the back of our truck and remembered that safely underneath the sodden bedrolls we'd packed my four boxes of archaeological remains – crammed with carefully marked paper packets containing plant and fauna fragments from a dig I'd done for my research up north. The samples were awaiting analysis by a colleague at Cape Town University and because my permit to temporarily export the material was taking longer to come though than expected, I had brought the boxes back to camp. Now they were a soggy mess of disintegrated paper and cardboard.

The area thronged with local people, busily retrieving all that had washed out of the Swakopmund trader's truck. Supplies included bottles of wine, hundreds of those small 250 ml bottles. One young man staggered out of the mud, moving strangely. The fingers of both hands were splayed: a little bottle jammed between each finger. More bottles were clasped under each arm and his T shirt, tied into a knot, bulged as though he was pregnant. Even his jeans pockets, back and front, were filled with small bottles. We couldn't help laughing as he disappeared into the dark.

Some older local people and children were, however, stacking the muddy, wet goods in a pile on the river bank. Dozens of foam pillows had been recovered. Rather bizarrely, a little hill of these white pillows – still dry inside their sealed plastic bag – was growing on the bank.

The Swakopmund son and father were in shock, and the older man's pre-occupation was finding a dry enough cigarette to smoke. We found the head of the household who lived on the nearest farm and gratefully accepted his offer to put people up for the night. We decided the two Germans and Tim and Rosie should go to the farm but that Garth and I would camp on the bank, looking after our piles of belongings. The farm, about 500 metres away, was too far to carry everything in the dark. The farmer also told us that there was a shop about five kilometres away that had a telephone that used to work.

Full of adrenaline and too miserable about the new Land Rover to relax, Garth and I set off along the dirt track in the dark for the Luck store. We found the little collection of ramshackle buildings in darkness – it was after 9 pm now. But barking dogs woke everyone anyway and we were invited in by the elderly Damara woman who ran the shop. She heard our story and commiserated, and insisted on fetching us two tepid cans of Coke from her store. She waved away our money. By candle light she indicated the telephone, standing on a box in a corner. It was obvious it had not been used for a long time; it was stone dead. We drank our Cokes, thanked the old woman and tramped wearily back to the river.

To add to our woes, it started to rain, a light patter just enough to make one uncomfortably wet but not enough to wash off the mud that covered us. We'd covered our luggage with a ground sail and now we made a place for ourselves underneath it as well. Our bedrolls were wet through so we used some of the rescued pillows to make a nest.

In an attempt to cheer me, Garth offered to fetch a few little bottles from the pile that lay nearby. He knew how much I love wine. But, like Garth, I was too dejected to eat or drink anything except some water from a recovered bottle. It was hot and uncomfortable under the heavy sail but at least it kept the irritating patter of rain off us. We slept a bit, talked glumly, dozed and talked some more, constantly re-organising our bed of pillows. We left the plastic on so as not to get them dirty but this made them uncomfortably sticky to lie on.

Neither of us could believe what had just happened. Our first new vehicle and we drown it with 400 kilometres on the clock! The experience was indeed a low point. We both knew we would eventually get the vehicle back on the road and life would move on. Yet, all night we were as mired in melancholy as were the vehicles in mud.

As always happens when one has a bad night, deep sleep finally buries you just before it's time to get up. Tim's voice, talking to Garth, woke me with a start and a heavy heart. The new day had arrived and we faced some serious challenges in this remote part of the world. We decided Garth would walk the seven kilometres back to the main road between Khorixas and Uis, while the rest of us waited with the vehicles, scooping mud out of the cabin and from under the bonnet. We could expect a few cars a day at best along the main road. And with rivers having come down, it was unlikely there would be any traffic at all on the track we were on.

Just after 6 am Garth strode off. He walked and jogged, expecting to have to spend a few hours on the side of the road waiting for a vehicle to give him a lift either the 40 kilometres to Khorixas or to Uis, which was about 90 kilometres in the other direction. His plans from there would depend on where he found himself. Somehow, he had to arrange to get the two vehicles out of the river as quickly as possible. Our base camp was about 120 kilometres to the west but we only had short-wave two-way radio for communication; it was unlikely he would be able to raise anyone at camp when he reached a telephone or radio. Our standby time was 8 am in the morning and he would almost certainly miss it.

As Garth approached the main road, he heard the sound of a heavy vehicle and he sprinted the last few hundred metres. Amazingly, a Department of Water Affairs truck was passing. Not only did they stop when a tall, bearded muddy man waved them down, but they also had a winch on the back of their heavy duty truck.

A few hours later, both vehicles had been dragged out of the river bed and stood forlornly on the bank, looking derelict under the mud that clung to every part of them. The Water Affairs men agreed to tow one of the vehicles to Uis where they were going, and the Swakopmund Land Rover disappeared down the road, with father and son, plus Garth who decided to take the lift to Uis to seek help for our vehicle.

I missed all this because in another remarkably lucky event, a vehicle had arrived from the west, soon after Garth had left for the main road. The two Herero-speaking men who worked for Rossing Foundation had spent the night with relatives on a local farm. Although they were en route to Khorixas, they immediately offered to turn round and drive me to our base camp. I grabbed the opportunity and jumped in the truck with the two strangers, leaving Tim and Rosie sitting in the sun, eating cereal from tin mugs. We managed to get through the Upper Huab although it too had flowed in the night and within three hours I was at Wereldsend. The men accepted a jerry can of fuel and went on their way. Later, I realised I'd left my jacket in their car and mentally wrote it off, but weeks later, it was returned to me.

People from our camp, including Matthew Rice, a young British man who was to become our first coordinator for our Caprivi programme – and later, a significant international figure in community conservation – drove immediately to the stranded vehicle. As soon as the half shafts had been disconnected so that mud and silt could not get into any moving parts, the Land Rover was towed to the nearest agent in Walvis Bay about 350 kilometres away. They picked up Garth in Uis on the way, and late the next night, Garth, Tim and Rosie finally arrived at Wereldsend with everything they'd been able to salvage.

Garth had phoned the British high commissioner from Uis and explained what had happened. Totally in character, Sir Francis did not bat an eyelid. He listened to the sad tale and remarked cheerfully, 'Well that's a story we'll dine out on for some time to come!'

Garth also phoned the insurance company – a local Windhoek agent who had been persuaded to cover the new Land Rover free for a year as his contribution to conservation. He received the news with less equanimity. Later he must have seen the funny side as he wrote up the incident rather humorously in an insurance industry magazine. It was a long time before we saw any humour in the situation.

The new Land Rover was eventually cleaned up and it did 15 years' service. Tim and Rosie got the job and spend a productive five years with us, before going back to the UK, then on to Australia and New Zealand. We continued to enjoy their humour. The trader from Swakopmund later thanked us for attempting to rescue his vehicle, but he made no reference to the fact that his father would probably have drowned if Garth had not remembered him just in time. As is his way, Garth modestly down-played my version of the story – that he had saved the old man's life.

In time, the story become part of our local history. But another far more tragic event about that river crossing lies further back in time. The next time we passed, we stopped at the farm to thank the family who had given us help and hospitality. While we drank tea, an old grandmother told us the river had claimed much more than vehicles. Four children were swept to their deaths when the river suddenly flooded about 30 years before. It had risen as quickly and as unexpectedly as it had for us. Ever since, she had avoided that river crossing when the river flowed because the sadness returned, like a low mist, she told us.

I recalled the deep wretchedness that overcame us that night and I wondered if somehow, as we lay on the banks of the Guantagab, wet, muddy and miserable, we were enveloped in sorrow from the past.

ELEVEN

High noon in Bushmanland

The more participatory the process, the stronger the facilitator needs to be – Lessons from the Field

IT'S NOT OFTEN THAT an opportunity arises to help undo racially discriminatory laws in a newly independent African country. So Garth and I did not hesitate to accept a request to do the community consultation (pro bono in the absence of a budget for consultants) in a series of socio-ecological surveys to be undertaken by the new conservation ministry after independence. These surveys in communal areas of Namibia where people still lived with wildlife aimed to inform new conservation policy and legislation. This process would eventually legally entrench community-based conservation, giving communal farmers equivalent rights over their wildlife as commercial farmers had enjoyed since the 1970s.

Before independence Garth and I were not only viewed as politically dangerous by some in the South West African regime, but were also regarded as the lunatic fringe by many orthodox conservationists. Today it seems remarkable that this community-based conservation philosophy could have been regarded as subversive. But in 1989, just before independence, even though Swapo had won the elections and there was already a new environment minister, the old guard were still very much in control. Thus the two Young Turks who wanted to change how conservation was practised in Namibia, Brian Jones and Dr Chris Brown, came down to Swakopmund in mufti to see us to discuss their brainchild – a socio-ecological survey in the West Caprivi Game park (now Bwabwata National Park) where about 7 000 San people lived.

If that survey went well, the plan was to do similar consultative processes in all the communal areas where wildlife survived. However, there was not much wildlife left in most such areas. An exception was the Kaokoveld where community conservation had been practised since the early 1980s and where wildlife was recovering well. In Caprivi, now the Zambezi Region, where IRDNC had started working in 1990, only remnant numbers of most species remained, and some – rhino and giraffe – had already disappeared. East Caprivi was worse off than West Caprivi Game Reserve where the Khoe and Vasekele San/Bushman people co-existed well with wild animals. East Bushmanland, home to Ju/'hoan San people, also still had some wildlife.

Working closely with local people and talking about empowerment of black communities in the political climate of the '80s had not endeared us to the colonial authorities and it was exhilarating to feel that at last our approach to conservation and development was coming out of the cold.

We made plans with Brian and Chris and yet again, I put my PhD Himba research on hold for a community-based conservation priority. I would have to explain this to the University of Cape Town's PhD committee and ask for an extension for another year... or two.

The two-week West Caprivi survey went well and taught us many lessons about the process. Based on the survey's results, a roadmap for the development of the reserve – with the plan to re-proclaim the area as the Bwabwata National Park – was eventually produced by the new Directorate of Environmental Affairs which had been created within the Ministry of Environment and Tourism. Importantly, the roadmap formally recognised that the San communities in West Caprivi had rights, even though they lived inside a game reserve. It acknowledged that they were the main reason there was still wildlife in the area and that they needed to benefit from it, especially as living in a reserve or park limited many other economic activities open to other Namibians. MET also undertook to ensure that people from other regions would not be allowed to come into the park with cattle.

Many twists and turns altered this plan in subsequent years (and continue to as I write these words) but, although the core vision remains true, new players in MET have needed to be reminded of it from time to time. Hundreds of people from across the Okavango River – and their cattle herds - have moved into the park and now dominate what is called the multiple-use area.

In the years following the 1990 survey, IRDNC assisted the people living inside the park to form the Kyaramacan Residents' Association, which later became a trust. The area's national park status precluded the formation of a communal conservancy as could be formed, since the 1998 enabling legislation, by people who lived on communal lands. Now that there was a representative community structure in the park MET was persuaded to allocate 50 per cent of trophy hunting fees to Kyaramacan. Many of us felt the trust should get 100 per cent but it was a start.

So the KA started receiving income from wildlife – and by 2018, the amount was several million Namibian dollars a year. But this lay in the future, as did the 2017 occupation of the park by the Namibian Defence Force, called in to tackle rising trans-boundary elephant poaching.

Back in 1990 Dr Megan Biesele, an American anthropologist, then director of the Nyae Nyae Foundation, which worked with the San communities of East Bushmanland, had joined our West Caprivi survey for a few days. She urged the new ministry to conduct a similar process in East Bushmanland where relations between the people and government conservation staff were poor. She was enthusiastic about the community-based natural resource management work we'd been pioneering and was sure a similar approach in her area could turn around a negative situation.

Thus in 1991, we found ourselves in East Bushmanland –

today the Nyae Nyae Conservancy. There were about 25 people on this survey, including some very senior conservation officials from Windhoek whose role was to oversee the whole process. In fact, their presence was a bit of a triumph for Chris and Brian as it meant that when the negotiations started at the end of the survey, we'd have some government decision-makers present.

Our core 'community' team was Brian, Garth and me, with Megan advising and translating. Applying a lesson we'd learnt from West Caprivi, we'd invited the recognised leadership of the San communities with whom we were consulting and negotiating, to join us for the entire survey, including at least two of them at all meetings. The idea of representational leadership was not something that most San communities were comfortable with in those days but thanks to the Nyae Nyae Foundation's work, a leadership group had already emerged.

With Megan, who speaks excellent Ju/'hoan, we started by sitting down with the five senior men who represented the people. By listening to them and forming a joint plan for the survey, we cut out many problems we would have encountered had we done it alone. We also stacked the odds in favour of constructive outcomes. If the San leadership co-owned the survey process with us, they would also be committed to positive results coming out of our 10 days of mutual hard work.

Brian, Garth and I had no doubt we had the hardest role – an average of two community meetings every day with large groups of people who despised most conservation workers, having experienced what they saw as arrogance and indifference from some such people. The others on the survey were doing natural resource inventories: wildlife numbers and species, insects, birds, trees and so on. Sounded like fun to us, to drive around in a 4x4 with your binoculars, viewing game, putting up nets to catch a few insects, making a few notes about the trees. One of the senior head-office officials did a large amount of his oversighting from his camp chair – in a shady spot at the base camp with a novel on his lap.

We would stagger into the camp at dusk, notebooks overflowing, exhausted and strung out after hours of listening to angry people's grievances about how government practised conservation in their area. Most of the other teams would have been back long enough to have showered and changed: they would be sitting around the fire, beer in hand, meat spiced and marinating, ready to go onto the coals. Each team catered for its own members so we had to prepare a meal each night and mostly we were just too tired to want to join the communal fire after eating. However, we knew that we needed to communicate with the 'old guard' government staff and not just with those who shared our views, so we usually dragged ourselves to the fire and joined the conversation.

On day four we faced a particularly difficult six-hour meeting in the nearby town of Tsumkwe with about 60 very angry people, including, as inevitably happens in town near liquor stores, a few inebriated individuals. The senior official who'd probably finished his novel by then decided to attend. It was time, he told us, to see how the community team performed. We wished he'd not chosen that meeting as we knew it would be a tough one. We were consulting with San people who lived in a town. Here alcohol abuse, violence and hopelessness were rife unlike in rural areas where people's lives offered more dignity.

The official quickly took exception to the extreme accusations made by people in the initial stages of the meeting. Had he attended earlier meetings with us, he would have known that we knew some of the claims made against government conservation staff were probably not true. But it was important to listen: it showed us how people were *feeling*. This anger and resentment was far better out in the open than simmering in people's hearts. As those involved in conflict management know, affirmation of people's feelings, even though one does not share them or agree with them, is the first step to real communication.

So we listened, and wrote down what people said. Our government official's face got redder and redder. He kept looking at Brian Jones who worked with, if not for, him, obviously waiting for Brian to defend the conservation directorate. When it became clear to him that we effete '*Engelsmanne*' were going to move on to another subject without putting the community straight, he stood up. We facilitators groaned collectively as he climbed into the people, telling them they should be ashamed of telling such untruths in public and that in his briefcase here on the ground next to his chair he had reports from the accused officials, which would prove the community version of these incidents wrong. And so on. All the positive energy we'd created at the meeting by listening while people shared their attitudes, if not always the facts, dissolved in moments.

People shouted at the official in Afrikaans – *We're independent now; you can't tell us what to do any more; we don't need to listen to the boere!* The San leaders with us made a half-hearted attempt to get us back on track but the meeting descended into chaos. The totally out-voiced official faltered, clearly out of his depth facing an angry horde. He sat down, torn between walking out – but thereby conceding defeat – or staying. He stayed, fiddling for a while in his briefcase. I saw Brian muttering to him but could not hear what was said.

Too angry to do nothing, I went and crouched next to the official. My furious whisper was something along the lines of: 'We all know some of these allegations are untrue! Do you think we're complete fools? But when you are conflict managing you start by listening to how the other side *feels*. You've gone and totally disrupted our process – and I'm not sure we can get back on track now!' I stomped back to my seat.

Brian, whose turn it was to lead the facilitation that day, did his best to calm things down. But the damage had been done. The trust and honest communication we'd been busy establishing was lost. Faces were sullen and hostile; youngsters catcalled from the back. A woman made a remark in Ju/'hoan that clearly amused everyone and their derisive laughter over-rode Brian's voice. We struggled on but the discussions had lost energy. Surliness prevailed. People in that part of the world tended not to confront but they were clearly antagonistic now whereas before they'd been curious and a bit suspicious. They evaded issues and muttered among themselves.

If it hadn't been so difficult to get people together to attend these meetings, we'd have stopped. Getting any kind of response to our checklist of open-ended survey questions felt like we were wading through thigh-deep mud. It was exhausting and dispiriting.

And then, as so often happens, out of the ashes came deliverance. The old man Bobo who rose to his feet had obviously been thinking about what he wanted to say for some time. His voice quavered with emotion as he spoke in poor but clearly understandable Afrikaans. He pointed at our still red-faced government official. He had something to tell him.

'You talk about things in your briefcase that will defeat us. You say these papers of yours contain the truth. I say bring them and come with me, come on foot into the bush for a week.'

There was total silence. Everyone waited for the old man's next words.

'Can you find food? Can you get water to drink?' He stepped forward, gesticulating at the official. 'Who will you turn to for help, white man? How much use will writing and reading the things inside your briefcase help you in the bush?'

He wasn't finished yet: 'Let me tell you who it will be that you follow like a small child. Me, and the other old Bushmen. You need us to help you live there. We who live with the wild animals. With just your papers you will die.'

With great dignity the old man sat. I wanted to leap up and applaud but the meeting did it for me. If there is such a thing as a standing ovation in Ju/'hoan culture, Bobo got it that morning. All eyes including ours were on the official. Brian started speaking and then thought better of it. We waited for what came next.

The official rose with as much dignity as his large belly allowed him. I held my breath. In Afrikaans he addressed the old man: 'It's true what you say, old man. In the bush, on foot, you are king and you would save me from hunger and thirst.'

I drew a long breath as he finished off.

'I think this is why we are here, holding all these meetings. We want to share what we know and what you know and make a good plan together that works for the wildlife and for the people.'

Brian, Garth or I couldn't have said it better. No one applauded but the meeting was back on track. We had to skip lunch and keep on going to be able to finish our check-sheet and it was worth it.

That evening we arrived back at camp before Chris, who had been wearing his ornithologist's hat for this survey and was tasked with a bird study. He drove in as the kettle was boiling and joined us for a cup of tea, looking less composed than usual.

'Long day, Chris?' I started, intending to tease him about the hardships of bird-watching.

'It's been a terrible day; you've no idea!'

Now Chris had our attention. He told us his sorry tale: He'd spotted a very rare bird – sadly I forget what it was – which was totally out of its normal range. An amazing sighting this far east (or maybe he said west) – definitely a first, he enthused. Now, as any ornithologist will know, what you have to do with such a rare sighting is catch or kill the bird to prove it was there. As a social scientist I found this remarkable but then, as I'd been told a few times on this and the previous survey, what does my discipline know about real science?

Chris got his .410 shotgun out of its case and set about stalking the bird.

'Damn thing kept moving. I had to crawl around, trying to get close enough.' He picked at the burrs in his socks and we all looked at his scratched knees and dirty regulation khaki shorts.

'Then finally, I had it lined up perfectly. I looked down the sights and just as I was about to squeeze the trigger, I realised the bird was sitting right in front of my vehicle.'

Chris jerked the shotgun up a split second before he blasted his car. But this caused him to topple backwards into a ditch, which accounted for the leaves in his red hair.

By now, Brian, Garth and I – who'd had quite an emotional and tough day – could no longer contain ourselves. We collapsed in mirth. Surprised and a bit wounded, Chris asked us what was so funny. That set us off even harder. We laughed and laughed, and eventually Chris too saw the funny side. Having attended a few 8-hour community meetings with us in West Caprivi, he was even prepared to concede that ornithology was not as tough as community work.

But an incident that was not at all amusing occurred towards the end of the survey. We'd finished our consultation work and negotiations for a conservation and development plan were due to start the next morning. First, we'd all be reporting on the results of our work. In our case that meant listing the key issues, problems and concerns we'd heard from the communities and giving a summary of aspirations and needs that had come up. Representatives from each community where we'd held meetings were coming in so they could hear that we truly reflected on what they had said. Once all this was on the table, there was a full day for senior government staff and community leaders to agree on a way forward – a joint plan.

Our role at this stage was facilitation. The part I enjoyed most was recording on a flip chart the common ground between the different 'sides'. We listed the conflicts as well, of course, and the group tried to address these but it never failed to surprise most participants how much consensus and shared views there actually were once everyone was given the opportunity to communicate their vision for the future. Megan was camping with the Nyae Nyae leadership group and like us had ensured that a few times during the survey she and the San delegation joined the communal fire in the evening to socialise with the senior conservation staff from head office. Huge quantities of meat were cooked and consumed by this Windhoek group, so much so that even the San were amazed.

We'd worked hard at explaining our community-based philosophy around this communal fire and seemed to have made a few converts, even among the most hard-core government staff. One of them in particular took to community conservation like a born-again Christian. Perhaps, having actually met some of the San people, and being given the opportunity to see and hear their reverence for nature, giving them conservation power rather than

TOP LEFT 1986 in Puros, then just 11 huts, no lodges or campsites. Me with Elias Hambo, Tukupoli Tjipomba and Tengape Tjiningire. 'Write that down' was a frequent reminder by people who could not read or write themselves but who liked the idea that future generations would be able to read about their world. Photo: Steven Fuller

TOP RIGHT With women at a homestead in the mid-1980s. Photo: Steven Fuller

MIDDLE LEFT In the days before schools in Kunene Region, children went out with their family's goat herds. Photo: Scott Ramsey

MIDDLE RIGHT Lineage head Heova shows how men dance during a celebration at Puros. Very 'traditional' Heova, who did not use a surname at that time, moved south because of war and drought. Photo: Steven Fuller

BOTTOM 2013: A group of Kunene conservancy rhino rangers at an early training session with soon-to-become CRR field coordinator Boas Hambo (third from left, standing), SRT director Simpson Uri-Khob, kneeling, and Jeff Muntifering, driver of the CRR initiative. The CRRs soon made their presence felt, specially after IRDNC and WWF Namibia provided two new dedicated rhino vehicles which contributed to 24/7 monitoring of conservancy rhinos. Since 2015 with local police, MET, SRT and IRDNC, the conservancy rhino rangers have played a lead role in stopping renewed rhino poaching in Kunene (see Chapter 18). The Rhino Pride campaign facilitated by IRDNC and SRT means few residents in Kunene are unaware of the importance of rhino. Photo: Jeff Muntifering

TOP LEFT *A wide-horned Ovahimba ox. Living with cattle that are free changed my perspective about domestic stock and how they are treated in the so-called developed world. Photo: Scott Ramsey*

TOP RIGHT *Without local communities, the Kunene Region may have lost its rhino. Community engagement stopped massive commercial poaching in the '80s, and in the last few years, team work by conservancy rhino rangers, NGOs, local police and the Ministry of Environment and Tourism has done so once again. Photo: Neil Jacobsohn*

MIDDLE LEFT *Women at Puros regarded my tent as inadequate so they built me a 'proper' dung hut which meant I no longer slept 'outside'. Photo: Neil Jacobsohn*

MIDDLE CENTER *An early documentary about community conservation being made by Joelle Chesselet and Craig Matthew. This team went on to make several more documentaries in Namibia including one on the Epupa EIA. Photo: Joelle Chesselet*

MIDDLE RIGHT *Jacobsohn family on a visit to the Kaokoveld in the '80s; with my 80-year-old father, brother Neil and his sons Triston and Craig. Photo: Garth Owen-Smith*

BOTTOM LEFT *Reading in bed is always a pleasure, even when living as a nomad. Photo: Neil Jacobsohn*

BOTTOM RIGHT *Elder Ngeve Tjihaku, a trustee of Conservancy Safaris Namibia, who represents Okondjombo Conservancy. Photo: Neil Jacobsohn*

TOP LEFT *Tusk award ceremony in London: The author with Matt and Stella Rice. Matt, now a well-known international community conservation specialist, started his conservation career as the first coordinator for IRDNC's Zambezi (formerly Caprivi) project (see Chapter 14). Stella is a lawyer. Photo: Getty*

TOP RIGHT *London 2015: Garth, winner of Tusk's Prince William Lifetime Award for Conservation, with sons Tuareg and Kyle, grandson Garth Owen-Smith Junior and Prince William. The Prince is patron of Tusk Trust. Photo: Getty*

BOTTOM *Dinner in a dry river bed in the Okondjombo Conservancy with Conservancy Safaris Namibia Himba host and guests. When you are being hosted by Himba people who are co-owners of the safari company, the cultural exchange tends to be mutually dignified and much more enjoyable than many other types of voyeuristic cultural tourism experiences. Photo: Neil Jacobsohn*

TOP *Dinner An ostrich inspects an old homestead. Depending on where rains falls and grass grows, the lineage that occupied it may one day return, so goods left behind should not be taken as souvenirs by tourists. Photo: Scott Ramsey*

MIDDLE *Dugout canoe on the Kwando River: Community-based conservation started in the Zambezi Region, formerly Caprivi, at independence in 1990. Game numbers have steadily increased.*

BOTTOM *Huab Valley elephants regularly visit this village, drinking water and sometimes helping themselves to tomatoes and other vegetables grown in small gardens. Remarkably, they are tolerated by these members of Torra Conservancy. Photo: Anton Esterhuizen*

TOP A British traditional leader, Prince William, with Namibian traditional leaders, the governor of Kunene Marius Sheya, IRDNC's director John K Kasaona, SRT's director Simson Uri-Khob, Kunene regional councillors, government officials, the founders of the Ehirovipuka and Omatendeka conservancies' Women for Conservation Movement, Kunene Regional Communal Conservancy Association members, Conservancy Rhino Rangers, Conservancy Safaris staff and IRDNC staff and trustees in the Hoanib River in 2018. As Tusk's patron, the Prince visited Namibia with Tusk founder Charlie Mayhew and Africa conservation coordinator Kenya-based Sarah Watson. Photo: Tusk

BOTTOM LEFT Elephant dung up cliffs indicates where desert adapted elephants have climbed up to drink from a high pool of water. Given the height of the rock ledges, one can only wonder how they did it. Photo: Neil Jacobsohn

BOTTOM RIGHT Giant annabooms dwarf CSN vehicles during a lunch stop in the Hoanib River. Photo: Scott Ramsey

TOP *The author introduces Jack Russell pup Katira to her first lion. The lion was darted and drugged so that Dr Fl* *Stander could collar it for research and for problem animal mitigation purposes. Signals from collared lion can ale* *conservancies when a pride comes into domestic stock herding areas. Staff can then warn herders to take specia precautions. Photo: Neil Jacobsohn*

BOTTOM LEFT *Me, then co-director of IRDNC, and IRDNC's Chief Lucky Kasaono with a Hoanib elephant. Th river had been flowing which made driving in it dangerous – hence the relieved smiles once elephants had bee located. Pictures of 'desert' elephant were needed for the British Independent newspaper's three-day trip to Kuner to gather material for a green Christmas appeal for funding for IRDNC. Photo: David Sandison*

BOTTOM RIGHT *Vengape Tjiningire in 1986. Many Himba women stopped using ochre because of the butterfa shortage during the recent drought, when the majority of their cattle died of starvation. Photo: Steven Fuller*

TOP LEFT *Mutjimbiko Mutambo, Kunene traditional leader and well-travelled Himba elder who has been to multiple countries for conservation and indigenous rights events, pledges his support for rhino conservation at a 2017 ceremony conducted by the Omusati governor, Erginus Endjala. IRDNC's John K Kasaona looks on, right. More than 50 councillors and chiefs pledged their rhino support. Photo: Jeff Muntifering*

TOP RIGHT *Garth Owen-Smith, in the rhino and elephant bone yard at Wereldsend, where some of the remains of elephant and rhino poached in the '80s are kept. In a politically unsupportive pre-independence climate Garth and a small team pioneered directly involving local communities and their leaders in conservation. At Independence in 1990 this approach was embraced by an idealistic new government, with legislative changes in 1998 giving communal area dwellers the same rights to wildlife enjoyed since the '70s by commercial farmers. Today there is a thriving government-supported country-wide communal conservancy, community forest and community fish reserve programme. Photo: Neil Jacobsohn*

BOTTOM LEFT *Sonia Hambo, chef extraordinaire and food and beverages manager of Conservancy Safaris Namibia, the safari company co-owned by five Himba conservancies. Photo: Scott Ramsey*

BOTTOM RIGHT *Basilia Shivute, IRDNC Kunene coordinator facilitating a conservancy bi-annual planning meeting at which scores of people took the Rhino Friend pledge. Photo: Jeff Muntifering*

Top LEFT *Jeff Muntifering, driver of the Conservancy Rhino Ranger project, with the first woman appointed as a conservancy rhino ranger – Natasha Gomez, of Huab Conservancy. A second woman rhino ranger has since been appointed by neighbouring Sorris Sorris Conservancy. Conservancy rhino rangers now total more than 60. Photo: Jeff Muntifering*

Top RIGHT *Garth Owen-Smith and the late Chris Eyre – two icons of Namibian conservation. While Garth pioneered community conservation with Kunene community leaders, Chris, as the government nature conservator in charge of the area in the '80s, had the courage to support what was then a politically unpopular approach. When he died Chris was honoured with a Himba funeral, attended by hundreds of people in the far north. Photo: Peter Sander*

Bottom LEFT *A younger Beaven Munali, Caprivi/Zambezi's first community game guard on the Kwando River in north-east Namibia. He rose to be one of two IRDNC-Zambezi assistant directors, with Janet Matota. Today, he is the chairman of the Zambezi Regional Council and a trustee of IRDNC. Photo: David Sandison*

Bottom RIGHT *Lions within a kilometre of a village inside Puros Conservancy. Sadly, this pride who were well tolerated by conservancy members, later moved north and were poisoned by herders outside the conservancy, indicative of the difference in attitudes between people in communal conservancies and those in non-conservancy areas. Puros residents were angry and upset to lose 'their' lions. Photo: Neil Jacobsohn* the new Swapo government seemed the lesser of two evils? Garth, always less cynical than me, preferred to believe that the community conservation philosophy made sense if you thought about it: people only become accountable if they have real responsibility, i.e., link rights and benefits to responsibilities. We had to tactfully rein in this official several times and explain that we were talking about equal partnerships, not handing all power to the community.

One government man who stood out was the late Ben Beytel who was to become the last white official of that group to remain in the ministry, a survivor who eventually was appointed to the post of Director of Conservation, only retiring in 2011. He had worked in Bushmanland and the San delegation knew him and really liked him. I found his views a bit Deep South and paternalistic but his genuine interest in and liking for the people shone through and as a result, he was widely respected locally.

On this last night before we got down to the important last two days, Megan and her group joined us all at the communal fire. A cold wind came up and one of the government officials insisted that she borrow his jacket. Gallantly he draped it over her shoulders. When the time came to leave, Megan tried to give the jacket back. But he refused, wanting her to stay warm on her 200-metre walk back to her camp. She could give it to him in the morning.

Thanking him, Megan left with the San leaders. As they walked away into the night, someone said sotto voce, *'Maar moet net nie die jas vir een van jou vuil boesmannetjies leen nie.'* (But just don't lend the jacket to one of your dirty little Bushmen). A few people laughed; some of us winced, and our group left shortly afterwards. Having grown up under apartheid we were used to such uncouth remarks from some of our fellow whites.

Early the next morning, as we were finishing breakfast, the San leadership came to see us. They were leaving they said, and just wanted to say goodbye and thank you. But the workshop, the most important part of the survey is about to start, we pointed out. Yes, they knew that but had decided not to stay anyway. Why, after all the work they'd done with us, after all the meetings and people we'd talked to? How could they walk away now, when we were ready to make joint plans for the future? They avoided making eye contact with us and insisted they needed to leave.

I quickly made them mugs of tea, knowing they were too well mannered to refuse to drink it, and that they would sit down with us. And hopefully talk.

We were horrified – the entire survey built up to these two days when the joint vision and plan would be developed. Without the community leadership the survey was dead in the water. And from the community leaders' point of view leaving now made no sense at all. Here was a real opportunity to link conservation to the development of their people, to turn around years of conflict, and they were walking out on it. What was going on?

It did not take too long for Kieviet, the senior man, to tell us. The group had heard the remark about dirty little Bushmen and the jacket made by one of the 'boere' last night. And the laughter. It had pained them deeply because they'd invested a lot of themselves in this survey. They had really believed the conservation people were genuine in trying to improve the bad situation in East Bushmanland. They'd sat around the fire with these men at night and talked together, swapping stories.

'We thought we were sharing our thinking. But last night we saw nothing has changed. These Afrikaners despise us and see us as dirty *bosmannetjies*. To them we are not people.' And so, Kieviet drained his mug of tea and stood up to leave with his group.

Before they could walk away Garth spoke: 'You do know you're all hypocrites, as bad as the Boere,' he said in Afrikaans which most understood well enough.

I held my breath. I knew and trusted Garth's great skills in conflict management. But where was he going with this unexpected remark? It stopped Kieviet and his party too. They glared at Garth, surprised and hostile – they'd expected us to understand their position, not insult them.

Garth was on a roll: 'Don't you believe me? Of course you're hypocrites. Just think of the names you've been calling the conservation officials behind their backs all week. "The *boere*", "the bellies that defeat themselves". You've been mocking them in an unkind way … so what's the difference between what you've been saying about them and one of them calling you names?'

One of the younger San men said the Ju/'hoan equivalent of *This is bullshit, let's go.* Our survey hung in the balance.

'We know you after this time of working together. And we know you're bigger than this,' Garth said quietly, turning back to the fire.

We all watched as he packed tobacco into his battered old pipe and then poked around the edges of the fire for a suitable ember to drop into the bowl. The younger man muttered something again. He and, it seemed, judging from the body language, others were impatient to leave. I was now watching Kieviet – he was the key to what happened next. He had been standing rigidly, obviously angry, while Garth called him and his group hypocrites.

The moment drew out unbearably. Garth placidly sucked his awful pipe and stared into the fire.

Then Kieviet laughed. 'You're right,' he said. 'It's true – we have names for them.'

It was over. The delegation sat down for another mug of tea, and a large box of rusks was quickly emptied while we all relaxed and shook our heads at how easy it is for people to misunderstand one another. *Boere* is a common derogatory name for white South Africans and Namibians used by many black people but the Bellies name had been new to us. Early on in the survey I'd written down the explanation I'd been given for this name. The men's bellies were so large that they had to keep eating to give them enough strength not to be toppled over by the weight of their huge stomachs. It was a wickedly funny name for the survey's massive meat-eaters.

Before we left the fireside that morning, I asked Kieviet what he called people like Brian, Garth and me.

He smiled and shook his head. 'No more names on this survey,' he said, leaving us in no doubt that we – and our weaknesses – had also been skewered by sharp Ju/'hoan humour.

And so the '*boere*, the bellies that defeat themselves' and the '*bosmannetjies*' sat down and planned together. Only a very few people in that big workshop knew it so nearly didn't happen.

TWELVE

Golden rules of the bush

He who has people will not perish – Namibian proverb

WE ARE TRAVELLING north, passing Tomakus, with three Conservancy Safaris guests on day three of a 10-day expedition when a group of Herero woman wave us down. Their frantic body language leaves no doubt there is an emergency.

We are taken to a sweating child, aged about three, lying under a tree across her mother's lap. She is badly blistered and burnt on the cheek, her chest and on one thigh. But it is her right hand which shocks us all. The skin on her palm and four fingers is in tatters, a deep oozing burn that is so severe we later find out there is no pain, almost no feeling at all in that hand because of third degree burns which have destroyed nerve endings. Her other burns, not as deep, are much more painful.

Our plans change at once. We tell the guests we need to turn back to Sesfontein – which we passed an hour and a half ago – and get this little girl to the clinic there. Apart from the risk of infection, she is in danger of losing use of her fingers as skin contracts with burns as acute as hers. The other burns are serious but nothing as bad as the hand.

We make space in our vehicle for mother and daughter, while hearing what happened. The child was hungry and plunged her hand into a large bubbling pot of porridge that was cooking on a fire – pap, *oruhere,* or as it is called in English, mealie meal. The burns on her face, chest and thigh were the result of her flapping her hand in agony, trying to get rid of the boiling porridge stuck to her skin. Her mother rode four hours on donkey-back, holding her daughter in front of her, to the main road that passes through Tomakus to get help. She'd arrived after dark last night and we were the first car that had stopped this morning. So nearly 24 hours have passed. One of our guests is a pharmacist from Switzerland, carrying a burn kit in her luggage. She offers to dress the worst of the burns there and then, and the mother gratefully agrees.

Our patient, who has been silent, almost certainly in shock, barely whimpers as the Swiss woman works over her. The rest of us wince and move away. Then we all pile into the vehicle and head for the clinic. Soon our patient starts crying; her mother asks if we can stop briefly. The child is very thirsty so we offer her some water with a packet of rehydration powder in it. She gulps down the mugful and wants more. She has a second mug but says she is still thirsty. Someone finds a coke for her and her mother and they drink as we continue driving.

At the clinic, the nursing sister is impressed with our Swiss guest's burn dressings and says she could not have done a better job herself. She decides to leave them on till they can get the girl to Opuwo Hospital the next day, the ambulance not being available today. We debate taking the child to Opuwo ourselves but the nurse tells us that the hospital wouldn't be able to do anything more than what we've already done. The most they would do would be to change her burn dressings – assuming they have burn kits in stock – and monitor her for infection.

We set off once again but after having to almost drag our pharmacist guest out of the clinic where she spent a fascinating few hours with the nursing sister and her patients, sharing knowledge and experience. Our plans and itinerary have changed. But this is what Conservancy Safaris is all about and no one minds, least of all the guests who are buoyed up by their non-touristic real experiences.

A few months later when passing through Tomakus again, I stopped to inquire about the child. She was back home, having healed well, including her hand. Later, I emailed the Swiss guests to let them know that their burn kit and our detour to the Sesfontein clinic had made a real difference to the life of one little girl.

Stopping to help anyone in need is not a big deal in rural Namibia, at least for those of us who live there. You always stop to help if you can because the next time it could be you in trouble. The other major reason is that the first step in community-based conservation is forging a relationship of trust and respect with local people which means being concerned about their needs and issues, not just your own conservation aims. I learnt this rule of the road early, while still in my research years, soon after I linked up with Garth, both personally and professionally. I knew he was a man obsessed with his conservation work but I hadn't yet realised the full impact this would have on my life.

It was my first Christmas with Garth. I was a bit sad that I would not be able to see any of my family – my ageing parents or my two brothers who were all in South Africa. There was no spare money to even consider the cost of flights. Although Garth and I had agreed that we didn't 'do' Christmas – the presents, fancy food, decorations and all that commercialised stuff – we hadn't discussed our plans in any detail. We'd been invited to Christmas lunch with good friends Dave and Alison Sandy in Swakopmund, a five-hour drive from our camp. We'd accepted, and I admit I was looking forward to just a little bit of festive consumerism, at least for the two children of the house.

I thought we could go into Swakopmund a day or two before Christmas – which fell on a Saturday that year – so that I could buy the kids a present each, some wine for the lunch, and maybe chocolates and flowers. Garth's plan was to work until the last moment – till about 9 am on Christmas morning – then leap into the Land Rover and head for Swakop. No shopping possible. When I realised this, we had a short sharp discussion. Why, I wanted to know, should his schedule and not mine prevail for once, especially as it was Christmas? The discussion ended with me telling him he was selfish and arrogant; he told me I was self-centred and always wanted my own way, even that I should consider moving to town if I couldn't cut it out here.

Suffice to say, there was not a great deal of Christmas cheer between us as we headed out at about 8.50 am on Christmas day. A reindeer would have been quite at home in the chilly atmosphere. I was angry and disappointed. He was superior and self-righteous.

I had yet to learn that my partner regards every minute spent in a town or city as some sort of admission of defeat on his part – or at the very least a waste of his time; whereas I quite enjoy having access to both bush and city life. I still do and he still dislikes towns and cities (but has softened his attitude a bit over the years). After more than three decades together, we've found a way that works for us both – most of the time. But in those early days, two strong wills often clashed.

We were already going to be late for lunch if it started at 1 pm so Garth chose the Skeleton Coast Park route, which is about an hour shorter than the Twyfelfontein–Uis road. ETA in Swakopmund was about 1.30 pm if we hurried. Twenty kilometres from camp, a Damara family, standing next to their old sagging truck, flagged us down. The problem, even a townie could see, was a flat tyre. Or so I thought.

Now after many years' experience, I know that a flat tyre is not a problem in the bush; it's a minor chore that takes a few minutes to do. The stranded family's real problem was that they had no jack, tyre lever or spare wheel. No puncture repair kit either.

Townie response: How irresponsible of these two adults to drive out here with four children, one of them a toddler, plus old Granny, without the above-mentioned equipment. The nearest garage at Khorixas is about 150 kilometres east of us through the desert. The government nature conservation camp at the Springbokwasser gate of the Skeleton Coast Park, which was 12 kilometres further west through the desert, may be able to help. But chances are all their vehicles will be out on patrol with their fishing rods and the gate guard will not have a jack etcetera lying around. It'll be 40 plus degrees out here in an hour or two. What on earth were these people thinking!

While I was thinking this, Garth was lighting his pipe and chatting to the man. I walked round the vehicle wondering where they kept their water container. A golden rule in the desert is never go anywhere without spare water. I asked the woman about this and was told they had no water. I shook my head, disapprovingly. How long have you been stuck here? About two hours – came the response.

A few cars had passed them – '*die boere wat visvang*' (white fishermen) – but no one had stopped except us.

So here was Garth's golden rule in action: You never drive past a vehicle in trouble in the desert; you always stop to help. Obviously all the farmers who'd passed the Damara family were new to the area . . . and so didn't know they should stop and help. But I assumed, having finally grasped what the real problem here was, and knowing we had a Christmas lunch date, that we would give the man a lift to the park gate and leave him there, for the park staff to sort out. I also assumed we would leave a bottle of water with the family, in case their wait was long. Garth, on the other hand, set about helping the driver fix the puncture with our puncture repair kit, jack and wheel spanner. Neither of our two spare wheels fitted the smaller truck. Getting the tube out of the tyre took the first 20 minutes. Then the men started the scraping -the-old-tube-and-looking-for-holes phase. I managed to catch Garth's eye and pointed at my watch.

'Can't we just leave them to get on with it?'

'No Maggs, they need our jack. I can loan them a wheel spanner because I've got another one but I can't leave the jack with them because then we could end up with a problem if we have a puncture.'

'Oh.' I check my watch again. 'This means at least another half an hour here. So we'll be an hour late for Christmas lunch, if we're lucky.'

'Maggs, it's Christmas day – you don't really expect me to leave a family stranded, do you? For a bloody lunch!'

'Ok Father bloody Theresa – you do your good deed,' I hissed. Now, not only did I feel furious at leaving our camp two days late but I also felt thoroughly ashamed of my superficiality and lack of compassion for others. I slunk off behind the Land Rover and had a bit of a weep. I missed my family thousands of kilometres away. The sun was already very hot in that treeless expanse of desert plains, and I was sweaty, dusty and very disappointed that we would not be able to share Christmas lunch with our friends. I hadn't had a meal with anyone except Garth and work colleagues in months and this lunch had assumed special importance. How rude the Sandys would think us, accepting their invitation, then turning up hours late. But I was also shamed by my city mind-set and lack of sympathy for the stranded family. I felt isolated and a stranger in this harsh hot land. And I thoroughly disliked Garth for showing me up.

A tap on my arm interrupted my self-pity. One of the children stood there with a juicy slice of ruby-red watermelon. She offered it to me solemnly and gestured towards where the people sat. I took it, and reluctantly followed her back to the truck where the men still worked. The family had put a blanket down in the half shade of the truck and everyone including Granny was sitting on it, eating watermelon. A place – the best and shadiest spot – was made for me on the blanket. Granny smiled at me and said something in Damara – quite a long speech.

'What did she say,' I asked.

An older boy replied, obviously summarising. She says: 'Thank you to God for sending you to help us. And bless you and Happy Christmas.'

Garth, crouched alongside us, eating a piece of watermelon while he watched his co-worker stick the last patch on the much-repaired tube, caught my eye. He was waiting for me to smile; I was waiting for him to show some empathy. We both looked away.

So there we all sat in the desert next to the old truck, having a sort of picnic. Three springbok watched us warily from a distance: a strange bunch – two men, three women and four children. And in spite of myself, I realised I was enjoying the moment as people talked, with the oldest son translating some of the conversation for me; we laughed and shared the watermelon while the wheel was put back on.

We arrived at our friends' around 3 pm. Of course, they had held lunch for us because, as Dave said, they knew us desert types. If we made it on the right day, we were doing well. We all laughed and eventually sat down to a large Christmas supper, turkey et al. There was wine, chocolates and a Christmas pudding. Young Laura and Christopher Sandy had received more than enough under the Christmas tree to not wonder about the lack of gifts from Garth and me.

Someone asked me what Garth had given me for Christmas. I explained we'd agreed we would not give gifts to one another. It was only later that I reflected on our day and realised he did give me a gift. A very valuable one – an understanding of the real Christmas spirit and an opportunity to see an important road rule put into practice as well. Since that Christmas day decades ago, I've practised this rule scrupulously, stopping to assist scores of people in all sorts of situations in remote places. But stopping to help doesn't mean always being kind and understanding. What's wrong with giving people a lecture when they need it?

Once, four large men flagged me down in the Skeleton Coast Park. I admit to being a bit nervous, as a lone woman, stopping on this isolated stretch of road. I didn't get out of my car; just rolled down the window to find out what they wanted. A not unusual story – puncture, but no jack or tyre lever to enable them to change the wheel. Sighing, I got out and gave them what they needed. While two of them put on their spare tyre (which luckily, not only did they have but it was full or air as well), I chatted to the other two. All from the north central region, it emerged they were members of Namibia's founding president's special guard. President Sam Nujoma liked relaxing at the government nature conservation camp on the coast called Mowe Bay. These men were on their way there to ensure the camp was ready for the president's arrival by helicopter the next day.

I couldn't stop myself and gave them a blast for being so careless not to check their government vehicle had the basics – at the very least a jack and a tyre lever. What sort of special guards are you?

How can you be trusted to look after our president if you are so irresponsible! The men laughed sheepishly. It wouldn't happen again, they assured me.

One February a few years later on a trip from Swakopmund heading north, I needed to cross the upper Guantagab, the same bit of the river where our first new vehicle had been drowned. It was déjà vu as I came over the hill and found a 4x4 firmly stuck in the mud. The river had flowed earlier that day and the three young German tourists in the car had rashly tried to cross.

There was nothing I could do to help as they were too far across the muddy track for my tow rope to reach the vehicle and after our previous experience, I was not prepared to reverse into the mud. The wire in the old fence that we'd used as a make-shift tow-rope all those years ago had long since disappeared. But I decided to cross the river at a different rocky place downstream that I knew would be okay and try to find a few men to come back with me to help the stranded tourists. I promised to be back within an hour or so. But I could find only older women and small children. I thought about my busy schedule and considered just driving on and leaving the Germans to their fate. But Garth's golden rule was too deeply entrenched, so I drove back. Parking safely on a high shoulder, I waded across the mud to where the unhappy trio sat in the meagre shade of a mopane tree.

By now, it was late afternoon. I knew it was extremely likely the river would come down again overnight or early the next morning as there was robust lighting on the horizon in the river's catchment. So I advised them to move all valuables out of their vehicle and camp on the river bank. They had borrowed the 4x4 from friends in Windhoek and the thought of having the vehicle damaged by a flooding river or worse upset them deeply. But there was just nothing we could do. I didn't have a high-lift jack with me and they were too deep in the mud for us four to push or pull. As it was too late for me to get back to Wereldsend, I decided to camp and at least cheer the tourists with a bottle of wine or two from my supply. We made a meal together and under the circumstances, our evening was quite pleasant.

At about ten, when it was time to go to bed, one of the group escorted me across the mud to the opposite bank where my car was parked. As we passed their trapped truck, I remarked that if only I'd had my high-lift jack here, we could have got the car out. The young man stopped in his tracks and told me there was a high-lift jack in their car. Somehow, he'd failed to hear me or perhaps understand my fast English when I'd asked them about jacks earlier.

It took us more than two hours in the dark but we did get the truck out of the river bed. Covered in mud, we drank another bottle of wine to celebrate that night. As expected, the river came down in flood early the next morning, which meant we were now on opposite sides of the river, so we said our farewells with a thumbs up and a wave. They were heading east towards Khorixas; I was going west to Wereldsend. I didn't expect to see them again, but two days later they arrived at Wereldsend with a thank you gift – 12 bottles of wine.

More recently, I was hurrying to a meeting in Windhoek, having left Swakopmund a bit late. A few kilometres outside Okahandja, I stopped to buy some mushrooms – *omayova* – from a man on the roadside. These are dinner plate-sized fungi that grow on the giant termite mounds in this region in the rain season, a much-loved seasonal Namibian delicacy. I was staying the night with colleagues and friends Len and Karin le Roux in Windhoek and knew a large mushroom or two would be a welcome addition to supper, if not supper itself.

The man gave me my two mushrooms – the last he had for sale on the road he said, then asked me if I would do him a *groot guns* – a big favour – and give him, and his family a lift to Okahandja. A bit impatiently, knowing I was already very late for my meeting, I agreed. Golden rule, et cetera et cetera. The family emerged from behind the bushes – ma, and ouma, oupa and three children. Seven people in all – plus four large boxes of mushrooms obviously destined for Okahandja.

By the time I'd made space for them all, adults in the back seat, and loaded the boxes, with the children, in the back of my double cab truck, I knew I was now seriously late. And I couldn't just drop the family and their boxes on the side of the freeway as we passed Okahandja. I'd have to turn into the town and take them to their destination, adding another 20 minutes or more to my journey. Grumpily, I did the right thing and took them where they were going. Ouma was especially grateful and insisted I take a few more mushrooms for my kindness. So there I was with six giant mushrooms on the backseat of my car, rushing to a meeting that had started more than an hour ago.

As I was parking outside IRDNC's offices, I saw Chris Weaver, head of WWF Namibia, walking to his car. He confirmed what I feared – the meeting was all but over, so he'd slipped out for another commitment. Oh well, at least I could endear myself to my colleagues with mushrooms. I gave him two large ones – which he gratefully accepted. I carried the rest up to IRDNC's office and managed to find homes for the others, apart from the ones for my hosts.

Later that morning, I received a phone call from a former colleague who now worked for WWF in Switzerland. Our paths hadn't crossed for years. He invited me to join him and his wife for lunch. Over our meal, he told me that it was by chance that he discovered I was in Windhoek – he'd been visiting the Namibian WWF offices and seen the mushrooms on Chris' desk. His Swiss wife had never seen such large mushrooms before and they asked Chris about them. Obviously, my name came up.

But the mushrooms were responsible for much more than re-uniting two old colleagues for a catch-up lunch. I was due to meet my brother Neil and his two daughters Bianca and Jade in France in a few weeks' time for a skiing holiday. Neil and girls were good skiers, having skied as a family since my now adult nieces were children; for me it would be the second time I had ever tried skiing.

This was not my normal type of holiday. But being a generous sort, Neil had told me all I had to do was get myself to Paris where Bianca lived. From there he'd pick up the tab. For the last week or so, I'd seen the email exchanges between my brother and the nieces about accommodation options in either the French or Swiss

Alps. My brother's largesse did not fully extend to his daughters as they had been raised to be financially responsible for themselves, and they were expected to contribute towards costs of this family holiday. I had been feeling quite uncomfortable about all of this, as it's not in my nature to freeload. But on the other hand, I would never have contemplated a skiing holiday unless Neil had invited me. My modern and social media savvy nieces had decided to wait till the last moment for online bargains in terms of hiring a ski chalet, or some sort of accommodation for us – a group of five, including Jade's boyfriend of the time.

My very beloved nieces have grown up with the impression that I was their eccentric and adventurous aunt, who was good at what she did and fairly famous in community-based conservation circles. They admire and respect me much more than I deserve. But to be frank, I quite enjoy this esteem from two remarkable young women, both of whom are high achievers in their chosen fields.

The mushroom episode was about to grow my reputation in their eyes.

During the lunch, I mentioned to the Swiss-based couple that my family and I were going to be skiing in their part of the world, and asked their advice about the finding accommodation at one of the resorts. As it turned out, they had a six-sleeper ski chalet at Chamonix and we were more than welcome to use it for our week-long holiday. My questions about cost were waved away – the chalet was not in use that week, and all we were to do was to replace any tinned food or wine that we used. They were so pleased to be able to assist a fellow conservation worker that they arranged to drive up to the chalet and show us around the day we arrived. Then, late afternoon, they would drive back to their home in Geneva. It was great emailing my brother and nieces with the news that, ahem, I had secured a picturesque double-storey chalet on the outskirts of a premier ski resort, as was telling them that it would not cost any of them anything except a gift for our hosts.

So doing a good turn for a poor family selling mushrooms translated into a week in a chalet in the Swiss Alps. If no good deed goes unpunished, as the saying puts it, this was a much-enjoyed exception. And the last of my giant mushrooms, prepared by my dear friend artist Karin Le Roux that night, (a chef of note) had never tasted better.

THIRTEEN

Inside an environmental impact assessment

Truth is stranger than fiction – Anonymous

THE MULTI-VOLUME environmental impact assessment (EIA) report has long ago been completed; the proposed Epupa hydro-electric dam on the Kunene River, on the border between Angola and Namibia, was not built. But there are many stories from this 1996/7 EIA that have never been written down, only shared around a few fires and dinner tables within small circles. This doesn't seem right given that the project polarised the region: it led to lawsuits, lies in high places, a pop song, various controversies and conflicts including a showdown with armed police in a dry river bed. There was a boycott plus some cross-cultural sexual abuse of young girls which caused a major diplomatic panic and a flurry of earnest emails around the world. Not to mention a Himba chief having his feet massaged with suntan lotion by a senior Swedish government official. Here then are some stories from the inside.

The Epupa study was the first big EIA done in Namibia. These days one is a lot more cynical about EIAs, having been involved in a few and seen the way data can be manipulated to make a case. But in the early 1990s there was more idealism. Signing my contract as a consultant meant giving the process wholehearted support. As a so-called Himba specialist, I felt I had little choice but to take part in what was a milestone EIA for our young country – setting precedents for fair environmental and social practice.

IRDNC was the main field-based organisation working with communities in the Kaokoveld and we'd already been drawn into the Epupa situation. Garth and I, with Chris Tapscott, then representing the Namibian Economic Policy Research Unit, had done the socio-economic and cultural section of the pre-feasibility study in 1992, four years before the full EIA started. So we were aware of the opposition to the dam by those who lived in and farmed in the impact area versus the pro-dam group in Opuwo and Windhoek who hoped to benefit from the development.

The Scandinavian consortium appointed to lead the EIA was a very experienced international group who hired more than 50 consultants to cover different aspects. I was one of three members of the social and cultural impact assessment team to work with the affected Himba communities. The other two were Professor Michael Bollig of Germany's Cologne University, and an Angolan consultant, who should better remain un-named, whose focus would be the few thousand Himba people who lived across the Kunene River in his country. We were delighted the study was to be funded by the Swedish government as this would ensure high standards being maintained.

Knowing how polarised people were about the dam, we weren't expecting an easy survey. But our role was to be impartial and ensure that our report truly reflected local views. Working with Michael was a bonus: he was well-known by the people in north Kunene and he was an academic Garth and I both liked and respected. Not always the case with some of the many researchers encountered over the years.

Wanting a transparent and model EIA, the Swedish Embassy in Windhoek and the project's Permanent Joint Management Committee (PJMC), comprising senior Angolan and Namibian government officials, accepted a pitch by Cape Town filmmakers Craig Matthew and Joelle Chesselet to produce a documentary account of the study. As the full EIA would take place over two years, Craig and Joelle would have to do a lot of coming and going to ensure the camera was present to record pivotal moments. Reluctantly, but realistically, they agreed that the PJMC would have the right to veto all footage before it was used. We'd worked with Craig and Joelle before and we trusted them as filmmakers with integrity whose final product would be creative and outstanding. We were glad to have them on the team.

After various meetings in Windhoek, my field work started. The first team I headed comprised Lina Kaisuma, a Namibian Herero-speaking woman who is a talented IRDNC facilitator, Tina Coombes, a South African social scientist who'd worked with me in the area before, my invaluable long-term research assistant, Shorty and a representative of the Himba traditional authorities. Most of the time, this representative was Mutjimbiko Mutambo, a tall councillor in his early 40s who carried himself with dignity and confidence, whom we met in 1992 during the pre-feasibility work. His insights, intelligence and humour added a lot of value.

His role in the Epupa study, and his leadership qualities in general, has meant that since the '90s Mutambo was invited to attend various international events for indigenous people and local communities. I happened to take him to the Windhoek airport for the first of these trips in the mid-1990s. It was to be his first flight, as well as his first time out of Namibia (apart from wading across the Kunene River into Angola to see relatives). So I fussed a bit and asked to see his ticket and passport while we stood together in the queue.

Not many Himba people travelled by air in those days, but if Mutambo noticed the surreptitious glances his attire was receiving, he was unfazed. I thought he looked rather splendid: car-tyre sandals, his long, muscular bare legs disappearing at mid-thigh into a brand-new dark-blue cotton erapi (a type of skirt), gathered stylishly and tucked into his leather hunger belt which he could tighten if he was not fed properly on his travels. A sleeveless purple T-shirt with a yellow surfer hanging ten on his board down Mutambo's chest completed the ensemble. Because it could be cold where he was going, he'd accepted one of Garth's warm bush jackets which he'd slung over one shoulder. Over the other shoulder was the small blue bag we'd given him for the remarkably few items he carried for his week away.

But I was staring in dismay at his passport: 'It's not your passport – it's Chief Kapika's. You've brought the wrong one!'

I knew my office had checked with him that he had an up-to-date passport and had liaised about the air ticket with the international organisation funding his trip.

Unperturbed, Mutambo insisted all was fine.

'But where's your own passport? You can't travel on this one.'

He didn't have his own, he informed me, and he didn't see why he couldn't use this passport, as the chief, his relative, had loaned it to him; the chief wasn't needing it this week.

I was speechless. Mutambo's ticket was in his own name. Would he be allowed on the plane? Today, post-September 11, he wouldn't have made it past the first counter. But things were more relaxed then, and I found myself explaining there had been a mix-up with the name on the ticket versus the name on the passport. That Mutambo was also a Kapika, which was a family name (true). I didn't actually lie and say the chief's passport was Mutambo's but I needn't have worried. The airways person who checked him in took it in his stride. A senior person was called and in minutes the air ticket had been changed to reflect the name in the passport. They were used to this sort of situation with rural people starting to travel since independence, he said cheerfully.

With boarding pass in hand, a composed Mutambo strolled towards immigration to catch his flight.

Mutambo later acquired his own passport and is now an experienced globetrotter. He's attended meetings and conferences in a number of African countries, been to Europe and to the United Nations in New York. He still wears car-tyre sandals, a T-shirt and an erapi. The last time I saw him before an air journey into a cold season he was wearing a handsome knee-length winter coat in charcoal grey wool over his traditional attire. He looked imposing.

A few years ago when Conservancy Safaris hosted members

of a United States archaeological society who were particularly interested in Himba culture we arranged for them to spend time with Mutambo. We shared a picnic lunch in the Omuhonga river bed and Mutambo held court, good-naturedly answering cultural questions he'd probably heard a dozen times before. But soon, as we'd told the group about his New York visit a few months earlier, he was asked what he thought of the city.

Tactfully, knowing he was speaking to people from the US, he started by telling them he'd met some friendly people in New York. And the doctor at the hotel was good. He'd given him strong pills that cured his back which was sore after his all-night flight.

But how did you like New York? What did you think of the city?

A direct question needed a truthful reply. 'I thought it was a terrible place,' he said.

The reason, he told the nonplussed Americans, was that you couldn't touch the ground. Only pavements and streets and floors of buildings. Even the plants he saw had to live inside pots. He felt sorry for the people there.

There was silence for a few moments while the Americans absorbed this. Then they rushed to tell Mutambo about Central Park and all the beautiful green spaces in the city. But he was unimpressed. He knew from his travels what a park was – an open place with some trees and grass surrounded by tall buildings. He'd seen how crowded the city was; all those people could never fit into even many of these parks. No one could argue with that.

Anyway, he assured the group, he was glad to hear there were some real places in New York and if he ever visited again, he'd ask someone to direct him there.

In Kunene, in our first six weeks in the field for the Epupa EIA, my team had to visit scores of *ozonganda* (homesteads) and work through a checklist of questions and discussion points. Where a number of *ozonganda* were in the same area, using the same water source, we could usually manage to get a representative group together, as long as we gave them a day's notice. We would send a youth ahead of us to inform people that we were coming *muhuka* (tomorrow). When this didn't work, we'd have to make do with the three or four people who were home. Once we were comfortable with the survey methodology, we split into two teams to reach as many people as possible.

Sometimes we could drive in but frequently we had to hike to the remoter temporary stock camps, enjoyable, but wasting many hours of our limited field time. A helicopter was in daily use by the big team of engineers working on the dam specifications, and infuriatingly it often flew over us as we slogged up a hill. I had asked Mr S, the head of the study, for use of the helicopters to reach areas too far for us to walk, but that request was not entertained. The social and cultural side of the survey was clearly not as important as the engineering aspects.

It was only some months later when we went back to do another part of the study that I was able to beg a few hours. Our helicopter flights into the most remote parts of Kunene such as Otijimborombonga had quite an impact on the Himba settlements we visited, and were talked about for years. Not because of us arriving in a helicopter – everybody knew people flew in these dragonfly-like machines called *ondera*. What amazed and delighted was the sight of our two Staffordshire terriers – Kumbu and Tjaba – calmly jumping out of the helicopter and then, after our meeting, jumping back into the cabin at my *ronda* (get in) command.

The pilot had needed a bit of persuasion to allow dogs into his bird: We had to promise to keep them under tight control and tie their leads to the back seats before he agreed, very reluctantly, to fly with them on board. Just one flight won him over. Kumbu would sit quietly on a seat so he could look out of a window while Tjaba who didn't have a good head for heights would curl up on the floor at my feet and sleep. In their long and eventful lives with Garth and me the dogs had travelled in all types of vehicles, light planes and boats, including many trips in a not-very-stable canoe on the Zambezi, so a dragonfly was no big deal.

Karine Rousset, a young Mauritian anthropologist who'd just joined IRDNC as a social intern was to work with Shorty and me this time, six weeks of field work being a good orientation. Apart from being air-sick into my hat – the only receptacle we could find in a hurry in the helicopter – she turned out to be a great asset who would go on to do outstanding work with San communities in West Caprivi. Eventually she married a co-worker, Nataniel Nuulimba, and they both left IRDNC after being head-hunted by a large Botswana NGO. Years later in 2010 when Garth and I were ready to stand down as co-directors, after more than 25 years in the position, Karine Rousset Nuulimba was appointed one of the three new co-directors, a post she held for seven years. I've never let her forget about my hat.

EIA consultants stayed at an attractive specially built tented camp on the banks of the Kunene River, a kilometre above the Epupa Falls. My team only came into the camp every five or six days to refuel, get punctures fixed and have a shower. Most of the time we camped wherever we found ourselves, near the *ozonganda* of the people we were interviewing. Often when we went back to the EIA camp, we took in a few senior Himba men or women who wanted to see this relatively luxurious new camp on their land. They didn't need accommodation as they always had relatives nearby but I usually invited them to join us for lunch or dinner. The young man managing the camp agreed with me that this was fair enough and he made sure there was enough food on the table for an extra two or three people when we came by. Our Himba guests were always fascinated by the sight of a dozen or more men – the dam engineers – hard at work on their laptops at the large table, which was also used for meals.

During one of our sojourns at the camp, we woke up to a new notice on the dining room board. It was one of those erudite quotes, supposedly by some native American chief, censuring people who only see nature as a commodity to use and who destroy great forests and rivers. This had nothing to do with me; putting it up would have been an unprofessional act on my part but assumptions were made by some.

Chris Bakkes, another new staff member of IRDNC, had come in for a few days to assist the social team with extra transport and logistics for some of our bigger meetings in a remote headman's area. Larger than life (I'd told him it was just as well he'd lost part of one arm to a crocodile because if he had all four limbs intact he'd be insufferable), Chris livened up the somewhat earnest mood of the camp. He took full advantage of the free beer in the camp fridge and from the first dinner-table discussion, he and Mr S did not take to one another. Later, he would go on to write several books in Afrikaans, the last one, a mixture of half-truths and his own opinion – and anyway out of date by the time it was published, annoying those of us who continue to work hard to make a difference here. One of Chris' other achievements is being the only person ever to be evicted from the EIA camp. This was the morning after he sat at the campfire after dinner and belted out a particularly filthy – and rather amusing – version of the Engineer's Song, specially adapted for Epupa Dam.

Not far into the study, we realised that our Angolan colleague wasn't producing much information. Although he came to our update meeting in Windhoek – where we were meant to discuss our results – and went back to Angola with his vehicle filled with goods of every description, including scores of soccer balls, he had virtually no data to share. Was he actually doing any field work?

Then I got a strange email from one of my Scandinavian colleagues. He wanted to know if it was 'customary' for 'senior status' men to touch and fondle young Himba girl's bare breasts in public? Was this a common custom? I noted that the same email had gone to a few other anthropologists around the world. It was not a custom I'd ever heard of after a decade of working among Himba communities, I emailed back. What was this about? The story emerged: Filmmaker Craig Matthew had accompanied the Angolan consultant on one of his field trips. Not a lot of social data collecting had been done, according to Craig. But he did have some film footage of other activities at the visited homesteads. The consultant had a fondness for the bare breasts of young Himba women. And he was so confident that he was entitled to indulge himself that he fondled several breasts even though he knew he was being filmed.

The leaders of the study and the Swedish ambassador in Windhoek had become drawn into this situation after a concerned Craig had shown them his footage, uncertain what to do with it and about it. I was called to a meeting with the Swedish ambassador who feared that the Swedish government, who was paying the consultant, could find itself embroiled in a sexual abuse case. My take back then – decades before the #MeToo movement – was simple: Fire the consultant for not producing data, as well as for his obnoxious behaviour. He was seriously disadvantaging the Angolan Himba people who knew little or nothing about the proposal to flood hundreds of square kilometres of grazing. Angolan Himba people urgently needed to catch up with the EIA so we needed to get someone else fast.

Breasts were not regarded as erogenous zones by the Himba women I knew, and after I consulted some of my Himba friends, I was pretty sure the girls who had been fondled would not be psychologically scarred or believe themselves to be victims of sexual harassment. Kata said if this man touched her breasts she would pinch his nipples back and then shove him hard in the stomach. He would be regarded as rude and uncouth but sex didn't come in to it. If the man had touched bottoms, it would have been a different matter: he would have been thrown out of the homestead and told not to come back.

Needless to say no groping of breasts was aired on Namibian TV or shown in the long EIA documentary which came out later. The Angolan was replaced, with Michael Bollig doing much of the undone work.

Then there was the mass meeting called by Nampower, Namibia's power utility, to be held over two days in Opuwo. It was supposed to give a public update on the EIA but the rumour went round that the government would make its decision on the dam at this meeting. I'd gone back into the field to collect some health data but everywhere we stopped people had gone to Opuwo. Almost no one was at home; they'd walked, ridden donkeys or hitched to town. So we returned to Opuwo ourselves. I was hoping that after the meeting we could find large groups of people still in town which would make our health survey a lot easier.

All stops had been pulled out by the organisers. Most of Opuwo, and what seemed to be the majority of Himba men and woman who lived in the proposed dam's broader impact area to the north, were gathered on a large open plot. A row of dignitaries sat under shade cloth on a big stage. I recognised the Swedish ambassador and her delegation and Namibia's Deputy Minister of Mines and Energy among other government and Nampower officials. Rows of chairs and some shade had been provided for some of the guests below the stage. These chairs rapidly filled up, with others sitting on the ground. We estimated there were easily a thousand people present. Hundreds of them, including Himba men and youths, were wearing white T-shirts with the slogan Vive Epupa in large black letters on the back and front. They were being handed out as people came in through the gates. Most people took one and many put it on. Garth had joined us and we were uncomfortable about this blatant manipulation. Few people would resist a free T-shirt but we knew most of the Himba wearing one were against the dam and did not understand that the slogan on their chests and backs declared support for it.

But the meeting was starting. There were rousing speeches from various pro-dam officials. Each talk was punctuated by a live band of Namibian musicians, complete with electric guitars and drums, whose very small repertoire mostly comprised a song called Vive Epupa. It didn't have many words but it clearly conveyed the message that the dam was a great and good thing. About 50 youths, both male and female, sat in front right below the stage. They leapt up enthusiastically to cheer and shout Viva Epupa after every speech. The word went round they were part of a rent-a-crowd initiative.

The first speaker set the tone: He talked disparagingly about foreign and white conservationists who were enemies of Namibia. They were anti-development and did not want people to get the jobs they deserved, he said. They wanted people kept backward and primitive and they had confused people with their lies so that a few Himba had been persuaded to oppose the dam. His words reminded me of those white South African officials in the early days of the struggle against apartheid who always claimed it was outsiders – foreign communists, hiding behind every bush – who were misleading the black majority to resist the Nationalist government's policies. As if black people couldn't possibly be against apartheid unless they were being influenced by foreigners.

Now the Namibian official was talking about a certain blue Toyota truck that he said had been used to bribe Himba headmen to be against the Epupa Dam. Garth and I, and other IRDNC staff there, were outraged. Our NGO had indeed facilitated the acquisition of the old blue truck. It was in direct response to the Himba leadership complaining that they felt like children in the EIA process because they had no transport and had to rely on NGOs or government officials to take them to meetings about the dam. We raised some money from a Dutch organisation, bought a second-hand truck and spent a few more thousand ensuring it was roadworthy. Then we held a meeting to help the headmen decide who their driver would be and in whose name the car would be registered. We'd pointed out that someone senior needed to be in control of the car – not a youngster who happened to have a driving license – to ensure it wasn't wasted on frivolous journeys. And then we'd left it to them. There was no doubt the infamous blue Toyota assisted the leadership to more fully participate in the EIA process so we thought we'd done a good thing in the interests of fair play and democracy in the country.

We should have been under no illusions about the official position on the dam. We'd had an unnerving experience in the Omuhonga dry river bed recently near Okongwati. Garth and I met Andrew Corbett, then the director of the Legal Assistance Centre (LAC), and Clement Daniels another LAC lawyer up there for us to give the Himba leadership an update on the study, and for

Andrew, as the Himba's legal representative, to discuss some other matters. We'd discovered that contrary to the agreed process, no one was keeping the leaders sufficiently informed. In particular, we felt it important that they be allowed to hear what the Angolan social study, back on track after its deviation, was producing.

By mid-morning more than 30 Himba leaders and elders were assembled in the river bed. As we were starting, all sitting on the sand in a large circle, an unknown film crew arrived. They were covering the Epupa Dam story, they told us, and wanted to film our meeting. Andrew explained the meeting was not public and asked them to leave. I noticed that though they backed off, they continued filming us while standing next to their nearby vehicle. Annoyed, I went up to them and asked them to please push off. They were disrupting a private meeting and by filming us they risked inflaming an already sensitive situation.

On our way through, Garth and I had just heard from IRDNC colleagues who worked in Opuwo that they were being accused of being traitors to Namibia because they were associated with us and the EIA. This intimidation by government workers may not have been official, but it was making the lives of some of our good staff difficult. It also put our conservation and development work at risk. So while we knew those who were harassing IRDNC workers were in the wrong, we were in no mood to stir matters up by appearing on international TV with no control over how the filmmakers presented the footage.

With ill-concealed bad grace, the film crew started packing up. I went back to the meeting and had just stood up to give my report-back on the Angolan Himba leadership's position on the dam when I noticed a line of about 20 armed police walking towards us from Okangwati settlement. I remember thinking, oh, they're on a patrol.

When I next looked up from my notes, the barrel of an AK47 was pointing at my stomach. We'd been surrounded by the group. I don't often run out of words but my voice just dried up.

Andrew leapt up and demanded an explanation. He also asked the group to stop pointing their weapons at us. An officer explained that the meeting was illegal and that we should disperse peacefully at once. Under what law was it illegal for a lawyer to consult with his clients, and for those clients to be given an update on an official government-sanctioned EIA study?

During this exchange, I was examining the lone policewoman whose semi-automatic weapon was pointed at me. She was short, a dinky-sized person who looked very fetching in her tight camouflage pants and shirt. I realised that deep inside me there lurked some embarrassing prejudice against women and firearms that made a mockery of my post-feminism. I confess she frightened me because she looked too young and attractive to be competent in weapons use. I kept trying to see if her AK47's safety catch was on. Later, some of the men admitted to similar feelings about this petite policewoman. I stayed quiet, pretending to be secure in my feminist ideology though it had failed me under pressure.

By now Andrew was in heated argument with the police group. The rest of us, Himba leaders included, had backed off a bit, keen to put some distance between ourselves and the AK47s. Andrew was in his element; the Legal Assistance Centre had done a lot of courageous work during the war in Namibia and its staff were used to the police trying to break up legitimate meetings.

To our delight we saw the film crew had rapidly unpacked their equipment and were again approaching. This time they were very welcome; presumably the police would hesitate to mow us down if they were being filmed. The senior policeman was not happy; he insisted they stop filming. Obligingly, the cameraman took the camera off his shoulder and held it against his hip. He was still filming, but the officer had returned to his argument with Andrew.

The police were adamant they were keeping the peace. They'd heard the Himba were threatening violence because of the dam and they had been instructed not to allow any gatherings. Andrew, who knew the Minister of Police well from their mutual struggle days, wanted to go to the police station to phone the minister, whose personal number he had. The TV crew obligingly produced a satellite phone, and there in the river bed, Andrew was able to contact the minister who then spoke to the head policeman. He was instructed to let the meeting take place. The line of police walked off, back to Okongwati.

After brewing some tea to calm our nerves we continued the meeting. A car load of familiar young men soon arrived. They were wearing plain clothes and sunglasses instead of their police uniforms, reminding me of Haiti dictator Papa Doc Duvalier's sinister special police. They parked within earshot and ignored Andrew's request that they move off. Eventually we decided to just go ahead as nothing we had to say was subversive.

The dramatic footage – of belligerent, armed police surrounding and confronting unarmed civilians, including peaceful, elderly Himba men sitting on white sand in a dry river bed – went around the world within 24 hours although I never saw it. It appeared on BBC news broadcasts and in the USA. For weeks afterwards, we got emails from friends and relatives, asking if we were alright and wanting to know when Namibia had turned into a dangerous police state. The police's ill-considered action to try to stop a legitimate meeting did the young country's image no good.

The confrontation triggered one important outcome. The LAC decided to challenge in court the section of a law that dated back to the apartheid government, under which government could summarily declare gatherings illegal. They won the case.

Back at the Opuwo mass meeting other speakers praised the government for its initiative to build the Epupa dam, which would bring many thousands of jobs to the area. Every house and hut would have electricity. Businesses in Opuwo would thrive; people would have cash in their pockets. Utopia lay ahead.

I was fuming and went and found the head of the Namibian engineering company contracted in the EIA. Was he happy with fellow Namibians being misled I asked?

Like me, he knew well that the jobs created by the building of Epupa would only last during the actual building phase, a few years, and then just a small team of technicians would be needed to run the dam. Other such dams had clearly shown the boom-and-bust scenario the Kunene Region would be facing. He also knew that the electricity generated would not bring power to Himba huts because it was unlikely that they would be able to pay for it! A decent man who was making a lot of money out of the EIA and who stood to make millions more if the dam was built, he agreed to stand up and give actual numbers of jobs (maybe 1 200 from both Namibia and Angola, many of them skilled and semi-skilled workers), and only for the building phase of the dam.

As the hot morning wore on and the Himba groups sat patiently listening to points of view opposite to the ones they held, some of the Himba leadership called a quick meeting with their lawyer, the fiery young Norman Tjombe, Garth and me. The former was attending on behalf of Andrew and the Legal Assistance Centre. Norman knew his clients were opposed to the dam and could see the snow job being done that morning. The concern was that the Swedish ambassador would be seriously misled. Norman was asked to intervene. He rose and with some difficulty got the meeting's master of ceremonies to allow him to ask a question.

When, he wanted to know, would the Himba leadership and those opposed to the building of the dam be given the chance to speak?

An agenda was waved in Norman's direction and he was asked to be patient. The schedule was very tight with many people due to speak. The Himba would have their chance tomorrow, Sunday.

Norman knew the ambassador and her team would only stay the first day, thus leaving with the false impression that the dam was widely welcomed. The Swedes were great dam builders but few dams were being built in Europe or US any more, and some were being de-commissioned as people realised that in some areas water was too valuable to be allowed to evaporate in huge hydro-electric schemes. This dam could provide many lucrative contracts for Swedish businesses if it went ahead. Thus the Swedish funding of the EIA was not just philanthropy.

Norman argued his case ardently, pointing out that the schedule was not too tight to have a pop group repeatedly singing the same

170

song between speeches. He asked the ambassador directly when she planned to leave the meeting. Having established she would be here after lunch but would leave Opuwo early the next morning, thus missing the second day when the Himba had been given their 'slot', he put pressure on the now-flustered emcee to reschedule the Himba leaders for this afternoon. He was sure, he said, that the Swedish party would be very keen to hear from the actual people whose cattle herding economy would be impacted by the dam, not just those who lived in Opuwo and Windhoek. The ambassador looked out at the sea of white Vive Epupa T-shirts, smiled and said she would indeed.

We had to wait till nearly 3 pm for the dignitaries who we assume had a big official lunch in town to remount the stage. The pop group tried to rally the crowd who were much quieter now. The youths in the front had dwindled to half their number, some of them probably nursing stomach aches from an unaccustomed overdose of junk food. We'd noticed they had plenty of cash to buy cold drinks, crisps and sweets all morning.

It was a hot afternoon. Norman had a short sharp argument in Herero with someone on the stage which ensured there were no more delays.

The first Himba leader Wahenuna spoke eloquently about why he and his people opposed the building of a dam which would flood the area from above the Epupa Falls to Nyandi, about 70 kilometres of river frontage, and an area of 250 square kilometres. Hundreds of ancestral graves would be under water and this was unacceptable to his people. He talked about the people fearing a big influx of job seekers; the government wanted the dam to give all their ex-combatants jobs. The Himba people, who could not speak English and had no schooling, would not get those jobs. He was concerned that the incomers would create a state of lawlessness. Would they listen to the Himba traditional authorities or would they do as they pleased on Himba land? These new people would keep their own domestic stock and may use up the grazing that Himba lineages reserved for the late dry season. So not only would people lose a huge amount of land under the waters of the dam and be pushed back into the gazing areas of others, they would also lose control of their land to strangers.

All this was absolutely likely and had been raised in the pre-feasibility study we did in 1992. These scenarios were listed as some of the major socio-economic and cultural impacts in that report. The crowd was attentive now, not just the Himba people, and only a few voices shouted Vive Epupa when the dignified traditional councillor sat down. A lot of people clapped loudly.

Mutambo was next. He wanted to discuss the blue Toyota he said, grasping the bull by its horns. He asked the crowds to look around the big field. They should count how many white Toyota Land Cruisers were parked nearby, having brought government and Nampower people from Windhoek. Everyone knew, he said, that these cars had been a gift to the government by the United Nations and other donors. Were these donors bribing the Namibian government? He paused and let the silence grow. Of course not, he continued, these donors gave these cars to help the country and the government. Why then was the old blue truck seen as a bribe? Surely the government could see that the old truck – just one old car compared to the thousands the government had been given – was meant to help the Himba? Or did the government speaker want the headmen to rely on NGOs for their transport? He also took issue with the government for treating the Himba people as if they were children who needed to be told what to think. His people had eyes and ears and could make up their own minds.

It was an inspiring piece of oratory. When he sat down after 20 off-the-cuff minutes, he received thunderous applause. The two Himba speakers had taken back the meeting. Even though not every word had been translated, enough of it had reached the ears of the Swedish delegation who were looking rather grim-faced.

Before the meeting ended – the second day having been called off as the Himba had already had their say – the Deputy Minister of Mines and Energy stood up. He announced that the Epupa dam would be built. Read my lips, he said, the dam will be built; the only decision still to be made is which of the three possible sites will be used. Strategically it was not a wise thing to say then as it, combined with the T-shirt fiasco that was about to erupt, was the tipping point in the EIA process.

Early the next morning Shorty and I went to the part of town where most of the Himba leadership was camping. We wanted a meeting with them to discuss a schedule for the health survey. Many people were still wearing their Vive Epupa T-shirts. I asked the men I was talking to while we waited for other headmen to arrive if they knew what the message on the shirts meant.

You know we can't read, someone said. What do our shirts say? I explained that the slogan declared support for the dam.

There was a stunned silence and then the headmen, one after the other, pulled off their Vive Epupa T-shirts and threw them on the ground. Some men spat contemptuously. A few youths were called and given instructions. In the next 15 minutes the pile of T-shirts grew till it was chest high. Everywhere you looked men and youths were taking off shirts. A score or so angry headmen were now grouped around the huge mound of T-shirts, talking among themselves, upset and excited.

'Er . . . what about my health survey? Could we just make a plan about that quickly and then we can leave the headmen.'

Shorty gave me a familiar look – which meant how can she worry us about such small things when something so important is being discussed – but he dutifully translated for me. After some more exchanges, a senior headmen who knew us well gestured at me and the shirts.

'You, who are working for the government on this dam story. Take these shirts and give them back.'

I shook my head. 'Oh no, not me – I'm just a consultant. You and your people took the shirts; you must take them back to one of the regional offices in town yourself.' I was already unpopular enough in pro-dam government circles without getting mixed up in the T-shirt debacle.

People were truly angry. They felt deceived and humiliated. As one old man put it: 'This government knows we can't read so they gave us these shirts to trick us.' The shirts coupled with the damage done by the deputy minister's statement that the dam would be built was the tipping point in the work towards the survey. The men told Shorty and me they had decided to withdraw from the EIA.

I was taken by surprise and started arguing against this decision. They should stay with the process, I said. That way they could influence what happened, especially in regard to the mitigation package if the dam was built, which still needed to be discussed. If they withdrew, they would lose that opportunity.

Minds had been made up and there was nothing I could say to change them. It was explained that they knew I was sincere in what I said, that I believed that the study would inform the decisions ahead. But surely I could see that I too was being deceived? The deputy minister had said very clearly in public that the decision to build the dam had already been taken. So the study was just a waste of time, a game the government was playing with the Himba people while behind their backs they went ahead with their plans to build their dam; a dam that would destroy the Himba, putting their ancestors' graves under water, and give their land to strangers.

We went back to town. I had to email the head of the consulting consortium about the boycott of the rest of the social study. Although we spoke to various Himba leaders again, the boycott stayed in place. I was asked to write up my incomplete report and did so. Apart from the health survey, the all-important mitigation section of the EIA – when decisions are made about how best to compensate the affected people for their loss of land and mitigate against other negative impacts – was not yet done. For the Scandinavian consortium this was disaster as an EIA without this section made the project un-bankable, as they put it. No one would fund the dam without a mitigation package in place. Many dams go ahead in developing countries where the mitigation section is inadequate to say the least, but to give the consortium and the Swedish Government credit, they wanted to do things correctly.

Thus we were called to a meeting in Windhoek early in 1997.

Most of the consultants were assembled. Results and data were discussed and then attention was moved to the undone mitigation report. Mr S's assistant proposed that we go ahead with a mitigation workshop, even though we'd have no Himba input. I objected and said that the EIA process required the input of the affected people – this was not negotiable – and that we should be discussing how we could get the Himba to stop the boycott.

Patiently, it was explained that the study was incomplete without the mitigation section; it was our responsibility to produce one. As someone who had worked with and studied the Himba people for a decade, surely I knew enough to speak on their behalf? I would not be comfortable doing this, I said, and suggested again that we explore ways to get the study back on track. Mr S's assistant sighed and suggested that I be a bit less militant and more co-operative.

Garth, who would have been a key player in discussing mitigation with Himba leadership, stood up and defended me. I was showing integrity, not militancy, he said.

Dr Chris Brown, on the permanent joint Angolan-Namibian governments' Epupa dam management committee, spoke next. With his usual eloquence, he talked about the importance of this first EIA to the new Namibia; how it would set the precedent for future EIAs and that we had to do it right and be seen to be doing it right. Thus he supported me and Garth fully. He asked me if we thought the Himba leadership would drop the boycott if the deputy minister was prepared to withdraw his statement in public.

I said I thought they might well.

Chris then suggested that instead of the proposed mitigation workshop, we spend some time drafting a suitable letter for the PJMC to sign asking the deputy minister to recant his 'Read my Lips' statement.

The Scandinavians disagreed and pushed for their mitigation workshop. Having been given a bad name, I may have become a bit militant then and I spoke about expediency versus integrity. With Garth and Chris on my side I almost felt sorry for our opponents. More support came from an unexpected direction. The Windhoek engineering consultants stood up and agreed with us, that a letter

be written trying to get the EIA back on track. Other consultants
– South African Dave Grossman, archaeologist John Kinahan
and several more – also supported this. It was actually a moving
experience to see that most of us, certainly all the Namibians and
southern Africans, irrespective of how we felt about the dam, truly
wanted the EIA to be of world-class standard. This meant doing
the right thing, even if it would delay the EIA's conclusion and
make us politically unpopular.

A letter was written but the deputy minister failed to take
back his statement. My consultancy contract was terminated
after I produced my report. I had a short sharp exchange with
the consultancy firm after a Swedish journalist phoned me to ask
why I had resigned. I said I had not resigned and narrated the
circumstances that led to the boycott; I was happy to resume my
role whenever the Himba agreed to continue the study. By then
Chief Kapika, formerly senior chief in the impact zone, had visited
Sweden and expressed his views against the dam very clearly.

An academic from the University of Namibia was appointed to
take my place. He held at least one large meeting at Epupa to discuss
mitigation. We heard about truckloads of bread and meat for those
who attended. The food was eaten but the Himba leadership was
unmoved. They were against the dam, and wanted nothing more
to do with the process.

As for the story about Chief Kapika having his feet massaged by
a Swedish minister who visited him to discuss his position on the
dam, this is what is supposed to have happened. I wasn't there but
a reliable eye witness was, claiming he filmed the meeting, too.

The Swedish government official (to spare her embarrassment
we'll not mention her portfolio) arrived with a government
delegation to see Chief Kapika at his *onganda* near Okangwati.
Their helicopter landed next to the homestead and no doubt
attracted quite a crowd. As his area would suffer the main impact
of the dam, the then chief was a key figure. Various government

players, right up to the president, had done their best to gain Chief Kapika's support. But he opposed the dam, irrespective of the government giving him a shiny new, red Toyota truck and even a ski-boat (so he could easily cross the dam to see his relatives in Angola). And he had a special grievance against the dam proponents.

We'd discovered during the pre-feasibility study that the chief had been misled about the dam's massive size, and he had given permission for it to be built. He'd thought it would be a nice big dam about 60 or even 100 metres across and he'd believed the officials who said the project would bring shops, schools, a hospital, electricity and plenty of water to the Himba. When he was told by Garth, Chris Tapscott and me the actual size of the dam and how much land it would flood, he and the elders with him were stunned and horrified. No way would they accept this project once they realised its magnitude.

Chief Kapika is well-known as a difficult man, even without feeling he'd been duped. Somebody should have warned the poor Swedish visitor. But perhaps the sophisticated Windhoek-based Namibian officials who accompanied her thought that a remote Himba headman would be over-awed by this important group helicoptering in.

Soon after the visitors arrived and sat down in the smart new camping chairs they'd brought, Chief Kapika appeared, carrying his own chair. It was a decrepit old canvas affair, the frame tied together with wire. Greetings were exchanged. Before anyone could go further the chief wanted to know what they'd brought him. It's not unusual for people seeking an audience with an important Himba chief to bring a gift but most are not as up front about it.

Consternation: no one had thought to bring anything. Then someone had a bright idea – he hurried back to the helicopter and rummaged in the big cool-box which contained the party's lunch. He returned with a cold Coke. This was presented to the chief. He tossed it to a nearby child. Then folded his hands in his lap expectantly.

As a politician, the Swedish minister was good at thinking on her feet even when sitting in a deck chair opposite a half-naked African chief wearing a cotton cloth round his hips and sandals made from car-tyres. She pulled her bright red Swiss Army Knife out of her bag and ceremoniously passed it to him. Chief Kapika found this gift acceptable although he owned several such knives. He examined it for a few seconds, obviously approving that the toothpick was still in its slot behind the scissors and tweezers, before giving it to one of his wives.

The meeting facilitator asked after the chief's health.

My foot hurts, he said. He kicked off his car-tyre sandal and stuck a dusty, callused foot out, presumably because the Swedish minister was the only woman there or perhaps she had been introduced as doctor somebody, although her doctorate was not in medicine. I need ointment, the chief said, gesturing at a small cut in his in-step and looking hopefully at her handbag.

I'm told she kept her composure but looked around for help. One of the party urgently asked if anyone had ointment, any kind of cream. No one did. Then, yet again, the minister saved the day. She had some sun-tan lotion. Would that do? It couldn't do any harm as the cut was nearly healed.

So it came to pass that the Swedish woman massaged lotion into Chief Kapika's foot. He lay his foot on her lap and seemed to enjoy her gentle touch. When she indicated she was finished, he was quick to swop feet so that she could give the other one a bit of a rub too.

The punchline to this story is not the chief's feet. It's that after talking for a while, the group said their goodbyes, shook hands all round, got back into their helicopter and flew off to find a nice shady place to have their picnic lunch.

My eye witness had a burning question for the group: Why didn't you talk to the chief about the dam? Wasn't that the whole point of the meeting?

Because the chief didn't mention the dam, was the reply…

The Epupa dam project petered out and while its merits were praised occasionally by a few of our leaders, the Namibian public heard no more about it.

Then in 2009/10 a new EIA was launched, this time looking at a site down-river of Epupa Falls, the Baines site. This wouldn't flood Epupa Falls and while the dam wall would be higher – 200 metres versus the Epupa's 163-metre-high wall, it could be argued by some that because it was in a high canyon, it was the least damaging of the two sites. I played a small role in the socio-cultural side of the new study and found nothing had changed. Those who farmed the area were still against a dam; those to whom the dam offered opportunity were for it. The socio-economic and cultural impacts would still be devastating for the resident Himba herders – apart from pushing them back into other people's herding areas.

At a Windhoek meeting, to which the Angolan delegation failed to arrive, a Nampower official proposed that the affected Himba be removed to a commercial farm that could be bought for them. This did not solve the ancestral grave problem, someone pointed out. She shrugged this off and stuck with her farm idea. At tea-time, I tried to explain to her why this would be impractical, given that the Himba are semi-nomadic pastoralists. But her cell phone rang; she needed to take the call. She didn't return to the meeting, having delivered her pearl of wisdom.

One of the mitigations I was able to propose in my section of the report was that the local people should get all tourism rights to the proposed dam's banks and to any islands formed by the inundation of the area.

Perhaps because the new site's geomorphology dictates that the dam-building town would have to be on the Angolan bank, meaning Angolans, rather than Namibians, would be in the frontline for jobs, and that supplies would logically come via Angola on an existing road, thus benefitting that country more than Namibia, there has been low interest in this project and like Epupa, it seems to have run out of steam.

FOURTEEN

Conservation in a war zone

Doing conservation work in a war zone requires changing one's strategy but not one's goal – Lessons from the Field

WAR CAME TO WEST Caprivi in 2000. Now part of Bwabwata National Park, this narrow strip of Namibia between Angola and Botswana is home to about 6 000 San people who call themselves Khoe, some Vasekele families, also San or Bushmen, and steadily increasing Mbukushu households from the Kavango Region across the Okavango River.

The strip is also vital elephant habitat, with populations of buffalo, impala, eland, roan, sable, tessebe, and small herds of red lechwe along the Kwando River. Sitatunga and waterbuck are occasionally seen. It is one of the last places left in the world where Southern African wattled crane can still be viewed and one of the last refuges of wild dogs. Other predators include lion, cheetah, leopard, hyena and jackals. Hippo and crocodile are plentiful in the Kwando and Okavango rivers, even though an anthrax outbreak hit hippo numbers in late 2017.

IRDNC had been working in former East and West Caprivi – now the Zambezi Region – since 1990. Our focus was similar to the work we did in the Kunene Region: community-based conservation with communities, their traditional leaders and government, and helping to improve management of natural resources by communities and facilitating ways for communities to benefit socially and economically from wildlife and other valuable natural resources. We wanted to show that community-based principles worked as well in this high-density population area in the north-east as in the sparsely populated north-west.

Our first foray into the north-east applying what had worked successfully in Kunene had not gone well, and taught us some valuable lessons: while there are common principles that underlie community conservation, there is no Holy Grail. You cannot just 'roll out' methods from one area to another.

The first of these principles requires taking the time to establish relationships, based on mutual trust and respect, with local communities *and* any other players who can impact on the resources you wish to see better managed and conserved. Also essential is rekindling a local vision of wildlife being valuable – culturally, socially and economically. In most African societies wildlife was valuable in pre-colonial days and historically Caprivi had a rich tapestry of cultural rules around hunting: sanctuaries where only hunters appointed by the chief could kill a limited number of a particular species, being just one example.

But we live in modern times and it's necessary to expose people to the ways in which wildlife can be a valuable part of the future. And not just economically. Over many years of working with different peoples in southern Africa – Namibia, South Africa, Zambia, Angola and Mozambique – and communicating with Africans across the continent, we've found that once this door – community conservation – is opened, it's an idea whose time has come. We've never had to 'hard sell' this concept to fellow Africans: different generations don't connect with the same aspects of community conservation but almost all see the potential and the value of ensuring that wild animals are not wiped out. Older people may see wonderful cultural links from their past which could enrich the future; the young may see opportunities for jobs and income but usually also the self-esteem and pride that goes with taking responsibility and being accountable. Don't all of us want to steer our own development?

Community conservation is more about *how* you implement than *what* you implement. You only discover the *how* when you are in a real partnership with the communities who live with the valued resources, and can mutually develop a methodology that is applicable to local conditions. Thus in Caprivi in 1990 my impatient nature walked IRDNC straight into a debacle.

Nothing happened in former East Caprivi in those days – and is still relatively true today – without permission and buy-in from the traditional authorities who are organised into traditional courts, or *khutas*. These are made up of the chief, the *ngambele* (a type of prime minister) and a number of *indunas*, representing different areas and villages. There are *silalo indunas* (sitting indunas – who attend the *khuta*) and *indunas*, who are village-based, and sometimes these men swapped positions.

After a fairly frustrating series of meetings with some of the main *khutas* we'd got nowhere. The Caprivians (now Zambezians) were suspicious and hostile about nature conservation – or, as we were sure, how it had been practised in the region. The then Directorate of Nature Conservation had taken a hard-line approach – walking into a village suspected of poaching and kicking over a cooking pot to see what sort of meat it contained, as one man told it. Communities retaliated: in an extreme case a postman was shot at because people thought he was from the directorate. We were warned directly at one *khuta* that if we built a house for 'our' conservation people in Zambezi, we might find it burnt down.

The key, obviously, was to change the 'our' to mean belonging to the *khuta* and their people and not to us. The community game guard system had worked excellently in Kunene to directly involve local people in conservation and to grow a sense of community ownership over wildlife. Accordingly, at a *khuta* meeting I attended with a young government nature conservation official from Katima Mulilo, who was supportive of community conservation, I pushed the *ngambela* and *indunas* hard – too hard, as it turned out.

Having been given the run around yet again by the roomful of old men, I stood up and made an impertinent and impassioned speech. I told them that as leaders they needed to look forward. It was true nature conservation had a bad relationship with local people, and had even taken away chiefs' traditional rights to have a limited number of wild animals hunted for certain annual ceremonies. But that was in the past. Now we had a new independent government and we were working together to forge a new type of conservation where people would find wildlife was more valuable alive than in a cooking pot.

So far so good. The next part was what got us into trouble. Indicating the 20 or so members of the public in the gallery at the *khuta*, I asked the leaders if they really felt they had the right to go on preventing their people from getting jobs as community game guards. Didn't people here need jobs and salaries out in the villages, as was happening in Kunene? I literally played to the gallery and asked a series of questions in a way that made it look like the *khuta* was holding back development in the area. My strategy worked and after discussion – without me and my government companion present – the *khuta* called us back in and told us we could appoint eight men as community game guards. Oh no, I said, you have to appoint them. They will work for you, not IRDNC or government nature conservation. We'll just raise money to pay them and work with you to decide their duties.

Elated, I looked forward to telling Garth when I got back to Kunene that I had kick-started the Caprivi project in one area. And surely other *khutas* would soon follow.

Setting off for Kunene, I gave a lift to a young British man Matthew Rice who had been helping to build a lodge in the area. We'd encountered him a few times and spotted real potential as well as liking him. Instead of dropping him off in Otiwarongo to hike on to Windhoek, I offered him a job – working in Zambezi with the about-to-be-appointed community game guards and further developing a community conservation project. We both drove on to Wereldsend. Matt spent a few months working with us in Kunene, and then moved to his new post in Zambezi. Thus we helped change the direction of his life.

The *khuta* duly appointed their game guards. One of them was particularly zealous, asking for hand-cuffs so he could restrain arrested poachers. Without dampening his enthusiasm, we explained he was not a policeman and while the community game guards would try to catch poachers, their primary job was to work closely with the *khuta* to *stop* poaching.

Naturally, within a few months, Matthew discovered that this game guard was his village's number one poacher, well-known for selling meat to his neighbours. The *khuta* knew this too and had set me up – after all I was just some woman who had come to the *khuta* two or three times trying to 'sell' an idea from the outside. This is typical of what happens when people rush in to community work, without first developing real relationships. In my case, we ended up paying a poacher to poach.

Additionally, it was my vision that I was trying to impose on the *khuta*, instead of taking the time to nurture a local vision of wildlife once again being valuable to the people who lived with it, not just to government, NGOs and owners of lodges.

Over the next ten years in the north-east, IRDNC developed the needed relationships and a local vision grew, as did a local version of how community conservation could work successfully. For seven of those years, Matt Rice coordinated this project, taking to community conservation like a duck to water.

Much of the progress we'd made was threatened – and indeed halted – by the spill over of the Angolan civil war into West Caprivi.

The war in Angola – over control of the country's valuable oil and diamond resources – was more than 30 years old when President Dos Santos' forces decided to deal with the small groups of men still loyal to Jonas Savimbi, most of whom were huddling in the bush in the region closest to Angola's border with West Caprivi. The Namibian government gave permission for Angolan troops to enter West Caprivi to clear these last rebel strongholds.

The first the people of Namibia knew of this was in 2000 when a French family from the Comores were ambushed in their hired camper vehicle on the West Caprivi highway. An IRDNC staff member happened to be first on the scene, his arrival possibly even causing the attackers to flee. Three children were killed and the father badly injured. The mother was found alive, shocked and bloodstained on the side of the road. Savimbi's men were accused of this brutal massacre, apparently in retaliation for Namibia allowing the Angolan army into West Caprivi.

Tourism had been building up nicely in Caprivi until August 1999 when there was an attempted coup by a small group of East Caprivians wanting Caprivi to break away from Namibia, and ally itself with Zambia. With this violent, brief and doomed secession bid followed a few months later by the fatal attack on the French family, tourism stopped dead in its tracks. Lodges and other tourism-related businesses were forced to close and as the months went by, scores of local staff lost their jobs.

With a decade of community conservation under its belt in Caprivi, IRDNC now faced some hard choices. Our first challenge was that we were funded by a grant from USAID. The Americans have strict conditions attached to their funding, and we were informed that none of the project staff would be allowed into the 'war zone' which is what West Caprivi had become, now occupied by the Namibian Defence Force, the Angolan troops and the rebels. USAID dropped its request for a staff evacuation plan once we explained that IRDNC supported more than 30 West Caprivian game guards, some field officers and a team of local women community resource officers (locally called *kwena chapi* – community keys who opened doors/opportunities for their community) and that they actually all lived in the war zone. But they stuck to their instructions to pull out all equipment that USAID had funded, including vehicles and two-way radios, and to cease using USAID funding to pay our West Caprivian team. A few staff had fled to Botswana to avoid the conflict but most had stayed.

Garth and I rebelled – we were not about to abandon West Caprivians when they needed us most, plus the area's wildlife would be under great threat from occupying troops wanting meat. We needed to find ways to maintain a conservation presence. Our appeal to USAID to consider continuing partial funding went nowhere. To be fair to the American officials in the USAID office in Windhoek, it was not within their power to change the rules, many of which were based on congressional decisions.

Our only way forward then was to find new funders. But who would be crazy enough to donate money to do conservation in a war zone? Fortunately, we knew just the right people. Two Swedish men – one of whom later went on to invest in Himba-owned Conservancy Safaris Namibia – were putting up to a million Namibian dollars a year into our Kunene work. We'd taken them out into Kunene a few times by then, and knew Anders Johansson and Staffan Encrantz to be progressive thinkers who'd become wealthy men by taking chances, not by playing it safe. I wrote to them immediately explaining the situation and its urgency. It took them just a few days to make up their minds – they were in. This was wonderful news, and as a result we were able to keep the community staff on half-salaries for the duration of the war. We also swapped round vehicles so that none bought with USAID funding were operational in the area.

An early morning UNITA attack on a road-building camp near where some of our non-Caprivian staff lived in West Caprivi prompted us to relocate them to the region's only town, Katima Mulilo, 130 kilometres away. Our local West Caprivian staff refused to move, even though it was very difficult for them to do their jobs, mostly being confined to their villages. They did not want to abandon their homes and their communities.

Richard Diggle, our Caprivi coordinator at that time, is British, a former banker who displayed that typically English characteristic of rising to the challenge in tough times. With staff, he developed a colour-coded operating system which could be assessed from one week to another and applied to our rural workers. Red – no travel, stay home. Yellow – limited work and travel but nothing after dark. Green, cautiously operational. West Caprivi, occupied by three armies, was obviously in a permanent state of code red.

The Namibian Defence Force closed the West Caprivi highway. If you had to traverse this area, you joined a convoy with an armed military escort which was provided once or twice a day. The only other way to drive to East Caprivi was through Botswana, via Gobabis on Namibia's eastern border.

We were very concerned about leaving the area's valuable wildlife to the mercy of the armed soldiers, especially since the Angolan government troops appeared to have no supply lines and were literally living off the land and the local people. Of the rebels we had little information. The Namibian Defence Force base was the Omega Military Camp which had been a headquarters for the South African and South West African troops – including Khoe and Vasekele San soldiers – during the liberation struggle.

One of our first actions was to transfer to Caprivi a Kunene IRDNC staff member who had fought in PLAN, Swapo's military wing. Mike's credentials and experience helped immensely with liaison with the Namibian military who had tended to be suspicious of the rest of us.

We learnt that we needed to change our methods to achieve the same conservation objectives, and that we had to take it step by step, first building relationships, in this case, with the Namibian military authorities. Not an easy task as senior officers tended to be replaced every few months, so we'd have to start all over again with a new man. But with Richard's leadership and careful attention to detail and Mike's record as a PLAN fighter, we steadily made progress.

Regularly, we used the military convoy to travel to Omega to meet with officers at the military base, and we got permission from senior officers there to be allowed to visit the villages of our staff to ensure they got their half-salaries and to keep up their morale. Richard had to take a day's unpaid leave to join us on these occasions as he was a third-party national, still funded by USAID, and as such he could not enter the war zone on USAID's funding. Garth and I, as Namibians who were in any case not paid by USAID but by the more robust British WWF, could decide to take risks as we wished.

And risk it was; more than 50 people were killed in West Caprivi during this period, either shot by the rebels or the Angolan government forces or blown up by anti-personnel mines. Roads were also mined with a pile of elephant dung, a common sight – a favourite way to disguise where a mine had been laid. It was difficult to tell the difference between the rebels and the Angolan government troops. Some of the latter definitely did not behave well, taking what little food local people had by force. A community game guard was shot dead after an Angolan government soldier was injured by an anti-personnel mine laid by the rebel Unita. Because the mine was near the game guard's village, the Angolans insisted he must have known about it.

Learning as we went along, we asked permission to do HIV/AIDS education at the Omega base. With bored soldiers as a captive audience, we discussed the epidemic and the ways the disease could be avoided. At the same talk, we discussed community conservation, mentioning the West Caprivian staff. We always stressed that our independent Namibian government had adopted community conservation as a strategy for development and so anyone poaching wildlife was being disloyal to the new Namibia.

Remarkably, this and other initiatives did make a difference and West Caprivi's wildlife was not decimated during these years, although undoubtedly some animals were poached. But it could have been a lot worse. We were also eventually able to get the military patrols to start taking community game guards with them, pointing out that these local men who knew the area well were a valuable resource. This stopped and started a few times, depending on who was in charge, but gradually we – and some of our staff – were being seen as a positive force.

We also got permission to use a small team of Namibian soldiers to assist us to continue IRDNC's monitoring of the impact of fire on West Caprivian vegetation. One of Garth's preoccupations is fire. The colonial banning of fires has turned out to be a disaster on African savannahs which have suffered severe bush encroachment wherever fire was removed from the system. But each ecosystem is different so there was no single fire strategy for all. Both East and West Caprivians had been burning for generations. The result – what the colonial government encountered when they arrived – was a productive open mosaic of grasses, trees, healthy floodplains and riparian forests, able to support a wide diversity of animals.

At independence, the new government had continued the South West African anti-fire stance and even strengthened it by accepting funding from the Finnish government to stamp out wild fires. This broke down local burning strategies, based on generations of local knowledge. Unfortunately none of the relevant government ministries or the Finnish donors seemed to notice that what the local people had been doing with their early burns each year had resulted in healthy veld. (An early burn simply means setting fire to the veld as soon after rains as possible – usually by April, May or June – instead of late year burns when a lot of fuel has had a chance to build up and the veld is very dry. The latter are hot dangerous fires that kill trees.) Nor did the authorities notice that the forestry reserve in East Caprivi, where fires had been actively prevented for decades – as we were told by proud forestry officials – had turned into an impenetrable bush thicket, severely limiting biodiversity and preventing all but a few very small species from using the area.

So there was some clear evidence that banning local burning resulted in bush encroachment and major build ups of fuel. Inevitably, late in the year, prevalent lightning or human error started fires. In areas that had been 'protected' from the local cool early burning, massive fires could now sweep unimpeded across huge swathes of dry veld, except around the small forestry station which staff worked hard at protecting. Elsewhere these hot fires killed wonderful mature trees, some of which had survived the local way of burning for generations.

Tired of hearing about fire from a variety of experts who based their opinions more on their own prejudices and academic paradigms than veld observations, we started the fire-monitoring project in West Caprivi that later linked us to Australian fire ecologists and communities. For 200 kilometres, every ten kilometres, we set up two marker poles, 200 metres into the bush to the left and to the right of the road. Three times a year at each pole we'd take four photographs of the vegetation: to the north, west, south and east. Satellite imagery provided an annual fire history, and in this way over a number of years, we could show the ground-truthed impact of early-in-the-year, and therefore cool fires, versus the later hot ones, or, if it so happened, no burning at all.

Early results gave us the impetus to facilitate a burning programme and IRDNC hired an Australian fire ecologist, Robin Beatty, who coincidently turned out to have studied under the key Darwin fire ecologists we later met. Robin worked with conservancies, traditional authorities and government to develop Namibia's first regional fire management plan. At the height of this programme, Robin had 60 per cent of the Zambezi Region being burnt early in the season by local fire teams – soon after the rains ended in April. The post-fire healthy green veld that benefited wildlife and domestic stock even started winning over the lodge owners, many of whom suffered from what we called the Bambi syndrome – Bambi being the sad little red deer whose habitat gets burnt up, and who has been used on stop wildfire posters. Bambi, of course, comes from an European ecosystem, not the African savanna. An outcome of the programme was that MET started early burning the national parks in Zambezi, thus also avoiding the late season dangerous hot fires due to build-up of dry reeds and grasses. MET also allowed the Khoe to openly continue their old burning practices in West Caprivi which was now Bwabwata National Park. The result was a large increase in grazing species – buffalo, sable, roan, zebra and lechwe.

It was quite a mission to continue our fire photo-monitoring after 2000. Lynne Halstead, a senior IRDNC facilitator, and I did the photogaphy together for a while. Almost all the Namibian soldiers assigned to us were terrified of wildlife. Usually Lynn and I ended up leading, with five or six reluctant armed escorts trailing behind. It was not that they were afraid of standing on personnel mines – our poles were not on a path – but that we might encounter elephant, buffalo or predators. I usually took our well-trained dogs with us on these bush walks, knowing they would be far better at early warning against dangerous wildlife, or other humans, than the timid soldiers.

Our biggest problem turned out to be finding our poles and we cursed ourselves for locating them 200 metres from the road when we could just as easily done 100 metres. For sure, a few poles were knocked down by elephant – we found them lying on the ground – but mostly it was just amazingly difficult to find a five-foot-high white pole in the healthy green (usually previously burnt) vegetation, including two-metre-high thatch grass.

My Jack Russell named Katira (Fearless in Herero) endeared herself to many of the men who drove with us as armed escorts. She regarded the front passenger seat of any vehicle I drove as hers. The lap of anyone sitting there was merely her convenient cushion, making it easier for her to see out and assist in navigation. A soldier with an AK47 on his lap was no impediment to this five-kilo dog with big attitude, and she would perch on him, or even on his firearm, causing much amusement in my car. Katira soon became one of the best-known members of our IRDNC team, helping us forge good relationships, as we traversed the war zone trying to keep a flag flying for community conservation.

The occupation of West Caprivi ended in 2002, within a few months of Jonas Savimbi being killed in Angola, with photographs of his body being circulated to prove he was dead. It took several years before the Zambezi Region got back to normal and tourism restarted very slowly.

With help from IRDNC, the residents of Bwabwata National Park had formed the residents' association and trust called Kyaramycan Association (KA) which was aimed at enabling them – as far as is possible – to achieve similar rights to wildlife as those enjoyed by communal conservancies outside parks on communal land. Eventually, MET agreed to give the KA 50 per cent of two lucrative trophy hunting contracts inside the park. Apart from their excellent stewardship of wildlife, this share of hunting fees was one way MET could contribute towards compensating the Khoe for agreeing, for example, to restrict their ownership of domestic stock. Sadly the few score resident Mbukushu did not, and over the years hundreds more people and cattle moved in from the Kavango

Region. The MET was unable to deal with this situation, although some officials, such as former MET director Maria Kapere, did try.

In 2017 the military returned to Bwabwata. Because MET was not coping with cross-border elephant poaching, it was decided to employ the Namibian Defence Force to take on the armed poachers. Life for the residents rapidly deteriorated. Several Khoe people were shot at while gathering in the bush, with one man killed and another badly wounded in the leg by apparently ill-disciplined soldiers. Women were told they could only gather veldfoods within a five-kilometre radius of their villages. But given the widespread distribution of veldfoods, this was as good as banning them from gathering – estimated to contribute up to 60 per cent of the local diet. People were also unable to harvest Devil's Claw, a local plant used in arthritis medicine, the annual sale of which had been earning harvesters around N$600 000 a year. The military occupation also prevented women from gathering palm fronds and plant dyes for their highly prized baskets, which are sold internationally, earning income for basket-makers. After the shootings many people were simply too afraid to leave their villages. Add to this an ill-timed anthrax epidemic which meant none of the game meat shot during trophy hunts in 2017 could be distributed as usual to Bwabwata's people – in case of contamination by this disease which can infect human animals as well.

All this meant real hunger, bordering on malnutrition and starvation, even though the Kyaramacan Association, which employs over 70 people, did a cash distribution of about N$900 000 to its 6 000 Khoe and 1 000 Mbukushu members. One or more corrupt KA members compounded the unhappy situation by stealing large amounts out of KA's bank account.

The government, MET and also IRDNC were sluggish in their reactions to this deteriorating overall situation in Bwabwata and an appeal by the Kyaramacan Association to get an own-use quota of game as much-needed protein was kicked back and forward by MET for months. In July 2018 a quota was finally agreed to provide some protein to Bwataba residents, and so-called protocols were eventually developed to assist gathering and palm frond collection.

Uno Dihako was one of West Caprivi's first community game guards. His energy and enthusiasm for conservation ensured that he quickly became senior field officer there, leading the other Khoe game guards. He was also a victim of the war. He wasn't shot or killed by a landmine; nor did he disappear as did about 20 other local men.

We met Uno during the new Namibian government's first socio-ecological survey in 1990, which Garth and I helped conduct. As about 7 000 San people then lived in West Caprivi game reserve, there was a vision – at least by an enlightened few in the conservation ministry – that conservation and human development could be linked. By then this was already happening in our community conservation project in north-western Namibia.

The Khoe and Vasekele people were quick to grasp this approach. Even though they had been banned from hunting, from their perspective they already managed their wildlife and they could not imagine living in a world without wild animals. What was lacking in this equation were real benefits. Those would come – eventually.

Uno was a larger than life character – short, wiry and turbo-charged with energy, a straight talker with a deadpan sense of humour and a huge infectious grin. Like hundreds of other Khoe men in West Caprivi, he'd been recruited into the combined South African-South West African armed forces in the '70s. He'd accepted the job, with its relatively huge salary from his local perspective, not because he was opposed to Swapo but because South African military recruiters convinced him that if he didn't help defend this territory, Swapo would over-run it and kill everyone who lived there.

The 'Bushman' soldiers were stationed at Omega. Their families were required to move to the camp as well. Omega was the only official army base in the country – perhaps the world – that was not fenced in. The Bushmen soldiers were prepared to live in the little square houses the army built for them but they were not prepared to live behind wire barriers that cut them off from their beloved veld. So Uno and others told us.

The Bushman troops were famed for their tracking skills and almost anyone who worked with these small, tough men fell under their spell. A former SADF officer tried to explain why: 'They're quick and intelligent with superb bush skills. Very tenacious – they never give up. But it's more than that – their loyalty and humour and a joie de vivre … it's hard to explain but you just enjoyed working with the Bushmen.'

By the time the war against Swapo was lost, Uno was a sergeant. His years as a soldier gave him an edge of discipline and efficiency. He had a keen sense of time, unlike many other community workers. If we were running late, he'd tap his watch and tell us we needed to hurry up.

Uno passionately believed in the vision of wildlife being his people's gold. Although he was a field man, more comfortable in the bush than at the front of a meeting, he became a fiery orator, persuading others to support the community conservation and development project.

He did not like to tell war stories. He said he'd had enough of killing and violence. In the '90s, IRDNC used to try to bring a feature film to our quarterly planning meetings so that field staff, many of whom had no access to television or cinemas, could enjoy some entertainment in the evenings. Our environmental awareness team which worked in schools had a TV, video and a small portable generator so the movies could be shown anywhere, and we used this equipment at planning sessions. The movies were a big hit in a world before connectivity, mobile phones, YouTube and Netflix.

One evening we showed the popular film *Braveheart*, starring some well-known actors, and about the early Scottish resistance to English occupation. Most of the staff enjoyed this epic film, dramatised from history. It contains realistic scenes of violence and bloodshed. Uno and his team walked out after the second graphic blood-shedding.

Later, I asked him why they'd left.

'We've seen real killing,' he told me. 'It's not something you watch in a movie for enjoying.'

His sense of responsibility led him to tackle all his assignments with extraordinary zeal. At one stage in the mid-90s the region became flooded with semi-automatic weapons: Savimbi's men were isolated and starving across West Caprivi's border with Angola and were swapping their firearms for food and clothing. Food aid was being provided in Angola by an American agency but the Angolan government was ensuring none of this reached the rebels in the hope of starving them out. Some of these firearms found their way into poacher's hands in Namibia, Botswana and Zambia which was of serious concern to Uno. Working quietly, he managed to persuade scores of people to give up the illegal firearms that they'd acquired for a few T-shirts and a bag of mealie meal or sugar. Uno personally was responsible for more than 100 semi-automatic weapons being handed in to the police at Bagani. The man deserved a medal.

Instead, a few months after the Angolan war spread into West Caprivi, he was arrested by the Namibian security forces and after being held for weeks in a prison cell with no outside contact, charged with treason.

Ostensibly, Uno was targeted, like others of our staff, because he had a project vehicle and a project two-way radio. But the Namibian special security forces were mostly ex-Swapo fighters who had no love for former Bushman soldiers.

Even though IRDNC quickly explained Uno's role in a Namibian government-sanctioned conservation project, and why he therefore had a vehicle and radio, the Namibian military said they had no jurisdiction over the special security team that had arrested him. Mostly, senior officers we spoke to said they knew some Bushmen had been arrested but they knew nothing about their cases or where they were. Weeks dragged by. All our inquiries hit a brick wall, including those of Mike, our ex-PLAN fighter. We had no way of knowing if Uno was dead or alive – just that he'd been arrested and taken away, not by the Namibian army, but by this 'special' security force.

With help from the chairman of IRDNC's board, Andrew

Corbett, and the Legal Assistance Centre, Caprivi coordinator Richard Diggle was eventually able to track Uno down. He was being imprisoned in Katima Mulilo.

We all wondered how he was coping in a cell – as a man who hated any kind of confinement, even a fence around a huge army base. Richard pushed and pushed till the authorities were persuaded to allow a lawyer and an IRDNC staff member to visit Uno. They found him in a terrible state: skin and bone, deeply depressed, confused and complaining of acute toothache. It took us days to get him some dental treatment. By then, probably because IRDNC and the LAC kept up the pressure, Uno had been charged - with treason. We were all incredulous. The charge was absurd and our lawyers demanded evidence. Uno's waking hours were filled with his conservation duties and those of us who knew him well would put our heads on a block that he was not involved in anything subversive. On the contrary, he was working for the development of new Namibia. As his handing over of 100 plus illegal firearms to the police, we would have thought, clearly demonstrated.

After about four months alone in a dank and dark cell, Uno was released on bail. Of course, the treason charges petered out. One could not help thinking about what Swapo's first Environment minister, Nico Bessenger, had said at his meeting in Windhoek about there being a choice – blood on the walls and behaving in the same way as had your oppressor or ensuring that such dark days could never happen again in a free and independent Namibia. Certainly, the security forces – those who detained Uno and a number of other Bushmen, some of whom were never seen again – had learnt well how to emulate the evils of the apartheid government.

We had got Uno's project vehicle back but the HF communication radio which had been removed from the vehicle disappeared. Initially we were told it was being held as 'evidence' but as the months, and then years passed we had to accept that this valuable piece of equipment, then worth just under N$10 000, had been stolen while in the custody of the security forces.

Uno never recovered from his incarceration. Although he tried to resume his job after we insisted he take some leave to recuperate, he was a broken man. The injustice of the charge of treason weighed heavily: he had believed not only in the vision of wildlife being valuable to the people of Namibia, but also in the policy of reconciliation that the country was supposed to have adopted after independence. He was deeply wounded that he could be accused of working against Namibia, a country that he thought had accepted him as an equal citizen. In his more lucid moments he could talk about these feelings, with pain and bitterness. He now believed that the Bushmen would never find a home with Swapo – they would always be hated.

A few times he said he wanted to sue the government to clear his name of the traitor slur. But mostly Uno was living in a world the rest of us couldn't see. He said things we didn't understand. His behaviour became erratic and he flew into rages that frightened his family. He was no longer reliable and several times just stopped doing his work for days at a time. We tried to get him to see a doctor, believing he was suffering from serious post-traumatic stress syndrome for which he could get help. He refused and talked wildly about being bewitched.

We gave him three months' paid leave to sort himself out. It didn't help and in the end, as he was not working and was refusing all offers of medical treatment, we had to put someone else in his critical post. We offered Uno part-time work, hoping he would eventually recover. He never did.

For another year or two we would occasionally see Uno at or near his homestead, a stranger who had aged. Then we heard he had died. I don't know what was put on his death certificate, if he ever had one, but there can be little doubt that being imprisoned for months, detained in solitary confinement without trial or rights, having his record as a conservationist ignored and besmirched broke his spirit. We can only imagine what he endured in a small dark room, cut off from all he loved – wild animals, trees, grasses, the sun, the moon and the stars.

We called it post-traumatic stress syndrome; one of his friends who had been in the army with Uno simply said: *Hulle het hom gek gemaak* (They drove him to madness). Someone else talked about Uno dying of a broken heart. There is some truth in all these opinions. What is also true is that Uno Dihako was a conservation hero as well as a victim of war – and racism.

FIFTEEN

Lost in the woods

A single finger cannot pick up even a grain of sand – African
proverb

RUNNING AN AFRICAN conservation and development NGO in the
two most remote corners of vast Namibia requires resilience and
unwavering optimism. And first-class highly motivated staff.

Community-based conservation may have been an idea whose
time had come but this did not mean it was easy to implement and
promote. And as the current directors of IRDNC would agree,
in spite of major achievements in Namibia and other African
countries, it is a work in progress and still fraught with challenges.
To be expected, of course, because community conservation and
development involves people, including politicians and the private
sector, the growth of a rural civil society and valuable natural
resources.

Looking back to the '80s, there has been steady and even
remarkable progress. The earliest days from 1982 when Garth and
some enlightened headmen started the community game guard
network – a bold and politically unpopular leap into what would
become a new conservation paradigm, giving birth to community-
based conservation; in 1996 when we were just four, then six people

with small amounts of donor funding, seemed very tough. It was the communities – and us – against the old monolithic colonial way of doing preservationist conservation. But as the programme grew and expanded across the country, with multiple partners and donors, plus party politics, we sometimes looked back with nostalgia on those hard but less complicated days.

By the early 2000s IRDNC employed 77 staff and worked in more than 60 diverse communities – people who made their livings as hunter-gathers, agriculturalists – both subsistence and cash cropping – plus fishermen and herders. Between us all we spoke 11 different languages and a spectrum of personalities and cultural perspectives had to be melded into teams. It didn't help that Kunene Region and Caprivi/Zambezi Region are more than 1000 kilometres apart – meaning Garth and I spent a lot of time on the road between the two regions.

On the other hand, although young people who have grown up with instantaneous mobile phone connection would find it hard to believe, there was something to be said for not being constantly interrupted by phone calls, emails and texts. An amazing amount of good work got done – with, for example, just a weekly radio call between Garth or me and Caprivi coordinator, Mathew Rice. Such planned and pre-scheduled communication enriched rather than handicapped our work. Instead of shooting off a quick email response to a colleague as one tends to do now, one prepared for these radio calls, with a list of considered issues and questions, what Nobel Prize-winning economist Daniel Kahneman calls slow thinking, as opposed to quick, instinctive thinking. Obviously we need both types of thinking in our lives but as Kahneman points out, many of the world's problems today are a result of people, including top decision-makers, applying quick thinking, based on what we think we know, to complex issues.

Fire makes a perfect example. Quick intuitive thinking tells us veld fires have to be bad – for the trees, the wildlife and for adding greenhouse gases to the atmosphere. Our Zambezi fire project and the cutting edge work in northern Australia, and now Botswana, demonstrates otherwise. And experience has shown, it is not just the layman who falls into these traps but so-called experts and government officials as well.

Over the years we stuck to our guns that IRDNC's focus would be the field – not the capital – and making things happen on the ground. This meant field-based staff. But we also needed to be able to make an input into policy at different levels, especially as we were promoting local community perspectives that would not normally find their way into centralised highly political decision-making. So a few technical, bigger-picture people were also essential.

Having studied African development anthropology and covered news stories as a journalist in different African countries before I moved to Namibia in the '80s, I knew Africa was littered with well-intended projects that fell apart as soon as the outside implementers and donors departed. As Africans, we were determined to avoid these pitfalls and build local sustainability into everything IRDNC did. So from the earliest days the policy was to hire local people in the project areas, and try to link them with a technically qualified person, one of whose major roles was to upgrade local staff skills.

Garth and I, who both came to the NGO world in our 30s from successful careers in other fields, also shared the belief that effective teams need diversity: different skills and a variety of outlooks and cultural values bringing resilience and creativity to an organisation. We thought we were being realistic and that we needed to level the playing field between local and outside competencies; undoubtedly some of our more technically qualified staff saw us as starry-eyed.

Within the organisation we built up, we ensured that local knowledge and experience was valued as much as formal education. Our vision was a team of people with complementary skills: some top staff undoubtedly 'under-educated' in conventional terms but highly qualified and experienced in other equally valuable ways; others with advanced internationally recognised qualifications as well as field experience. Working together, interdependent, they should make an outstanding team. That was the theory – in practise this was often hard to achieve and could lead to tensions.

Much depended on the personalities of the individuals and how they managed conflicts. An efficient grants manager, necessarily having strong formal education facing tight donor deadlines and his/her own field commitment, will take strain when a colleague who is skilled at networking, while handling various important, strategic issues, misses a report deadline because of differing priorities. The grants manager fears that the NGO could lose its funding if it becomes unreliable in the donor's eyes; the networker argues that there would be nothing to spend funding on if crucial strategic engagement in the field did not take place. Both are right. What is needed is mutual respect, good communication and perhaps a bit more discipline and planning on the part of the networker, and some built-in flexibility from the grants manager.

While our majority rural Namibian staff could live at their homes in the regions, we were always short of people with good technical skills who were prepared to live and work in the field. Government and private sector snapped up the qualified Namibians and an NGO without pension funding, generous medical aid and interest-free housing loan policies could not compete. Nevertheless, we were able to attract some idealistic and very competent young technically qualified people over the years – Colin Nott, Anna Davis, Anton and Wanda Esterhuizen, Nils Oosterhuizen, Ed Humphries, Aino Paavo, Richard Fryer and Basilia Shivute to name just a few who lived at Wereldsend – but never enough to cover the ever-expanding work. Life for non-local staff in Caprivi/Zambezi seemed a bit easier as it's a much smaller region and the town of Katima Mulilo was just a few hours away. But they too faced the challenges of living in a very remote region far from family and friends. Many staff and the directors were often stretched to burnout levels.

Work permits were needed for non-Namibians, a slow and onerous process, which meant we sometimes lost a good applicant in the months while we waited for a work permit to come through. That all our outside workers played a major training and mentoring role of local rural Namibians did not always seem to impress the Home Affairs ministry.

One of the solutions was volunteers through government-accredited volunteer organisations such as the British VSO or the similar Australian or American organisations. Australian volunteers turned out to be particularly suited to Namibian conditions; the two Aussies we took on were used to living in a hot climate in a remote area and knew how to be self-sufficient, quite apart from their qualifications. Another advantage of these organisations was that one could advertise the specific skills and qualifications needed plus the time period of two years, with the possibility of extending by another year or two, was long enough for a volunteer to make a real input.

Over the years scores of young people have offered to volunteer for three-month stints but mostly we did not accept these short-termers. From experience we knew they would probably benefit more – in terms of gaining a great life experience – than the NGO did. Mostly, we were too busy, under-resourced and short-staffed to cater for the needs of these adventurous young people, as much as we would have liked to. It takes a most remarkable volunteer to achieve much in a remote field situation in a few months. He or she needs to be looked after by local staff as the volunteer does not speak a local language or have a 4x4 vehicle. Of those we accepted, I can recall only four who were outstanding, adding value to the work, all of whom went on to successful careers in their own countries.

So when you get a good volunteer, you look after her. Thus when Angela Howells, recruited in 2003 through British VSO as a human resource development specialist, had settled into her cottage on the Fish Farm on the banks of the Zambezi River, I started observing how she spent her off-duty time. We didn't want her going back to the UK because she was lonely.

Angela, a former British Telecom human resource development manager, was exactly who we needed to coach and mentor some of our Zambezian senior staff. Motivated and mature, she took early retirement from a high-powered job to fulfil a life-long ambition to live and work in Africa. She ended up staying on with IRDNC, year after year, and eventually became a permanent resident in Namibia, with her own small human resource development company, doing consultancies for IRDNC, Save the Rhino Trust and others. A number of IRDNC's senior black staff benefited immensely from her coaching, including John K Kasaona, currently one of two directors of the NGO and Janet Matota, Assistant Director: Zambezi. Angela also managed Conservancy Safaris Namibia for a critical interim period, after the investor withdrew.

I need not have worried about her in Katima Mulilio; a social animal, she quickly made friends within IRDNC and in town. The only spare time she seemed to have at weekends was in the afternoons between lunch and drinks before dinner. So I invited her to join me on a walk one Saturday afternoon, not just because we both needed the exercise but also to catch up on how she was doing.

We drove about 30 kilometres out of Katima to where the mopane forests were at their best. Elephant still ventured into this area, avoiding the occasional village. I turned into a small dirt track off the main road, drove a few kilometres, then parked in a clearing. It was a warm May day and the dappled shade of the big mopanes made walking pleasant. My dogs roamed around as Angela and I strolled out. After about an hour we thought we'd better start heading back to the car. But there was a problem. We'd been talking non-stop, and as someone with a terrible sense of direction, I was not 100 per cent sure exactly which way was back. Mopane forest in all directions as far as the eye could see, and the ground was too hard to show footprints. I knew we'd not walked in a straight line – we'd changed direction twice to look at some old elephant dung.

'How's your sense of direction?' I asked casually.

'Not too bad – when there are street signs,' Angela told me cheerfully.

I decided not to make her nervous by looking irresolute and set off confidently in the general direction we'd come from. Trouble was after another 45 minutes of walking we were still deep among mopanes. By now the sun was almost down and the forest had acquired a gloomy aspect. Angela was also sweating and looking tired.

'We've been walking a lot faster on the way back . . . we must be close the car?' Her tone was hopeful. Then she looked at my face. 'Are we lost? We're lost, aren't we?'

One of my father's sayings seemed appropriate: 'No we are not lost; being lost is a state of mind. We're just not exactly sure where we are.'

Angela laughed, scoring a lot of credit.

'But the car can't be far. That track must be very close too. In that direction don't you think?'

I could see Angela's mind working as she looked around the darkening forest where elephant and other wild animals lurked. She tried to be helpful: 'I think we've been curving a bit to the left so the track should be in front of us.'

Ten minutes later, now walking in twilight, we stopped again.

'I think we'd better stop looking for the car and the dirt track and head in the direction of the main road. We'll be able to find the track we took then.'

We were discussing the main road's exact direction when my dogs barked and we heard voices. Two local men appeared out of the shadows. The older one carried a shotgun and the younger a large panga. Filled with relief, I stepped forward and greeted them; Angela had hung back, sort of stepping behind a tree. The younger man spoke a little English. I explained we were looking for our car.

'Where?' he asked.

'Um, I'm not sure. Maybe you can point us towards the main road to Katima?' He indicated with his panga slightly to the right of the direction we'd been walking. 'How far?' I asked. 'Five, maybe eight kilometres.' My jaw dropped. Surely not!

Angela had joined us now, having realised that in spite of how threatening they looked with their weapons, the men were friendly. I looked at her red face, and worried whether she'd be able to cover that distance.

The young Zambezian kindly insisted on coming with us. As I hoped, his estimate of distance was way out and the main road was less than a kilometre away. Now it was dark. No traffic at all on the road. Angela sat down on a log. Our guide stood around helpfully while I considered our options. I was 95 per cent sure that we'd come out to the main road above the dirt track off which our car was parked. But what if I was wrong and the track – and the car – was in the other direction?

'Are there many dirt tracks off this road,' I asked, knowing the answer. A series of parallel chopping motions with the panga indicated there were many. So I'd have to take a chance. 'I think the car is in that direction.'

'Angela, you stay here with the dogs while this young man and I fetch the car.' However, the usually well-behaved dogs refused to co-operate and followed us each time we set off. And no way was Angela going to stay alone on the side of the road at the edge of a forest in Africa in the pitch dark.

'But you're too tired to walk any more and we won't be long.'

'Oh yeah? If you've chosen the right direction,' Angela observed accurately. 'But forget it. I'm not staying here alone. Just give me a minute or two to catch my breath.'

While she was taking her minutes, we heard a car. I stepped to the side of the road and waved them down.

'Hi Margie!' In one of those amazing coincidences that life offers now and then, the cheerful face of Janine, the older daughter of the owners of the Fish Farm where Angela lived, was framed in the window. Her mother, Katy Sharpe, was driving her and some friends back from boarding school in Zimbabwe for the holidays.

Too relieved to be embarrassed, I explained our predicament. The car-load of girls cheerfully climbed out to wait with Angela while we fetched my vehicle. We turned up the next track, drove for a few kilometres, and there it was where we'd left it. I borrowed some money from Katy to pay our guide for his time and thanked him sincerely. I doubt he knew how grateful I was.

Later, over a glass of wine, Angela expressed embarrassment at how terrified she'd been at the sight of the two men, armed to the teeth, as it seemed to her. Embarrassed myself for getting so lost, I was easy on her: 'I guess you don't meet many men carrying pangas and shotguns in England.'

'And you also don't take walks where there are elephants in the forest,' Angela added.

'All the elephant dung was weeks old,' I assured her, wondering if she'd ever believe anything I said again.

But what Angela refused to believe was that the whole afternoon hadn't been a setup.

'You planned this all. You were never lost and you arranged to meet Katy. It's too much of a coincidence. You were just seeing what I was made of!'

I smiled and denied it . . . but not too much.

Ed Humphries, our first Australian volunteer, ended up marrying a Namibian woman, Aino Paavo from Tsandi, whom he met while she was doing her conservation diploma practical at IRDNC. We enjoyed watching Ed's courtship of the beautiful – and very smart – Aino. My theory is that it all started the night she beat him and all the others at darts. He was smitten. They both worked for IRDNC for some years, based at Wereldsend, and we were sorry to see them go. However, as Aino was headhunted to be personal assistant to the Ministry of Environment and Tourism's permanent secretary, and Ed went into community-based tourism, we knew they would continue to play valuable roles in Namibia. They still live and work in Windhoek, raising their daughter. Aino now works in the Ministry of Trade and Industry; Ed serves as the Honorary Australian Consul as well as doing community tourism work.

IRDNC's other Aussie was a competent young post-graduate anthropology graduate, Pam McGrath. She was ardently leftist in her views, in that very Australian way. We enjoyed her idealism but knew that a few years in rural Namibia would knock the edges off any naivety.

Early in her two-year volunteering stint (which she extended for another year or two), we stationed her in the village of Hupula in

East Caprivi alongside the home of Janet Matota. Janet had started her career with IRDNC as our first community activator/resource monitor. These were a small team of local women whose role was primarily to ensure that the majority of other local women, often working in the fields when important meetings were held with men in their villages, received important information that had been discussed at these meetings. This meant they could contribute usefully to decision-making.

The idea to hire local women as community activators/resource monitors had arisen while I did follow-ups of the village meetings and was surprised to find that men did not routinely pass on information to their wives and/or other female family members, even when it directly affected women – such as ways to mitigate against elephant damage in the fields where women toiled for hours each day. In the early '90s, very few Zambezian women had jobs outside the work they did at home and in the fields so we were unsure how the all-male *khutas* and *indunas* would receive a proposal to hire a team of women.

Having learnt my lesson with the poacher-game guard, I was very careful when I went to the various *khutas* to discuss this idea not to impose my Western gender ideology. My strategy was to present the results of my gender surveys, done at all villages, which clearly showed that many of the traditional roles of women involved use of natural resources – veld foods, water lilies, thatching grass, palm fronds and bark for dyes – as well as the majority of routine tasks in the gardens. Would it not therefore be sensible, I asked, to appoint a small team of women to monitor how such resources were used, and to ensure that women were kept up to date about community-based conservation issues? Everyone knew women were usually too busy in the fields to attend meetings so the women's team could go into the fields and hold small meetings there. The NGO would pay them but they would work for the community, in the same way that community game guards did. After a short discussion, the first *khuta* agreed this was a good idea. It was easy once one traditional court had agreed, to get buy-in from the others, though there was no love lost between different tribal groups. *Indunas* put up the names of women who the community thought were suitable, and who were interested in a part-time job. I interviewed the first group, only rejecting one woman as unsuitable, as I recall. Janet was our first hire.

We were fortunate that a young American elephant researcher, Caitlyn O'Connor was working with us as she was able to give the community activators their first important role, as well as provide them with good field training. Caitlyn was testing different methods of keeping elephants out of fields, which was of great interest and concern to the women too. But as my surveys had shown, men were not passing on such information to their women. This was partly because some of the men were using the elephant problems as a political football in a political party context.

The women, on the other hand, just wanted to keep elephants out of their fields so that their crops could be harvested, providing their households with food and cash. They were outraged to hear that they had not been informed about the offered mitigation methods. Told that men in her village had refused to assist in the cutting of poles for a test solar electric fence around a group of gardens, one woman had us all laughing at her solution. There was only one way to deal with these lazy men, she said. Let them sleep alone till they changed their minds and helped built the electric fence. The first of our test fences went up soon afterwards.

I was delighted when the LIFE (Living in a Finite Environment) project which funded IRDNC Caprivi at the time appointed Barbara Wycoff-Baird, another social scientist, to a key position. Experienced and insightful, she understood our approach, as did her boss Chris Weaver, and this made them both a pleasure to work with.

It was a few years later that Australian volunteer Pam was assigned to work with Janet who by then was leading the community activators as well as running the first craft development project in the region. University graduate Pam, highly literate and numerate, would assist Janet to acquire some of her sharp-edged skills while Janet would be training Pam in community-based facilitation and action.

Janet felt it was a good idea if Pam lived in Hupula with her, and a tent under a shade roof with an adjoining kitchen shelter was put up close to Janet's homestead on the outskirts of the village. The final touch was a fence of sturdy reeds, providing Pam with a circular courtyard and privacy, but more importantly, discouraging elephants from visiting at night. Filled with youthful energy and enthusiasm, our volunteer moved in.

A few weeks later, Garth and I were woken at 2 am by a car hooting outside the cottage where we slept on Fish Farm. It was Beaven Munali, senior field officer working with the team of community game guards, in his IRDNC vehicle.

We stumbled blearily outside. Ever courteous, Beaven first apologised for waking us by hooting, explaining that he and the others with him were nervous of the Fish Farm dogs at night. The men were regularly at the IRDNC office, also on the Fish Farm, so the dogs knew them. But in the early hours of a dark morning, they did not wish to put this to the test.

They had just dropped Pam at the Katima Mulilo State Hospital, in a serious condition, after she fell seven metres down an abandoned well. We rushed to the hospital and found Pam, scratched, tearful and dirty from her ordeal, groggy after a pain injection. The hospital planned to X-ray her first thing the next morning but it was obvious her lower leg was broken – and there could be other more serious injuries.

Beaven elected to do the two-hour drive back to his village, now that he knew Pam was in safe hands. We thanked him for bringing her to the hospital but were yet to hear the central role he had played in her rescue as he was too modest to tell what is, in fact, a very dramatic story in which a young woman could have been far more severely injured or even killed. This is what I was able to piece together from accounts given to me by Pam herself, Janet, Beaven and others who were there – as recorded in my field book at the time.

It was all because there was an eclipse of the moon, avers Pam. She was outside her courtyard, looking at the moon. In the dark, she lost her way and strayed onto an overgrown path. Looking upwards and not at her feet, all it took was a step backwards, overbalancing on a log, then taking another step, into a void and a horrifying plunge into the black hole of the long abandoned well.

Thorn bushes had been wedged into the mouth of the well to prevent children and domestic stock from falling in, and it was probably these bushes that saved Pam from more serious injuries. They caught around her, hooking painfully into her skin and clothes as she fell, but keeping her more or less upright, and possibly even slowing her fall. Thus she did not smash into any of the wire steps that protruded at one-metre intervals from the well's inside walls.

With a jarring thud, feeling her left leg collapse under her, Pam remembers landing at the bottom which was covered by a few centimetres of water. Jammed half-upright, with her body painfully pierced by thorns, and in pitch darkness, she briefly blacked out. The throbbing pain in her lower left leg brought her back to consciousness. Looking upwards: far away, she could see a small circle, not of light, but of less intense darkness. For a while, she remained still, trying to assess the extent of her injuries. Her leg was definitely broken, her back hurt and she could feel her skin was pierced in numerous places. Salty tears stung the scratches on her face. Although she didn't know it, one of her eyelids was swelling rapidly where a thorn had punctured it but miraculously missed her eye.

As her eyes adjusted to the dark she saw the narrow wire steps that offered her only escape. She reached for the nearest one and tried to pull herself upright. The searing pain in her left leg took her breath away and put paid to any thoughts of climbing out. So sensibly, she called for help.

But the well was at least 100 metres from the nearest homestead and her throat was raw before someone eventually heard her screams. A crowd of shocked villagers gathered around. A flashlight was found and shone down at her. Realising that Pam could not climb up herself, Janet's husband went into the well to see if he could help her up. But the confined space and her injured leg made this impossible.

Reassuring her that he would be back soon with a rope, he clambered out to the waiting crowd. Some of the older men were keeping people back from the hole to stop soil falling in and in fear of a more serious cave-in.

Several lengths of rope were tied together. A man climbed down and tied a double loop under Pam's arms, round her chest, and went back up with the end of the rope. A group of eager men heaved on it. The rope tightened then someone yelled at the men to stop pulling. Chunks of earth and vegetation slid into the well, raining down onto Pam. Pulling her weight with the rope cutting against the sides of the old shaft was too dangerous and could cause it to collapse.

Those who were there told me they stood around suggesting different ways to pull Pam out. The recent case of a cow that had fallen down another well at another village was discussed at length. The technique used there involved a vehicle and shooting the frantic cow before it could be hauled out. An old *induna* kept insisting that the police be called but the nearest police station was 140 kilometres away. The closest telephone was at the school and locked up for the night.

Then Janet decided to call Beaven – he had a truck and she knew he was a good man in an emergency. They would also need him to drive Pam to hospital. Two youths were dispatched to run to his village, about seven kilometres away. They left immediately, running like hares in the dark.

Beaven arrived and climbed down to Pam, finding her white-faced and shivering, in spite of the stuffy warmth of the shaft.

'It's okay, little sister,' he reassured her, 'we'll get you out soon.'

He quickly assessed the situation, noting the instability of the soil around the well's opening. So he drove to Lianshulu Lodge about 25 kilometres to the north to seek help there; they had a winch on one of their vehicles.

Two hours later, with Beaven taking charge of the rescue, willing hands laid Pam onto a mattress at the back of his truck. Janet covered her with blankets and held her hand as Beaven drove her slowly – two hours – to the hospital. Then they came to call us.

A puzzling codicil to this story was the Russian doctor who was stationed at the Katima Mulilo Hospital. I went with Pam to have her X-rays done early in the morning and then took them to a well-known private doctor in town, Dr Andre Birkenstock. Pam was insured for medical emergencies and did not need to be a state patient. In any case, as Andre pointed out, the nature of her fracture with the two bones of her leg shearing apart above her ankle meant she needed a titanium pin inserted to hold them in place. No such pins were available in Katima. He advised stabilising her for a day, then flying her to Windhoek for the surgery. He was also keen for her to have a second round of X-rays in Windhoek, particularly of her spine, as the well-used X-ray plates at the hospital were scratched and thus difficult to interpret.

It was about 8.30 am when I went back to the hospital to tell Pam the plan. As I walked down the corridor, I heard her unmistakable Aussie voice raised in protest.

'No, leave me alone, don't you touch me', she yelled. 'Call Dr Jacobsohn (me).' I ran into the ward to find Pam fending off two bemused hospital orderlies who were trying to load her onto a gurney. Turned out the Russian doctor had decided to operate to repair her broken leg. Garth went off to find him and tell him that Pam was not a state patient, and that the bones needed a titanium pin.

The Russian took exception and assured Garth he was a very experienced doctor: 'Why don't you trust me? I have fixed many bad injuries, on the front line of not one, but two wars.'

Tactfully Garth pointed at the long queue of local people waiting for the doctor's attention: 'You've got more than enough to do with all these patients – so we'll be transferring Pam to Windhoek tomorrow.'

The Russian was unmollified but called off his orderlies.

Later that morning I had to phone Pam's parents who were in Indonesia. I rehearsed what to say so as not to unduly frighten them. Her father came on the line. I explained that Pam had had an accident, a fall down a well, but that she was fine apart from a broken leg and some scratches – and everything was under control.

'What was she on?' Her father's immediate question, rendered me speechless for a moment. I assured him his daughter, who it turned out was somewhat accident prone, was not on any illegal substance – just looking at a moon eclipse. Hmmmm, he said.

Garth and I went to have a look at the well at Hupula and update everyone there about her injuries. We were shaken when we saw how deep the narrow circular shaft was and how easily her injuries could have been a lot worse. As it turned out, one of her vertebrae was damaged – the first X-rays was too scratched to reveal this – and Pam had to wear a spinal brace as well as cope with a broken leg and crutches for the next few months. Undaunted by her injuries, she returned to continue her work in Zambezi as soon as she could.

While we were looking at the well, I noticed a broken pair of men's shoes lying near the top. I asked whose they were.

'Mine,' said Beaven. 'I went up and down the wire steps so often, my shoes broke.'

Very grateful for his cool head during the rescue, I offered to buy him another pair of shoes.

Beaven drew himself up and looked at me with mild reproach. 'No Director,' he said. 'In my culture, you don't get rewarded for helping save someone's life. It is what people do for one another.'

Beaven rose to become IRDNC Zambezi's assistant director, with Janet, making a major contribution to community-based conservation in Namibia. For many years he did a popular weekly radio programme about community conservation. He interviewed scores of people, discussed conservation issues and broadcast conservancy information and news. It was no surprise to any of us when IRDNC did some work in neighbouring Zambia that even there he was well-known, and as the voice of community conservation, he was treated as a celebrity. In 2015 he left the NGO to go into politics, and is now an elected Swapo regional councillor. Today Beaven is chairman of the Regional Council of Zambezi Region, an influential leadership position, alongside the governor of the region. He has not lost his passion for conservation and is a trustee on IRDNC's board.

As for our volunteer who fell down a well, Pam went on to do a doctorate and teaches at Brisbane University in Australia. There is definitely one moon eclipse she will never forget.

SIXTEEN

Police trouble, dirty tricks and goat droppings

Action always beats intention – Anonymous

'YOU'VE BEEN CHARGED with breaking and entry and malicious damage to property. Police left Opuwo this morning for Swakopmund to arrest you. They'll bring you back for a weekend in the cells … not a good idea. You got a lawyer?'

I thank my colleague for his tip-off and put the phone down on a Thursday afternoon in 2013. I am shocked and distressed. There's been a mistake. I'm not guilty. Well yes, I did climb over a fence and spray-paint the back wall of the new Onyuva clinic which had stood empty due to a dispute between the builder and the donors for more than two years. But I had permission from the US donors who funded the clinic. It wasn't malicious damage – I was merely trying to make the building's back white wall a little less visible from the deck of Etaambura Camp. The US official I'd spoken to said she couldn't see any reason why we shouldn't paint the wall and the shiny silver tin roof of the building; ochre for the wall – the same colour as the ground and the building's own trim – and a camouflage green for the roof, to fit in with the green mopanes.

I'd waited patiently for nearly two years for the clinic to open.

Building started in 2009 – an election year when an amazing amount of public work got done, showing what the government could do in ordinary years if it wanted to. The builder who got the contract is an Afrikaans Namibian living in Warmquelle, an acquaintance.

The clinic didn't bother Garth at all. As usual, he hears different music: 'The area is not a game reserve or a wilderness; it's real Africa where people and wildlife live together. Let Etaambura's guests see the clinic: it's an entry point for talking about African conservation, done the African way,' he tells me.

I agree with Garth about many things. But this does not mean I believe that the big, squat white building with a silver tin roof reflecting the sun on the edge of the view from Etaambura's wonderful decks adds anything to the experience. What makes it worse is that months pass without the clinic opening and becoming useful to local people. The donor refuses to hand it to the health ministry because of some alleged structural defects in the virtually completed building. The builder maintains that if the donor pays him the last tranche of his funding – 25 per cent being withheld till the job is complete and it passes inspection – he will be able to rectify the problems. A stalemate – he can't fix the building without some of the last 25 per cent; the donor won't pay till the building passes inspection. So, he gets his brother, a Windhoek lawyer, to represent him. One of the first things the lawyer brother does is take out a builder's lien on the clinic – which means the building becomes the property of the builder, not the donor. Trouble is, I didn't know any of this when I decided to paint the back wall and roof.

It was January 2013 – and I was helping to lead Conservancy Safaris' first yoga safari: eight guests, plus Caroline Pajewski, our India-trained yoga teacher from Recline Studio in Swakopmund. We'd planned three nights at Etaambura so we could really get into yoga and meditation, plus a few overnight camping stops in memorable landscapes en route. So far we'd done a bit more game viewing than yoga.

Garth at 6.30 am in the Hoanib Valley, as we are laying out our yoga mats for our sunrise meditation: 'I don't want to interrupt but elephants are just down-river and I'm driving there now. If anyone wants to come...' A moment's hesitation, then sand gets kicked on yoga mats as we scramble for cameras and binoculars and head for the vehicles. Isn't watching elephants a lot like meditation?

It rained the first morning at Etaambura and our practice was cut short because wind blew rain onto us and the newly thatched roof leaked in a few places. We decided to give up, enjoy the rain and resume mid-afternoon. This left me – and Caroline – with a few spare hours. I had bought two cans of camouflage green spray paint to see if this was the right colour for the clinic roof.

I am a very experienced spray painter. No racist apartheid-era beach sign was safe from my spray can of black paint in the Cape Peninsula in the '70s, ever since, as a young reporter, I covered a story where police with dogs ordered two black families off a 'whites only' beach. I saw fear and confusion on the children's faces and the adults' impotent rage as they left Muizenberg's sands. I was hooked – every time I saw a 'whites only' sign on a beach, I blasted it with black paint, sometimes going back at night, sometimes right there and then if I thought I could get away with it. In the larger scheme of things, it may have been a very trivial strike against apartheid but it certainly was my very own small personal protest.

Painting the clinic roof and back wall was quite different. There was nothing furtive about it and I even invited Caroline to help me when the rain stopped that January morning. I had permission. We drove down the hill and looked for the clinic caretaker. We found a young man and he found a rickety short ladder in a store room. No key to the gate in the clinic's high fence so he helped us and the ladder over the gate and then drifted off. We tried to get on the roof to test the green paint. It was just too high.

So we decided to see what the paint looked like on the back wall. As two cans were not enough to cover the wall, we got the bright idea to break up the stark whiteness by spraying a curving zig-zag sort of pattern, up and down, across the whole wall. That might at least break up its visibility from Etaambura's decks till I could arrange for some ochre paint. Remember this back wall could not be seen from the road. It should also be mentioned that Etaambura is in the far north-west, two days 4x4 drive from Swakopmund, the same from Windhoek, and five to six hard hours' drive from Opuwo. My visits there were infrequent – maybe once a quarter – so I thought it very efficient to at least make a start on camouflaging the back of the clinic. But when we got back to the lodge's deck, we saw the green paint had made little difference. Ochre was definitely the colour needed.

Now a few weeks later, I am about to be arrested. I phone around for the builder's cell number. I tell him there's been a mistake. I had permission to paint the wall. To my dismay he is adamant that I have broken the law, cost him many thousands of dollars and he wants me to speak to his lawyer.

His brother-lawyer stuns me with his immediate hostility, and he cuts short my explanation. He tells me to write a statement and he will consider it. But he refuses to call off the police officers who are en route to Swakopmund.

Feeling somewhat desperate at the thought of a weekend in a crowded cell in Opuwo, I phone the chairman of CSN's board, Advocate Andrew Corbett. We share a long history, even faced an armed posse of police together in a dry river bed but it's the first time I've had to ask him to help me not get arrested. Having dealt with far more serious issues, Andrew is unfazed. He'll phone the lawyer, whom he knows, and get him to be more reasonable. He urges me to write my statement. He phones back and says his colleague has agreed to withdraw charges.

It's not quite over; later I find out that the lawyer-brother intends suing me for costs incurred when the builder had to go to Onyuva to inspect the damage to his building, *and* he wants me to pay for the costs of the caretaker travelling to Warmquelle to inform him of the vandalism. The caretaker is apparently the builder's son, not the young man who helped us over the fence. The brother names a large sum that makes me go pale.

By now Garth has returned from some fieldwork. He recalls meeting the builder in Sesfontein and hearing about the 'damage' I'd done. Garth explained that I had permission and that my intent was camouflage not vandalism but the builder had already set his brother on the case. Even though I feel like a weak and feeble woman depending on my man for help when the going gets tough, I swallow my pride and ask Garth to phone the builder – they have known each other for about 40 years and I have a feeling he'll be more reasonable, man to man. At the same time I consult a lawyer, not my chairman, this time. The legal advice given to me is not to admit to anything or pay anything.

Garth, of course, has totally the opposite viewpoint. He believes I do owe the builder something. Obviously not the inflated amount the lawyer is claiming. But by leaping in without doing a proper investigation into the situation, I have cost the builder a trip to Onyuva. As we have found out the caretaker son got a free lift with an IRDNC vehicle, we can forget about those costs.

But I had permission, I bleat again.

Garth shrugs. 'Either you take responsibility for your actions or you don't. Your call.'

I glare at him. It's a pain having a partner who is usually right.

All ends reasonably amicably after Garth and the builder talk and when I agree to pay his fuel costs to Onyuva. We meet for a meal at Etaambura later in the month and he gives us permission to paint the green-striped wall an ochre colour. A few months later, the job is done, the ochre paint making the clinic a lot less intrusive. The builder promises that as soon as his legal dispute with the US donors is resolved, he will paint the clinic roof green.

It took four more years for the clinic to open – in 2017. The builder seems to have forgotten his promise to paint the roof green, but one of these days I'll get round to it myself. At least this health facility is finally benefitting local people in a very remote part of the country.

The confusion and fallout around a clinic wall was not my first encounter with the police in north-west Namibia. A thin layer of goat dung was once all that stood between me and the heavy hand of the South West African security police.

It was the mid-80s, with the guerrilla war between South Africa and Swapo lurching painfully towards its inevitable conclusion in Namibia. I had been studying prehistoric pastoralist remains along the west coast of the Cape in South Africa but as I wanted to work with living, modern pastoralists in north-west Namibia for my doctorate – on the edge of the liberation war – I had to apply for a security and research permit from government. Months went by after my letter of application for the permit was sent to the authorities in South Africa. Telephone inquiries were deflected; I re-sent a copy of my application, to no avail. Perhaps my 'record' had caught up with me.

Before studying archaeology, as a journalist, I worked for several newspapers of the *vyande Engelese pers* (hostile English press) in South Africa. These included the *Cape Times* which broke a paradigm by blatantly publishing an interview with exiled Oliver Tambo, even though he, and the African National Congress, was then still banned. I was the only other journalist who knew in advance that the editor Tony Heard had flown to London to meet the ANC leader. Tony faced a three-year jail sentence, with no fine option. On his return, in early November 1985, with a State of Emergency in force because of township unrest, I helped him prepare the interview for publication. We worked in the garden to avoid being overheard by security police taps inside the house we shared. If they were tipped off we feared an urgent interdict to prevent ANC's views being published in the next morning's paper. They could also have raided us and confiscated the interview tapes. Tony was arrested but in the end not jailed.

I'd left the *Cape Times* by then and was at university, moonlighting as a foreign correspondent for 18 Dutch newspapers. My reports to the Netherlands could not have been published in South Africa, particularly since the State of Emergency clampdown on reporting on any police action in the black townships. So mine was not the kind of career path likely to endear me to the former South African regime. But I was such small cheese in the big picture that I did not expect to be refused a security permit to do research in Namibia.

After six months of hitting a blank wall, I sought the assistance of an Opposition Party MP who offered to table my plight as a question in parliament. Why was a bone fide academic who had never been convicted of any crime being denied a permit to undertake valid research? Coincidentally, the permit came through shortly after this question was published in a list to be tabled.

Soon after starting my research in north-west Namibia, I was called to Opuwo, capital of the region and the location of a large SADF army base, by a certain lieutenant, then head of the security police. The tall, blond man warned me that my background as an ANC supporter was well-known and that I was being watched. If I tried any tricks my research permit would be cancelled and I would be thrown out of the country, or worse. He hoped he had made himself *purrr-fectly* clear, he said several times.

Formalities over, I got on with my research. Some months later I returned to my university for a few weeks. I left my bakkie parked at the Khorixas rest camp, and obtained a lift to Windhoek from where I flew to Cape Town. After about a month away, I went back to Khorixas. Everything seemed exactly as I'd left it as I packed my supplies for four months' fieldwork into the canopied back of my truck.

In my first week out I encountered Venomeho. This Himba family head was in trouble because a windmill had broken down. The nearest alternative water that year was a day's walk away. No problem for the people and their stock, except for an unusually large crop of kid-goats who would need to be carried. Only three people were at the camp – the old man and two youths. They could carry about half the kids, but feared, with good reason, that jackals would kill the remaining baby goats as soon as they left. No thorn-bush enclosure cannot be breached by the wily jackal, given enough time. Without water, there was no time to lose. The only solution was to use my truck to transport the kids.

We unloaded some of my gear under a leadwood tree and about 40 small bleating goats went into the back of the vehicle. While we were at it, we took everything else the group needed to be transported which was not much, especially compared to what I travelled with. Shorty, Venomeho and I drove; the youths set off on foot with the adult animals.

We spent a night at the new camp and returned to Tomakus to collect our goods and travel on to Puros. The closed canopy of my truck smelled like a goat kraal, so soon after we reached Puros we drove down to the spring that rises in the Hoarusib River, downriver from the village, to give the bakkie a thorough cleaning. Shorty unpacked everything and started removing the goat dung- and urine-besmeared heavy-duty black rubber matting that covered the floor while I went to fill two buckets with water. Then he called to me, asking what he should do with my papers.

Puzzled, I went back up the sandy bank. And there, arranged in neat stacks of about 25 each, was a layer of what the lieutenant at Opuwa would call 'subversive literature.' The crudely printed papers were all in Oshivambo but I could pick out words such as Kassinga, boere and Swapo. I had seen such pamphlets before and knew they sought to recruit Namibians to join the struggle.

We had given a number of people lifts in the back of the truck in the week we'd been on the road. But it was quite impossible that any such hitchhiker would be able to lift the matting on the floor of the heavily packed bakkie – containing tin trunks of foods, a tent, boxes of books, tools, my bag of clothes and so on – and arrange this tidy display. I had slept next to the truck every night. It didn't take a genius to work out where and when the revolutionary literature had found its way into my vehicle.

Obviously, I had not been subversive enough for the security police, as I went about my research, mapping homesteads and asking endless questions about people's daily lives, so someone had decided to help things along. Enough 'evidence' had been planted in my truck to get me kicked out of Namibia – or worse. It could have happened anytime during the month the truck stood in Khorixas. I'd left the canopy locked and found it locked but breaking into the back of an old truck would have posed no challenge for some. It was a clever place to hide the pamphlets as in the normal course of events, one does not lift up a bakkie's rubber floor matting, and the papers could have remained in place, undetected, for as long as it suited the dirty tricks squad.

Shorty and I discussed the implications of his find, and on his advice, we called Headman Matheus to bear witness. We burnt most of the pamphlets. There seemed no point in doing anything else as people in the area were illiterate, and in case, they spoke Otjiherero, not Oshivambo. I packaged samples – one of each pamphlet – in a sturdy plastic bag, wrote a brief statement about the incident which Shorty and the headman signed, the latter with a X. I added my signature and the date, and hid the package. By then, the women of Puros had built me my own dung-plastered hut. I moved in and settled down to my work, wondering what the security police's next move would be. They took a few weeks to get back to me by which time we'd almost forgotten the pamphlets.

A truck load of black and white men arrived one morning. They were courteous and intent on paying me a visit. I made some tea and chatted to the two officers, while some of the others drifted around, apparently enjoying the scenery, and talking to people in nearby homesteads. The two with me were intrigued with my hut and asked to look inside.

'Feel free,' I said, busying myself with the kettle at the fire. Both men disappeared inside behind the curtain covering the door. There was very little to search inside the small shelter, and they were soon back out in the bright sunlight, purporting to be surprised how cool the 'primitive' dwelling was.

'Cool in the heat and warm when it's cold outside,' I informed them. Still they wanted to know why I chose to sleep in a hut without a door instead of a good modern tent that could be zipped closed against the insects and elements. I explained that the women here were unhappy about me sleeping in what they saw as a flimsy tent which was the same as being outside to them, and they had volunteered to construct a hut for me. We sat under my shade tree and drank tea. Shorty was lurking around, keeping an eye on my truck which was parked nearby under another tree. Later, he confirmed that two men had checked inside the unlocked back, lifting the matting and peering at the now empty truck floor.

Eventually, the men left, presumably perplexed and wondering,

I hope, whether I had not put the pamphlets to good use.

I couldn't help laughing as we talked about how a good turn and a layer of goat dung had foiled a dirty little trick that could have had a serious impact on both our lives, as Shorty could have been viewed as my accomplice. But Shorty didn't see this as a joke at all – he remained indignant about the dishonesty of the security police. I intended making a complaint to the authorities, using the package and statement, as evidence. But life moved on and I forgot. The pamphlets remained hidden in my shade tree, a few metres above where the men sat and drank tea.

Years later, long after I finished my doctorate, and Swapo had formed the new democratically elected government, heavy rain in the Hoarusib River catchment caused a particularly large flood. Fast flowing water eroded the river bank on which my old hut stood. Its remains eventually fell into the river bed; my shade tree also slid down the embankment. The next year's flow took away the tree, and presumably the little plastic package of Swapo literature too. Perhaps it still exists, buried in silt and debris, slowly decaying, somewhere in the Hoarusib. Or perhaps goats ate it and turned it into goat droppings.

SEVENTEEN

Veldskoene in the palace

WINNING AWARDS FOR one's work is gratifying, even though it is very often a team who deserves the recognition. International attention makes the award winner less vulnerable personally and politically when confronting corruption and greed in powerful places, and can give you a more authoritative voice. Awards uplift, motivate and make fund-raising easier. We've received more than our fair share of international recognition since Garth was deservedly selected as the rhino conservationist of the year by the South African Rhino and Elephant Foundation in the early '90s. IRDNC's staff and Namibian conservancies have also won a number of international prizes.

The 1993 Goldman Grassroots Environmental Prize for Africa was our first – awarded to us jointly; this was followed the next year by us each getting the United Nations Environmental Programme's Global 500 Roll of Honour award. In 1997, WWF Netherlands recognised us both as Knights of the Order of the Golden Ark. A unisex award that does not discriminate against women, I am a knight of this order, not a dame. A few years later the Cheetah Foundation of Namibia gave us a special conservation award. The last award came out of the blue in 2015 – Tusk Trust's Prince William Lifetime Conservation Award.

A bonus of most awards is interesting international travel, meeting other winners and learning about their inspirational work. Of course, it's not just the winners who are doing worthwhile work. At a Goldman Prize event in New York an American woman came up and told me how much she admired me. I asked her what she did. Oh, she said, just a very small project, aimed at trying to get consumers to buy more sustainably. With sincerity I was able to tell her that her work was just as important as ours – she was targeting one of the causes of the mess our world is in, and I wished her all strength.

For the Goldman prize we travelled to San Francisco where the Goldman Foundation has its headquarters. We spent a few days there and then did a whirlwind tour of New York and Washington. Garth had never been to the US before and was not sure it was an experience he would enjoy. He was also troubled by the timing of the week in the US because, given his tight work schedule, it had meant putting off spending time with his son Tuareg who had just started a post-school volunteership with IRDNC.

So he was not the most cheerful travelling companion as we flew to the US. Fortunately, our first stop was San Francisco, a beautiful city with its hippie anti-establishment history that Garth could relate to. There were four other winners, one for each continent: JoAnn Tall, of the Oglala Lakota tribe who'd spearheaded a campaign to stop toxic and nuclear waste contamination in the Black Hill Badlands in the USA, Dai Qing of China who had opposed the Yangtze Dam on both environmental and social grounds, Sviatoslav Zabelin, a Russian who had made a major impact on environmental policy in his country, Juan Mayr of Colombia who went on to become that country's Minister of Environment and the late John Sinclair who successfully headed off mining in an irreplaceable island ecosystem in Australia. Spending time with these remarkable people was a privilege.

Our schedule was hectic: media interviews, lunches with various VIPs, receptions and dinners each evening. Within a day or two we'd heard our co-winners' interviews so often that we joked about swapping places and giving each other's stories to the media.

A lunch that stands out was with Caroline Getty, who'd visited our project in Namibia and contributed some funding for rhino conservation. She had camped with us and Blythe Loutit for a few days, and apart from Caroline having a hair-raisingly close encounter with a rhino – fortunately keeping her cool and backing off calmly at Garth's side, it had been a great trip. Like most of us who've had overly close experiences with dangerous wild animals, she enjoyed the encounter much more afterwards, in the telling and re-telling, than at the time.

In San Francisco, Garth and I excused ourselves from the group lunch and were picked up by Caroline. To our great pleasure, no restaurant: she'd brought a picnic and we drove across the Golden Gate bridge and shared a delicious basket of deli food while sitting on a blanket on a hill overlooking the ocean in the San Francisco Golden Gate National Park. Perceptively, Caroline had decided we probably needed a break – and to be in nature – from all the hype of the city. It could not have been a more thoughtful gesture, sending us restored into the fray.

Coming from southern Africa, we were used to street people begging for money. San Francisco has plenty of those – often Vietnam War veterans, we were told. Some of their signs, giving reasons why they needed money, were intriguing. Our favourite was a long-haired, bearded man who slouched against a wall at a busy intersection near our hotel. His large sign offered free advice on anything for $1. Many people, including us, gave him money just for making us smile. Garth – tall, lean and bearded, and in his normal bush clothing – was easy to be mistaken for a street person and some of us teased him that he should put a hat on the ground for money when he went outside to smoke his pipe. This was before smoking even in public spaces such as pavements had been banned.

In New York, we met the mayor for lunch and were hosted at a 'green' restaurant for dinner by Robert Kennedy Jr, son of the late Senator, brother of the late President Jack Kennedy. We arrived early at the venue which boasted it only used recycled paper. While the rest of us went inside for a drink, Garth stayed on the pavement for a quick puff of his pipe to help him deal with the next few hours. As a 100 per cent introvert, every social interaction takes energy from him, even though he may enjoy it – unlike extroverts who actually gain energy from interacting with others.

Within moments he was accosted by the restaurant manager who asked him to move away, and not smoke there, obviously assuming he was a street person. Garth took exception to her tone and asked her if she owned the pavements of New York. (He could have added – but didn't – that the mayor of New York had, in fact, that very day, given us 'freedom of New York' for our brief stay in his city). The manager continued to try to hustle Garth away, getting increasingly annoyed with this tall man in a bush jacket. At that moment, a limousine drew up and two men emerged. One was Ray Bonner, Pulitzer prize-winning author and investigative journalist, who'd visited us in Namibia the year before while researching his book on conservation, *At the Hand of Man: Peril and Hope for Africa's Wildlife*. His companion was the host of our evening, Robert Kennedy.

Ray recognised Garth and greeted him like a long lost friend. He introduced Garth to Robert who shook his hand with enthusiasm and congratulated him on winning the Goldman award. The now scarlet-faced manager was left speechless on the pavement as the three men swept past her into the restaurant. When she recovered, she found Garth and offered profuse apologies, positively grovelling. Garth punished her by telling a humorous version of the story at dinner.

All the winners in our year were remarkable people. The South Lakota native American JoAnn Tall was in a wheel-chair, crippled at a young age with arthritis, and she travelled with an entourage of three of her brothers – tall, unsmiling men wearing traditional dress. She'd won the award for the North American continent by forging a network of native American tribes and getting them to work together against big industry's plans to defile the Black Hills in South Dakota.

At first she and her party remained aloof. But slowly, as we all travelled together in limousines, had meals together and talked among ourselves, she warmed to the group. One afternoon we were all taken on a visit to Muir Woods, near San Francisco. Walking under the massive and magnificent redwood trees was a near religious experience for many of us who'd never seen so many tall trees. JoAnn was deeply affected. She was moved to climb out of her wheelchair – being pushed by one of her brothers, and leaned on another's arm as she slowly tottered along, drinking in the trees.

I can feel their spirits, she told me, black eyes shining with tears, her whole body conveying rapture.

She boycotted a congressional visit in Washington, as a protest about the way colonial Americans treated native Americans. Some of the paintings on the walls inside congress – naive historical art depicting native Americans as savages being slaughtered in battles – underscored her point.

But JoAnn and her group gave a wonderful gift to her co-winners, and most of all, to the colonial Americans involved in our week. One evening, before an event, she asked if she could speak. She told us that she and her brothers had listened to our hearts over the past few days and knew now that we were good people who loved and respected the earth. She was thus proud to be among our numbers. As a thank you to us all and to the Goldman Foundation, her brothers wanted to show their appreciation with a short Lakota ceremony. Drums were produced and the group treated us to an interlude of drumming and singing, so beautiful and meaningful that it raised goosebumps. Many were moved to tears.

Five years later the Goldman Foundation invited us back to San Francisco for a reunion of all prize winners to date. Meeting them all – about 40 men and women from countries around the world – and having the opportunity to spend a few days together on Berkley University campus, sharing and learning from one another's work, was a stimulating experience. As the award targets grassroots work and activism, we all had a lot in common.

A big reception was held at the city's large Presidium one evening. All winners were given gold-coloured badges to wear: name, continent and the year we'd won the award. There were hundreds of guests, many of whom would come up and ask about your work, usually just as you'd put something from the lavish spread into your mouth. It was hard to talk and hear in the buzz of animated conversations. Naturally, Garth made an escape as soon as he decently could.

Taking his can of beer with him, he went outside and stood on the pavement, smoking his pipe. Well-dressed guests, San Francisco's elite, continued to arrive in limousines and most barely glanced his way. Just another street person. A young man walked past and seeing Garth's beer can, he stopped to talk. This is my reconstruction of what happened, based on what Garth told me because I only met the man half an hour later when I went out to find Garth and bring him back in as the speeches were about to start.

Hey dude, the man asked, did you get that beer inside? Yep, replied Garth. Plenty of food and drink in there.

This real street person or someone who was certainly poor, judging by his tattered clothing, then walked in, but was escorted out very soon after.

Nah, he said, they say you need an invitation. Pity. I'm starving.

Garth promptly took off his gold badge – Garth Owen-Smith, Africa, 1993 – and told his not-very-clean companion, he could borrow the badge to get some food.

In strolled the man with Garth's badge pinned prominently on his polar-necked jersey. I have no doubt that while he was cramming food into his mouth, he was accosted many times by guests wanting to congratulate him on his great work for conservation in Africa – after all he was a black man. I wonder what he told them. Half an hour or so later, with a beer can in both pockets of his jeans and as much food as he could carry, he came out. This was the point at which I met him, and saw him return the badge to Garth. All I could do was laugh and hope the man had represented Africa well.

Among the group of first Goldman winners is Nobel Peace Prize laureate – the late Wangari Maathai of Kenya. We happened to be in Kenya when it was announced that she won. That night when we were dining in a restaurant in Mombasa, the band called for requests. I sent a note asking that the band leader announce

Wangari's Nobel award much to the delight of the Kenyans there who might never have known. We all stood and applauded.

Three winners have been assassinated for their environmental cause and many more imprisoned unjustly.

I went to London alone to get Garth and my UNEP Global 500 certificates from Prime Minister John Major and enjoyed the experience, which included tree planting and meeting budding young conservationists at a school. The Namibian ambassador to the UK attended the award ceremony and sat next to me. He was so proud of Namibia getting these two awards that he held my hand and beamed through most of the ceremony. I looked at our hands, one black, one white, and beamed too.

Two awards stand out for adding immense value to our family life. Working in remote parts of Namibia for decades has meant sacrificing close contact with family – and friends for that matter. When we did manage to get together, it was often hard for a city-based parent or sibling to relate to our lifestyle and the kind of work we were doing. For Garth's two sons, their father's work meant they didn't see him for months at a time, and he lost out on much of what modern fatherhood is about. We had the boys for part of their school holidays each year and tried to share important days like Christmas, for example, with them and their mother June, Garth's ex-wife. But even then, our work sometimes took precedence. June, with some help from Garth, and just a little from me, did a sterling job in raising two strong-minded, intelligent men who have forged their own paths in life.

In 1996 we were invited to Holland for our WWF Knights of the Order of the Golden Ark awards. We were told we could bring a guest to the Soesdyk Palace award ceremony where Prince Bernhard would be doing the presentations. My mother had died two years previously – without me being able to say goodbye because I put off going to see her in hospital in Pretoria to quickly finish some important fieldwork. She was 86 and had fallen and broken her hip so I did not think it was the end. I was wrong and she passed away before I, her only daughter, could get there. After nearly 60 years of marriage my father's grief was overwhelming. I stayed with him for two weeks after the funeral, helping him learn to cope alone. But then I had no choice but to get back to work in Namibia.

I worried a lot about him in the next months and was glad both my brothers were near enough to see him regularly. Nevertheless, it was obvious my father had fallen into a serious depression, especially after Judy, his beloved collie, died a few months after my mother's death. On the spur of the moment, I phoned my brother Neil. I asked him if he would pay flights for our father to join Garth and me in the Netherlands for the award. He thought this was an excellent idea.

I had expected my frugal 88-year-old father to be very resistant to the idea of flying to Holland for four days but with Neil's enthusiastic encouragement he accepted our invitation. What helped was that my father had a good friend in Pretoria who was Dutch: when the friend heard Jake had been invited to attend his daughter's award ceremony at the royal palace, he told my dad he would be crazy to turn down the opportunity and urged him to go – and come back and tell him all about it. So my dad flew to Holland.

Good friends of ours, journalists Leo Enthoven and his wife Carla, drove Jake, Garth and me to our charming hotel near the Soesdyk Palace. The award event required fairly formal clothes and as my luggage had been lost by the airline, I had to find something to wear. I managed to buy an outfit I could afford – not having had time to make a claim against the airline – but totally forgot about my footwear. All I had was what I was wearing: a pair of clumsy waterproof walking boots that I thought would be fine for wet Europe in the daytime. They kept my feet dry when it rained but they didn't look so hot with the tan, gold and black tunic and skirt I wore to the palace, as photographs of the event attest! Garth, who has never owned a suit in his life, was the epitome of sartorial elegance in a beautifully cut dark blue suit, borrowed from Sir Francis Richards, former British high commissioner to Namibia, the same high commissioner who gave us a Land Rover and our NGO's name shortly after independence.

We'd visited Jill and Francis at their home in the UK en route to the Netherlands. It was not the first time Garth had borrowed that exact same suit – first was in the early 1990s when Queen Elizabeth and Prince Philip visited Namibia. Rather mischievously, knowing how little we liked pomp and ceremony, Jill and Francis insisted we come to the royal reception they were holding at their embassy home in Windhoek. We'd met Prince Philip at a conservation discussion earlier in the day with a dozen or so other conservationists but we didn't expect to actually get to speak to the Queen.

Like all the guests, we'd been given strict instructions about royal protocol. We had to arrive before the Queen, and form two lines in the avenue in the garden that led to the embassy residence's ornate front door. The Queen would be led by Francis, entering the line at one end, speaking to just a few people before exiting at the other end and going into the building. We should not speak to the Queen unless spoken to, only responding to what she said to us.

Garth and I placed ourselves right at the end of the line of at least 80 people, chatting casually and looking forward to a glass of wine, or at least I was, when – naturally – Francis brought the Queen to a stop in front of us, and introduced us. She looked as tired as she probably felt having flown in from a day in the north-central part of the country an hour before.

Francis mentioned we lived in a place called World's End (Wereldsend) that was located in a desert. She perked up and told us England had a World's End but no doubt it was quite different from our desert home. She seemed to run out of anything to say after that and Francis was about to escort her inside. But Garth was feeling sorry for this weary, hardworking monarch. So he breached etiquette and started a conversation, asking her about her World's End and telling her about ours. The Queen seemed delighted to be addressed and chatted away for several more minutes, asking lots of questions and replying to Garth's. Neither seemed perturbed that they had caused a delay as President Sam Nujoma, the First Lady of Namibia and Jill had to stand around at the door of the residence waiting for this animated conversation to end.

In Soesdyk Palace, a few years later, Garth and I were swept into media interviews and discussions with conservation colleagues before the awards ceremony and I didn't have much time for my father. I kept checking he was okay, and saw he was in a corner talking to a woman about his age. Good.

It wasn't till quite a bit later that I went up to them and overheard part of their conversation. Having been on their feet for an hour, they were agreeing that these events where you had to stand were quite trying, that their feet hurt and it was no good circulating, as one probably should, because it was too noisy to hear a damn thing. The old woman put her hand on Jake's arm and told him she was glad to have found him to talk to and he must give his Dutch friend in Pretoria her best wishes. I stepped forward to introduce myself and was flabbergasted to recognise the old Queen Juliana who was married to Prince Bernhard. What a lovely story my dad would have to tell his Dutch friend back home.

My dad enjoyed every moment of his unexpected last overseas trip – and spending time with the former queen was as much a highlight as seeing Garth and me get our badges pinned to our chests by Prince Bernard. It was wonderful for Garth, Neil and I to be able to provide him with such a great experience at the end of his long life. He died two years later at 90.

Many years later, we briefly hosted the British queen's grandson Prince Harry at Wereldsend when he was doing some rhino tracking. He live up to his reputation as a charming, high-spirited and irrepressible character.

As Namibians, we never expected to have anything more to do with British royalty till an email arrived from Sarah Watson of Tusk Trust in 2015, saying that Garth had been chosen as their Prince William Lifetime Conservation winner. We'd no idea that Garth had been nominated. He was in the field so I made the decision on his behalf to accept Sarah's invitation to both of us to fly to London to accept the award from the prince, who she told me was Tusk's patron. But I had one condition.

It had immediately occurred to me that as both Garth's sons,

Tuareg and Kyle, plus our grandson Garth Owen-Smith Jr lived in the UK, we could surely invite them to the awards ceremony. The boys had never seen their father receive an award and because they both lived overseas we rarely saw them. Garth Jr was almost 14 that year and we'd only met him four or five times in his life. I told Sarah that we would come as long as we could invite all three Owen-Smith boys. I wanted Sarah, Garth Jr's mother to come too but Tusk's Sarah felt that four guests was pushing it a step too far, given the limited space available at the Claridges ballroom where the gala dinner was to be held. Several hundred well-heeled guests would be paying a lot of money to Tusk to attend the prestigious event.

So we went to London. Tusk did us proud with the way our boys were treated, being welcomed to our Sloane Square hotel before the event, meeting the other award winners – a conservationist of the year award and a young ranger award, plus two finalists. Although the Tusk Conservation award and the Young Ranger award went to Dr Emmanuel de Merode for his DRC work and Edward Ndiritu of Kenya, the other two finalists were also most impressive people – Mary Molokwe, a Nigerian working in difficult circumstances in Liberia and Cosmos Mumba of Zambia. Mary later used her prize as a finalist to visit the Namibian community conservation programme with some government officials from Liberia. As a lover of all non-human primates, I was fascinated to hear about Cosmos' work to protect them, including the less charismatic ones such as monkeys and baboons.

This large group and our three boys, all impeccable in formal evening attire or traditional dress, were driven to Claridges where we had to exit our black Land Rovers onto a red carpet. Crowds of people lined the streets, obviously waiting to see the royals arrive. But we got some clapping and flashbulbs going off. Mary and I got the giggles as we strolled down the red carpet and swept into Claridges. It was just like on TV although no one tried to interview us about our (very non-couture) gowns. Mary looked spectacular in her brightly coloured modern Nigerian attire and I wasn't too bad in a borrowed red evening dress.

We'd met Prince William the day before at Kensington Palace and were pleased when Charlie Mayhew, founder and CEO of Tusk, steered the tall prince to where we stood and introduced him to the three Owen-Smith boys. Garth Jr watched and listened wide-eyed while his father Tuareg and William chatted casually about surfing. Later our grandson declared the Tusk dinner as the best night of his life.

It was a glittering occasion with many celebrities, and we recognised film stars, an opera singer and met some of the top names in conservation. One of those was Matthew Rice, with his future wife Stella. Sarah had deliberately not told us Matt – whom we regard as our third son – and Stella were coming, and it was a wonderful surprise. We'd not met stunning Stella before so we enjoyed telling her about Matt in his early days in Namibia. We are proud to have given him his start in community conservation. And we are also proud to see that Matt has surpassed our work in what he has achieved in multiple African countries in the last 30 years.

For dinner, Garth and I were seated at the main table with the prince, Charlie Mayhew, his wife and four of Tusk's major donors. Garth was preoccupied because he knew he had an acceptance speech to make and while he has no trouble holding the floor round a campfire, he was not at ease in this sophisticated setting. He was only a few months out of major surgery – a quadruple heart by-pass – caused, his doctor reckoned, by stress and smoking. Garth agreed about the stress and did give up his pipe – for a while. But he was not at his best that evening and was struggling to cope with the rapid-fire questions about our work coming at him from the guests on either side of him. He barely touched his food.

I was enjoying myself, deep in conversation with remarkable Charlie on one side and the charming, erudite prince on the other. William's passion for conservation was evident. He'd just returned from China where he had met with the Chinese president about banning ivory trade. He told me about his job as a rescue helicopter pilot in the UK. Why on earth, I asked, didn't he work full-time as an ambassador for conservation as this was obviously where he could make the most impact. There must be many other excellent helicopter pilots in the UK who could do his job. The prince said there was nothing he would like more than to work for conservation.

We talked about other things including his brother's visit to Namibia the year before. I told William that when we mentioned to young black Namibian colleagues that Prince Harry, grandson of Britain's queen, was coming, none of them knew who he was. But when we said he was the youngest son of Princess Di, then faces lit up as everyone knew her. I was touched by William's reaction. He thanked me for telling him that story because it made him happy to know that his late mother was still remembered and loved around the world.

At one stage Garth excused himself from the people sitting next to him and left the banquet hall. The prince looked disconcerted. 'Where's he going?' he asked. I explained he'd recently had heart surgery and probably just needed a few minutes' air before the award ceremony which was due to start soon. William suggested I follow him and check he was alright. But I assured him this was normal behaviour for Garth – at some stage during any function held indoors, he would bolt for the hills. Later, we found out that it was a breach of British etiquette for Garth to leave the prince's table without asking his permission. And of course, he didn't manage to get outside the hotel into the fresh air – security was tight and no one, not even the Prince William Lifetime Conservation Award winner, was being allowed in or out.

William duly gave out the awards and speeches were made. Garth graciously started his acceptance speech by asking me to stand up, telling the audience that I should be standing next to him and that he shared the award with me, as his co-worker and partner for 30 plus years. He spoke for a few minutes more, not his best speech, under the circumstances. But then knowing how incredibly articulate he can be I was probably more critical than the other listeners. At the end, he remembered to do something we'd discussed. He asked his sons to stand up and told the audience that he wanted to acknowledge his boys, now both fine young men, who had grown up without a full-time father and had thus paid the price for their father's obsession with his conservation work. Claridges banquet hall erupted into applause. It was a moving moment that meant a great deal to Garth, the boys, our grandson and me. Nothing will ever compensate the boys for often having to do without Garth as they grew up but I hope seeing that his work was important enough for it to be internationally recognised made them proud of who their father is.

When we had time to read newspapers we saw that Garth's brand-new tan veldskoene which he'd worn for our afternoon visit to Kensington Palace had made headlines in Namibia and gone viral online. Photographs of us with the prince had been released and one newspaper gleefully used the headline: 'Vellies in the palace.' To our great amusement his vellies even got a picture and mention in a British newspaper's fashion page as a different fashion statement. Garth was unimpressed with all this attention to his shoes. He thought newspapers should be writing about our conservation work. Besides he could not understand what the fuss was all about when we were told we could wear our traditional dress.

I was intrigued to learn that many young Namibians avidly follow the UK royal family's lives on social media. This emerged when Prince William visited Namibia in late 2018 as Tusk's patron. IRDNC and SRT, both recipients of Tusk funding, helped host him and his group. After rhino tracking we arranged for him to meet a small delegation of rural Namibians involved in the Ombonde People's Park – an African version of a park which is a partnership between two conservancies and government. Traditional leaders, conservancy representatives, the Women for Conservation movement and the support groups – a total of 20 people – were to discuss their work with William under big shade trees near the spectacular little Natural Selection lodge in the Hoanib River valley where the party had overnighted. The governor of Kunene was also invited although he had been warned no speeches: this was an occasion for the prince to listen and learn about how ordinary Namibians were doing conservation.

We'd all done a sterling job at keeping the royal destination confidential as is normal for such visits, but the governor's office must have leaked it at the last moment. He turned up in a seven-car convoy, filled with regional council members and other government officials. Garth and John Kasaona had to drive out to meet Tusk's Charlie Mayhew to warn him the group had suddenly tripled in size in spite of the remote location, in case this was viewed as a security issue. John pointed out that having all these local politicians and government officials present was positive for community conservation efforts.

While we waited for Tusk entourage, I asked some of the young officials who'd turned up with the governor why they drove at least five hours – each way – just to see a traditional leader from another country. Was it because he was a relatively rare international celebrity to Kunene Region? Obviously that was part of it but people were remarkably well informed and spoke warmly about 'Harry and William and Kate and Meghan'. I learnt more about the private lives of modern British royalty under trees in the Hoanib than from years of watching their occasional newsworthy activities on BBC and Sky. I just hoped that some of these Namibians would emulate a British traditional leader and take an interest in environmental issues.

EIGHTEEN

The real threats to Africa's wildlife

When we talk about or speak to large groups or family in Lakota we use the term mitakuye oyasin *which means all my relatives – and we are also addressing the plants, trees and animals. Basically all living on earth as they take care of us* – Dani Morrison, member of the Oglala Lakota Nation and Masters student, Bozeman campus, Montana State University, 2019.

LIVING IN A DUNG hut on and off over several years changed my perspective about wildlife and how it should be conserved outside parks and reserves. It also reaffirmed what I already knew – that a world without wild animals would be unthinkable.

It's a thrilling experience to see dangerous wild animals from inside a sturdy 4x4 vehicle. Hearing lions roar while you're in your bedroll on the floor of a door-less structure made of branches plastered with sand and cattle dung or encountering elephant when you are on foot gathering firewood or fetching water are different experiences altogether. They make your heart pound and your mouth go dry. Ask me – or any of the countless ordinary people across Africa who live with wildlife.

At first I was amazed that most of the Himba people I was

living with were so accepting of dangerous wild animals in their back yards. Like me, most were afraid of close encounters, and older men and women gave me lots of advice on how to avoid such mishaps. That's how these encounters were perceived by the older generation, as mishaps because, as someone put it, it meant you were not looking or you were drunk. Unlike many in the 'developed' world, these people accepted responsibility for themselves; they did not look for someone else to blame or sue.

Younger people who had got used to very little wildlife – most had been poached out in the '70s and early '80s – were less tolerant and much more afraid as wild animal numbers increased. I came to see that older people felt connected to the natural world and its wild inhabitants in a direct and fundamental way. This relationship – their feeling of being part of the web of life – had much to teach me and most of us in the modern world.

It has long been recognised that the remarkable resilience of nomadism as a way of life is underpinned by social relations and *socio-ecological relations* that are responsive to the arid and semi-arid terrains nomads usually inhabit. I had to go beyond my research focus on built space and material goods to understand the Himba people's powerful awareness of their place within their social, symbolic, economic and physical cosmorama. I invented terms such as 'bio-geography' in my attempt to make sense of a daily life in which people truly perceived themselves as a part of the ecosystem, not at its apex.

My contact with young people who had gone to school and received a Eurocentric education made me pessimistic that this communality of people and nature would continue for much longer.

I wrote in my 1995 doctoral thesis that 'as Kaoko communities integrate into the central state economy, it is predicted that they will join the Western world and much of modern (and impoverished) Africa in viewing the natural landscape as a series of unrelated resources to be exploited in order to make money. This changed relationship with the natural environment where humans are alienated (for a variety of different reasons) from natural resources can be shown historically to be the first step towards the massive environmental degradation visited on the world in the name of development and progress.'

Fortunately, I was only partially right: community-based conservation has given tens of thousands of rural Namibians – not just the Himba people – the social, economic and spiritual space to keep alive and pass on a set of values that implicitly acknowledges the intimate relationship between humans and nature.

But let's not be starry-eyed about this. No one wants to turn back the clock. All rural Namibians want and need money, jobs and many of the benefits of modern technology. Community conservation plays a major role in diversifying local economies beyond subsistence livelihoods and therefore contributes to modern aspirations. By reinstating nature as culturally and spiritually part of us, by opening up respected posts for rural and urban people to be able to work in or for nature protecting and monitoring wildlife and valuable trees and plants, it also holds the possibility that the values of an older and wiser generation will survive into the future.

And as I have said before, that may well be the Namibian conservancy programme's single greatest contribution.

So my initial city dweller's amazement – that so many modern rural Africans were prepared to share their land with wildlife, in spite of the economic damage to farming livelihoods and the risk some species pose to human life – was slowly replaced by deep respect. That a Damara farmer can rant about the elephants who damaged the pipes at his borehole-fed water tank so that there is no water for his cattle and goats – or his family. Yet, when asked if he'd like to see the elephants shot or removed, he is nonplussed by the question. Of course not, he told Garth: these are our elephants, even when some of them are '*stout kinders*' (naughty children). Others are not so tolerant and over the years at least 20 Kunene elephants have been shot while raiding fields, particularly in areas where there are no conservancies and no vision of sharing the future with wildlife, or where conservancies earn no income.

We can react emotionally to these elephant deaths, or we can focus on the longer-term survival of the 400 plus so-called desert elephant. It would be helpful to their survival if certain social media 'conservationists' stopped applying their Eurocentric attitudes to Namibia's communal lands where people and wildlife live together. As if a Kunene farmer who has lost 27 goats and sheep, plus two donkeys, inside a kraal, in repeated lion raids, should not shoot a member of this lion pride as a deterrent to the rest. A strategy that has proved itself many times.

Are those who were so vocal about this 2018 event saying that this individual lion's life is more important than the farmer and his family's attempts to make a living? Glibly, as though they are talking about picking up a pet cat and putting it in a cage to drive it to the vet for its shots, some of these people suggest that problem lions be darted and moved, with no idea of what this entails in a conservancy that is 3 522 square kilometres in size, besides the enormous difficulty of finding a safe haven for such lions. And remember too that these are not a few lions clinging onto survival: Namibia's desert lions are the only free-ranging lion population in Africa that are increasing – from about 20 in the 1980s to about 150 plus in 2018.

Mostly one should ignore such absurd crusades on social media except when this is putting the long-term survival of lion, rhino and elephant at risk, as some of these campaigns do. And Namibia has been attacked in recent years, with calls for tourist boycotts, by individuals and groups both within and outside the country, who sentimentally individualise wild animals, misrepresent facts and totally miss the big picture of a *long-term* conservation strategy that requires balancing the needs of people, wildlife and tourism.

I have to ask, as I did in a letter to *The Namibian* newspaper, after urban complaints about a tourism-habituated lioness being shot in Torra Conservancy: How many of you would tolerate a lioness lying within 200 metres of your children's school playground? After this skinny lioness was shot, it was discovered she had badly broken teeth and would have been in constant pain. This was why she was seeking small, easy prey such as baby donkeys and even a chicken. A child could have been next. And how many of the parents among the social media mob would be prepared to let their children walk to school (in the absence of other options such as mom driving them in her fancy 4x4) across the Zambezi-Chobe floodplains where elephant and buffalo roam?

To quote Namibia's Minister of Environment and Tourism in June 2018, self-proclaimed conservationists use social media to prey on well-meaning but uninformed people in society. 'Because conservation biology is complex and difficult to explain in sound bites, they prefer to project simplistic approaches and solutions which (have) failed worldwide . . . a more western urban short-term animal rights approach which is highly counterproductive to long term conservation.'

What use does it do to save one desert lion from trophy hunting – by procuring enough donations from a gullible public to buy and then not use the hunting contract – when that lion could slowly starve to death anyway in a post-drought lion over-population situation when the much-reduced wild prey species disperses far and wide? And even worse, while this 'saved' lion is desperately trying to stay alive by killing cattle, goats, horses and donkeys, his actions are starting to erode a farming community's support for wildlife conservation in general – including protecting rhino and elephant – and specifically – whether they are still prepared to live with lions. By saving that one lion, the whole population of desert-dwelling lion is being put at risk. Far better that the lion is killed by a trophy hunter and the income to the conservancy is put to good use compensating farming losses.

People who think they are supporting conservation by donating money to those who claim the right to express their extreme preservationist views on the best way to conserve a wild species – without bothering to research and understand the context and background, or by manipulating facts to suit their case – would do well to stop and think. They are doing more harm than good.

Notably it is not Dr Flip Stander, Namibia's internationally known lion researcher, who is calling for individual lions to be 'saved'. He understands the realities on the ground when predators and people live together. The community-based conservation programme has ensured there *are* still lion and elephant in north-west Namibia, even if some individuals have to be shot to balance the costs of living with wildlife, and to demonstrate that people and their livelihoods matter, not just lions.

The areas we are discussing are not game reserves or parks. They are communal farming lands where hundreds of thousands of ordinary rural people are trying to feed their families, to clothe and educate their children, and to have some surplus cash to buy a TV and a cell phone.

It is some of these same rural people who have chosen to form conservancies to ensure space for wild animals on their land. They have *chosen* to live with wild animals even though there are real consequences that impact on their livelihoods. In just one week in November 2017, a pride of lions killed more than 171 goats and sheep in Torra Conservancy. This was after farmers had endured the worst drought since the 1980s, being forced to watch most of their domestic stock starve to death. Admittedly, the high stock losses to predators in the north-west in 2017–18 are not normal nor what happens every year. From 2017 when the drought was partially broken in a few places, we experienced the impact of the over-population of predators.

The same cycle occurs during every major drought in the north-west. The predators – lions, hyena, leopard, cheetah, jackals – increase to an unsustainable level because of the easy pickings of wild prey around permanent water. If the drought continues for several years, numbers of prey species reduce due to starvation, predation and low or no breeding rates. At the same time, farmers move their stock into these wild areas where there may still be fodder in an effort to keep their animals alive.

But, counterintuitively (Kahneman's fast thinking versus slow thinking neatly illustrated) it gets worse *after* the rains.

Already lowered numbers of gemsbok, zebra and springbok are able to leave the areas around permanent water and disperse into the hills and valleys where there is now new green grass and temporary water. Hunting thus becomes more difficult, so predators turn to what remains: domestic stock. The correct management in such a situation would have been to reduce the numbers of predators during or after the drought. I believe MET was reluctant to do this because of the social media outrage that would have erupted. So the people who really count – those who live with wild animals, including lions – were forced to bear the economic costs.

From 2014 onwards, IRDNC facilitated a coordinated emergency drought response aimed at reducing stock losses in Kunene Region. NGOs, conservancies and private sector tourism worked together to fund lion-proof kraals and pay special lion guards. MET oversaw the development of a human–wildlife conflict mitigation strategy. IRDNC now has a special human–wildlife conflict unit to work with conservancies – which took time to set up because funding had to be raised.

In the north-east of the country farmers in communal conservancies routinely cope with hippo and elephant trampling and eating crops, as well as predators killing stock. Electric fencing, trip alarms, chilli smoke bombs – you name it, it's been tried.

We once tested an electric fence barrier between Mudumu National Park and neighbouring village fields in north-east Namibia, the same one that local men had to be persuaded by their women to help erect. It all worked, for a while. Then the elephants discovered they could break the fencing with their tusks without getting shocked. One old bull couldn't be bothered: he was observed pushing a teenage bull into the fence so that it broke, shorting the electricity. Then he strolled through to the fields, with his slightly shocked but none-the-worse-for-it young companion.

Crocodiles live in the rivers, which are the only water supply for many people, so cattle are at risk every time they drink, as are women doing laundry and fetching water. The conservancy movement has helped communities develop and share strategies to manage some of these risks, often drawing on elders' memories – such as reviving the sensible old practice of fencing off small areas in rivers where cattle can safely drink and people can access water. In the past thorn bushes were used as a barrier in the shallows; today it is sturdy poles and wire fencing.

Without rural people supporting wildlife conservation there will be no wildlife. It is these rural people in Namibia – and in many other African countries – who hold the future of wild animals in their hands, not individuals and groups on the outside promising that your funding will save the last black-maned lion in Damaraland or save desert elephant from extinction.

It is just common sense, therefore, to link wildlife conservation to improving the lives of the people who live with or neighbour wild animals.

The two biggest current threats to Africa's wildlife are loss of land for them to live on and the fact that the majority of Africans, and most of their leaders, do not view, or experience, wild animals as one of their most valuable resources. This is about attitudes, not just economics. You can break these threats down into habitat degradation and/or the conversion of wild lands for agricultural and other human uses, pollution, poaching, human wildlife conflict and other very real problems. But at the heart of conservation's failures across the continent are these two fundamental issues. The others listed are their symptoms.

Corruption in high places is the oil in the machinery. But if enough ordinary African people, both urban and rural, cared deeply about wildlife and saw it as valuable to their lives, the paradigm would change. Those who facilitate wildlife product trafficking would no longer be able to operate with impunity.

Wildlife does not have to be valuable purely in a monetary sense: I have never met anyone who cannot be moved in some way by the world we have not manufactured.

As elder Japie Uararavi told us in the late 1980s, a decade after virtually all wildlife had disappeared from Puros: 'In the old days when I rode my donkey from Puros to Otjivatenda, it was a short road. Now the giraffe and gemsbok are gone and the road has become very long.' Japie has lived long enough to see the return of abundant wild animals to the area. He has also seen wildlife numbers decline in the recent drought up to 2018. But populations are already picking up. Conservation requires a long-term perspective.

Implementing community-based conservation has more than doubled the land under wildlife conservation in Namibia to over 40 per cent with communal conservancies adding nearly 166 000 square kilometres (20 per cent of the country) by the end of 2018.

No community has ever been coerced into forming a conservancy; rural people chose to share their lives and land with wildlife. A few deep thinkers in a community may start the process but when strategies to activate the key principles of community conservation are implemented, inevitably majority support follows. We should never forget that people can choose to de-proclaim their conservancy; if for example, the burden of living with lion or elephant became too heavy. It seems we cannot remind some social media conservationists enough about this. Or that conservancies are not parks. They are multiple-use areas, zoned by the residents themselves for farming, mixed farming and wildlife, tourism and core wildlife areas.

But rural people can do more than provide space for wild animals to live; they are also the key to anti-poaching efforts. If the majority of the local people are against the minority who are poaching, or who are colluding with poachers (or criminals of any kind), the poachers and as importantly the dealers will face an unsupportive milieu.

Thus by focusing on the good guys – the 98 per cent whose attitudes can be changed to be on conservation's side, instead of the 2 per cent who are incorrigible, there is a good chance of stopping illegal hunting. As the saying goes, where you put your attention is where your energy goes.

This is not theory – it is a tried and tested approach which worked 30 years ago to stop massive poaching across the north-west. It has again worked in the past few years against modern rhino poaching in north-western Namibia, coupled with rigorous on-the-ground monitoring by local conservancy teams, NGOs and government, working together.

It is also notable that in Zambezi, elephant poachers quickly learnt to target the national parks, rather than the conservancies where people live and are vigilant.

Namibia hosts the world's second largest black rhino population so it was inevitable, with neighbouring South Africa losing up to three rhinos a day, that poaching would spread here. This had long been anticipated by NGOs, conservancies and MET. Garth pushed for several retired, elderly community game guards from the earlier poaching era to be re-employed as consultants to do some mentoring of young conservancy game guards who had never faced poaching. Other partners brought in various specialists from South Africa and elsewhere.

Garth stood up at a national rhino security workshop in Windhoek in 2011 and made a strong case for conservancies not to be left out. Any successful rhino security plan had to involve the people who lived with the rhino, he said. A few months later in May, Save the Rhino Trust did an internal strategy review. This was the first time the impending poaching crisis was discussed at their board level and a pivotal decision was made to draw on and build conservancy capacity rather than hire more SRT trackers. Thus the two NGOs – IRDNC and SRT – were united in an approach that saw communities as lead players.

In February 2012, a meeting was held at Wereldsend at which conservancies called on the government and NGOs to assist them. We need help to protect our rhino, they said.

An outcome was the Conservancy Rhino Ranger project with each of the rhino-hosting conservancies appointing two or more rhino rangers. Some worked on a volunteer basis until funding could be raised. The first conservancy rhino ranger was signed up in August 2012 by the project's driver Jeff Muntifering, a quietly competent American who was living at Wereldsend, married to IRDNC's Kunene coordinator, Basilia Shivute. Jeff is affiliated to the Minnesota Zoo and is SRT's science advisor.

Four months later, in December 2012, after many poaching-free years, a rhino was killed in a communal conservancy. Within 48 hours conservancy members had apprehended the poachers and recovered the horns.

In spite of this quick conservancy success, the knee-jerk

response of the authorities was to turn inwards. Almost none of these officials were in office when community involvement stopped the 1980s rhino and elephant poaching, and no one seemed to think the past had anything to teach them. So they ignored their single greatest anti-poaching resource – the conservancies and their members.

The national police's Special Protected Resources Unit roared into action, driving up to the rugged north-west in a small saloon car, needing to borrow a 4x4 to visit the first crime scene. They were totally inexperienced in rhino-poaching cases but nevertheless excluded conservancies from investigations, even though these are legal bodies set up by communities to manage and benefit from their wildlife.

For the next two years, conservancies and NGOs stood by and watched while the north-west lost 10% of its rhino population without a single arrest, apart from after the first rhino was killed. In our worst year more than 20 rhinos died. We called it the Yellow Tape era because police officers would put a yellow crime-scene tape around a rhino carcass and prevent conservancy game guards and rhino monitors from coming near in case they contaminated the crime scene. Even though, on occasion, these local men could identify boot tracks, and knew where the owner of the boots lived, and importantly, for whom he worked.

MET did not engage with conservancies when a decision was taken to dehorn rhino in conservancies. This reinforced the anger and alienation communities were already feeling about being excluded from anti-poaching efforts, after decades of support for conservation, and now being treated with blatant mistrust by the national police. Dehorning had proved ineffective in other countries where poachers had shot the dehorned animal anyway – either for the remaining piece of horn or so as not to waste time tracking it again – but there was panic in government corridors and the dehorning was understandable. It's a quick and instinctive response.

I had an exchange with Colgar Sikopo, MET's capable and committed Director of Parks and Wildlife, about dehorning. From his perspective, de-horning would buy time for rhino security strategies to be put in place by government. We couldn't meet minds on how the many millions of dollars spent on each dehorning operation, involving helicopters, vehicles and vets, could be better spent.

It wasn't long before poachers went to work in Etosha National Park. Only after more than 60 rhino had been killed would park staff start finding carcasses. Senior park people scurried around trying to find a forgotten copy of the rhino security plan that had been drawn up several years earlier.

However our focus is not Etosha but the communal conservancies and their tourism concessions.

By 2015, five years after stepping down as co-directors of IRDNC, Garth and I could no longer tolerate the situation in our backyard. We raised enough money – a series of small grants, a tiny fraction of what was spent on dehorning rhino – to re-activate community engagement in rhino poaching mitigation. A grant from Goldman Foundation was enough to host a four-day traditional leader trip into the rhino-poaching area, led by IRDNC's John K Kasaona and Garth. Till then some of these men were unaware of how serious the situation had become. Like the 2012 meeting, this 2015 event was to be a catalyst for turning round a seemingly hopeless situation.

Police, MET, IRDNC, SRT, conservancy leaders and private sector tourism joined the expedition which exceeded 40 people in more than a dozen 4x4 vehicles. Conservancy Safaris did the camping and catering logistics on a cost recovery basis. On the last day, a joint action plan was developed by all.

Traditional authorities, shocked at what they'd seen and heard, committed to stopping rhino poaching in their areas as they or their predecessors had done before, asked for 'an old-fashioned' four-day meeting with conservancy leaders at Wereldsend. No slick facilitation or cards to be pinned on boards, please – just a flipchart and some pens to write down the final plan.

NGOs, police and MET were excluded from the first two days of this large gathering at which, we're told, elders gave younger

251

leadership a history lesson – that there would be no wildlife for the conservancies to benefit from if their grandparents and parents had not agreed to conserve wildlife in the 1980s and 1990s. We were allowed in for the last two days when action plans were discussed and adopted. The energy and commitment in this meeting was inspiring.

A comment by a young conservancy chairman stands out. He had not spoken before in four days, not because he was not paying attention he said, but because he was learning so much. Even as a chairman of a conservancy he did not know the history, how it was communities and their leaders who had stopped the elephant, rhino and other poaching of the 1980s. Only now did he fully understand the importance of his role as head of a conservancy.

'And,' he concluded, 'the weight of this role is now heavy on my shoulders.'

The commitment of all community leaders and the jointly developed action plans led to the conservancy rhino rangers doing joint patrols with MET and police. Our funding was also used to improve liaison between community leaders, IRDNC, SRT, police and MET. Now, finally, there was a team.

By then the conservancy rhino rangers under the field coordination of Boas Hambo were proving themselves a force to be reckoned with – unarmed, not afraid to walk for hours and highly dedicated. Boots on the ground coupled with appropriate technology.

Boas had been working as a guide and logistics manager for Conservancy Safaris who had poached him from IRDNC where he was a junior field officer. One of our protégés, Boas has benefited from mentoring from both Garth and Russell, as well as Angela, Jeff and me. After loaning him and a Conservancy Safaris vehicle to the conservancy rhino rangers a few times, it was evident that his passion lay with the rhinos. So CSN seconded him to where he could do the most good. Jeff, his supervisor, and Simpson Uri-Khob, director of the SRT, have nothing but praise for this emerging young conservation leader and the conservancies' teams of local men and women.

IRDNC and Garth, with assistance from Chris Weaver of WWF Namibia, raised additional funding to provide more support to the Conservancy Rhino Ranger Project, boosting what SRT and Jeff's donors had provided. Thanks to a US family, the Keanes, we were able to buy two 4x4 vehicles – one for the SRT and another for the conservancy rhino rangers. This latter vehicle was critical. Up till then the rhino rangers had to share SRT's vehicles and could not operate independently. Once they were in a position to do their own patrols, coverage of rhino areas greatly increased.

In 2015, the year of the traditional leader tour and four-day meeting, only three rhino were killed in the conservancy and concession areas. But, unlike previously, arrests were made each time, thanks to community support. Since then no further rhino have been shot in our project areas in conservancies. Touch wood.

A breakthrough at the edge of where we work was the arrests in 2017 of people allegedly responsible for killing 11 rhino over two years, on the southern boundary of a tourism concession, south of the veterinary cordon fence.

On the monitoring side, sightings of rhino are up 500 per cent from ten years ago – up to 350 rhino sightings a month compared to 50 or 60 a month when SRT worked alone. According to a recent analysis by Jeff, the conservancy rhino rangers account for two out of three of these sightings. They have thus emerged as invaluable to Namibia's rhino anti-poaching effort. And importantly, by 2018 in more than ten separate cases in different conservancies, community information has *prevented* rhino poaching, with police able to intercept armed poaching groups before they were able to kill rhino.

A contributing factor to Namibian conservancies' successes in stopping modern rhino poaching is the outreach project called Rhino Pride. Supported by both IRDNC and SRT, this work has involved schools and different sectors of the Kunene public in various activities, including even pop concerts.

In a recent conversation with Jeff about the high-quality pre-emptive intelligence coming from ordinary members of the public, we agreed directly involving communities and their leaders in anti-poaching efforts at different levels – from conservancy rhino rangers to traditional and conservancy leaders – had been the decisive factor. If you want people to act responsibly, they first have to become accountable. Add to this a broad outreach to the public, including youth, fostering a modern vision of rhinos – alive and thriving – being valuable to us all.

As Garth said at that rhino security workshop in Windhoek, people don't buy into a plan drawn up by others in the capital. They need to make input into it and preferably come up with their own plan, owning it and taking responsibility for it. Had various early schemes by government been implemented – such as bringing in the army or special units of armed men from outside the region – we may have lost our rhino. Few non-local groups could have the same motivation as the conservancy rhino rangers to monitor and protect *their* rhino. Similarly, both IRDNC and SRT, the two active NGOs, are largely staffed by local people.

MET and others have worked at national level, alerting the public across the country to the threat against our rhino. Penalties for poaching and being in possession of horn have been raised significantly.

Sadly, while the local police have definitely proved to be good team players, one cannot report that the national police have yet been effective in cracking cases which involve outsiders as the buyers of horn. Even where journalists flag unexplained sudden conspicuous consumption by individuals in certain north-central villages, investigations have come to nothing. Allegations of corruption in high places continue to be made in the media.

More than 35 years' experience of implementing community conservation has convinced us that community-based approaches are the best way to achieve a thriving and sustainable African way of conserving wildlife, both outside national parks and inside, where the focus would be on neighbours.

In spite of their devastating rhino losses, there has been low interest from South Africa in Namibia's approaches to conservation. Well-known South African conservationist and artist Clive Walker in his book *Rhino Revolution: Searching for New Solutions*, coauthored with Anton Walker, actually writes off community engagement as a failure, and talks about a 'shocking reversal of prior successes of state and community-based involvement in conservation' in the Kunene region. The book, published two years *after* Kunene community-engagement turned round the situation, could not have got it more wrong.

It's different, we've been told – your human populations are so low. If we point out that Zambezi Region, with the highest density of people in the broader territory, across the borders into Botswana, Angola, Zambia and Zimbabwe, has seen a remarkable wildlife recovery since conservancies have been formed, the next point made will be that Namibia does not have the big cities with criminal gangs. Another excuse is that many traditional leaders and community leaders have been corrupted in South Africa – as if this is not also the case in parts of Namibia. No one would claim community conservation is easy or quick – it is a long, hard slog with many obstacles. The key is to get *below* the leadership to the ordinary people. Of course, the situation across our borders is different. But there are principles that apply everywhere and this is where we believe Namibia has lessons for other countries. Let's not waste time re-inventing the wheel while we lose wildlife.

Some South Africans are taking note, however. In 2017, Jeff and I nominated the conservancy rhino rangers for a South African rhino conservation award. They received second prize.

The first principle of all community action, whether it is about conservation or not, is that every context is different so there is no holy grail that can be rolled out. The plan must be home-grown from the bottom up with relevant communities as partners. This could be a township or a town, a rural area with many villages or a community of parents living in different places but linked by their common interest in their children's schooling. The other principles are not sequential and strategies to implement them usually overlap. I list them below because they are as applicable to, for example, a campaign against crime or plastic pollution as for community conservation.

- Focus on developing real relationships, based on mutual trust and respect, and addressing community needs as well as conservation (or other) needs.
- Nurture – with all players – a mutual vision of how wildlife, as applied in our case, can benefit both local communities and the country. Social media can facilitate this in many cases. But often, there are no short cuts to direct engagement. Every group, who can impact on the resources we want to be better managed, needs to be engaged and involved which means learning the local social geography, if necessary via social surveys.
- Consultation is never enough – it's a negotiation.

Garth was once asked at a large meeting of conservationists what he regarded as the best community 'extension' tools. People had been discussing technological outreach all morning but Garth, with his vast experience, had not said anything. Hence the question. 'My most useful tools are my ears,' he told the gathering, making perhaps the most important point of all. That meeting was a few decades ago but who would dispute that hearing others, specially today, remains an invaluable aid to addressing any challenge, not just in conservation.

- In the case of wildlife conservation, local people have to develop a sense of *local* ownership – and gain legal rights – over the resources (not necessarily the land). If this happens, communities will also take ownership of solutions and actions with their partners, of which government should be a major one.
- It is also essential that local people, women as well as men, are directly involved in action. In Namibia, this has been via conservancy game guards, rhino monitors, lion guards, local women working as community activators and men and women playing various roles within their conservancies.
- Local social structures with capacity to plan, make decisions, collaborate with partners and act may need to be

created or adapted from existing community institutions. Communal conservancies, a residents' trust in Bwabwata National Park, communal forests and communal fish reserves play this role in my country. We're now pioneering a new African type of park – a people's park – which is a partnership between conservancies and government.

- It may be necessary to level the playing field to facilitate real partnerships, another principle. The weaker partner may require additional information or capacity building.

When IRDNC helped what became Torra Conservancy to negotiate with the investor who built Damaraland Camp – Namibia's first joint-venture lodge between a community and private sector – none of the local residents had any idea how valuable their land was. It was 1995.

Anna Davis, Colin Nott, Bennie Roman and ourselves held a training session at Wereldsend. Garth and I role-played the investors – offering the community team a flat fee of N$25 000 for use of the land and its water. They all accepted immediately. It took a discussion for people to realise that spectacular land on which wildlife roamed free was a hugely valuable asset for this community and that the investor should pay an annual rent and bed-night levies linked to the lodge's increasing profitability. In the end, with assistance from Colin Nott, then IRDNC's Kunene coordinator, and other partners, they negotiated a model deal with Wilderness Safaris which has earned and continues to earn this community millions of dollars over the years.

- We always mention equitable benefits as the last principle: social and cultural as well as economic benefits must be generated from and linked to the natural resources. Putting it last is deliberate to make the point that if you start with this one, community-based conservation won't reach its full potential. Without the other principles, community poaching is likely to continue even though some monetary benefits are flowing from wildlife. Elite capture of economic benefits is an on-going risk – not just in conservation; here is where NGOs can help facilitate forums for democratic processes.

These principles may be slow and hard to achieve but with home-grown and contextually creative methods they lay the foundation for modern African conservation outside parks and with parks' neighbours. No conservation problem cannot be overcome if a majority of local communities are supportive. Politicians don't lead; they follow – if there is a big enough lobby. Any type of conservation project should therefore have community involvement and action as a key component.

Community conservation has boosted Namibia's economy (net national income) by nearly N$1 billion a year. Thousands of new formal and informal rural jobs have been created and direct returns of well over N$130 million a year are being earned by conservancies and their rural communities. At last count, nearly 170 local natural resource enterprises were hosted by 58 of Namibia's 80 plus conservancies. Some conservancies have proven to have dishonest committees and leaders. Hopefully, members of the corrupt conservancies are learning from the honest majority that it is the members' responsibility to hold their leadership accountable.

Wildlife recoveries have been outstanding although in Kunene the recent four-year drought, coupled with the related increase in predators, hit the upward trend of wildlife hard. In the years before the drought some of us complained that conservancy hunting quotas were too high; others point out that such animals would have probably starved to death anyway in the drought. Recovery is already being seen where rains have fallen with some species producing young for the first time in several years. Conservancy own-use or live sale quotas have been stopped, notably with many conservancies coming to this decision themselves, ahead of government.

In the high human density Zambezi region in north-east Namibia, conservancies provide much needed wildlife-friendly buffer zones around small national parks. And, despite increasing numbers of people bringing more challenges, wildlife continues to thrive, which is a complete turnaround from where we started in 1990. As stated, the upsurge in elephant poaching from neighbouring countries in recent years occurs mainly inside the parks, not in conservancies where the poachers get caught by community staff.

It is a great pity that environmental awareness projects fell out of favour in past years when donors became increasingly metric about results and outputs from their funding. You cannot do justice to EA in this way. How do you quantify the future value of children learning to respect nature?

Some years ago Garth and I gave a seminar for a post-graduate group of conservationists, all involved in human–wildlife conflict in their countries, at Oxford University. We started by asking each of the 20 or so students to briefly outline their own work: we heard about working with Indian communities of several million on the edge of a tiger reserve; a similar situation in a Russian area. Almost every student faced a million or more people trying to make a living on the edges of their wildlife areas. A seemingly impossible task – doing community-based conservation with human populations of that size?

Most of the students were already hard at work with a variety of community strategies – a common one was working with schools, and taking children to see the high-value species. All parents love their children's education and life experience being enhanced. And only if you expose children to wildlife and nature at the right age in the right way, can you create adults who care about species other than themselves.

And then we come to trophy hunting and legalising the trade in ivory and rhino horn, the topics that most polarise conservationists today.

Some aspects of hunting – such as South Africa's iniquitous canned lion industry – are easy to deplore. In Namibia where professional hunting is reasonably well managed (not perfectly), its considerable contribution to community conservation is quantified each year. While most hunters pay on time, disgracefully, a few hunters owe conservancies considerable amounts of money for hunts already conducted. They need to be named and shamed. In most conservancies photographic tourism alone simply does not earn enough to justify stopping hunting. Even though the situation is much improved with the private sector sharing some photographic tourism income, most of the big profits still go to outside owners and shareholders, not to the conservancy members who live with the wildlife. This was our motivation for Conservancy Safaris to be conservancy-owned.

My truth, therefore, is that my head understands that trophy hunting is necessary now – at this stage in this part of developing Africa to add local jobs and income into the equation so that we don't lose our wildlife and wild spaces. But my heart says no to killing animals for sport. So I am saying yes and no in a similar way that I say yes and no to some modern technology.

Ian McCallum's passionate and poetic Ecological Intelligence has helped me come to terms with such contradictions as have decades of field work. Working alongside many thinking African conservationists, not the least being Garth, has grounded me in the practical realities of helping to build, stone by stone, paths along which people can rediscover or invent anew a non-utilitarian relationship with nature. We don't and can't all walk the same path but they are all going to the same place. I hope trophy hunting is just one of those stones along an African path that in due course, we can leave behind.

A strong economic case for trading in rhino horn can be made in African countries by harvesting the horns without killing the animal. Yet, is it not a step too far? Some of my colleagues have called this a question a triumph of emotion over logic. I have been asked by Dr Chris Brown: How many countries in the West would put fences around one of their most valuable resources (rhinos) and earn a bit of money from people coming to see them? What we know Western countries would do is lop off the horns (which regrow) and sell this product.

Those promoting the case for legal trade believe it would undercut the illegal trade by bringing down the price. If such illegal trade was no longer profitable, presumably the poaching would stop. Trade in rhino horn has been banned for 40 years. In that time black rhino populations have declined by 95 per cent The price of horn has increased from US$50 a kg to around US$65 000 today, which makes it more valuable per kg than gold. Clearly the ban has failed to protect rhino.

At current prices, it is unlikely that the poor Chinese masses can still afford to use horn for traditional medicine. One of its modern uses is as a prestige product. Some super wealthy Asians provide powered horn at parties for guests to sniff or add to a drink. Garth and others also point out that horn is undoubtedly being used by speculators for investment, in the same way that property, gold, diamonds and the stock market is used. Stock piles of horn will have created billionaires over the last four decades and will continue to do so while the price remains so high.

For me the devil is in the detail. Who will monitor this trade and keep it honest? We can set up structures but the world is not an honest place – arguably more corrupt than it has ever been. There is also the issue of growing and feeding the appetite for horn instead of throwing massive effort into exposing users of horn to a different way of thinking? And what if a corrupt cartel or two arranged to purchase all horn on sale and re-sell it at high prices?

The pro-trade side points out that all these red flags could be overcome with sufficient long-term dedication by a courageous team prepared to be vilified by the Western social media. A board of reputable conservationists, not corruptible politicians and the profit-motivated private sector, would have to monitor such trade, with all the necessary checks and balances.

Money raised by trading could be used for conservation, not the least to help fund serious environmental education locally – so that hundreds of millions of Africa's children are exposed to the natural world and thus develop a reverence and respect for nature. Only if a majority of ordinary Africans care about the continent's wildlife will there be any hope.

As a white African, I share the resentment Africa feels when the rest of the world dictates how we should protect our wildlife – perhaps it is time for us to take some risks and test some new approaches. At the very least, we need to buy time.

Trading means supporting the West's flawed economic systems and practices. While there is no doubt such systems, and technology, have made life easier than ever before for those of us with access, we also need to acknowledge the terrible cost to our world and to ourselves. Ian McCallum points out that technological progress is a misleading gauge of successful adaptation. Believing that the different species on earth exist in hierarchies of dominance is to totally misunderstand natural selection. We dominate because of technology. The fittest species co-exist with others and 'successfully fit into and with the environment'.

The evolutionary jury is still out but as a species, we the human animal, the new boy on the block with our maladaptive strategies and technologies, are in danger of proving ourselves unfit to survive.

It's important to realise that our current state of ecological emergency is not merely the inevitable result of humans doing what humans do. In their intelligently seditious critique of capitalism, *A History of the World in Seven Cheap Things*, Patel and Moore contend that the destruction of nature has largely been the result of an economic system organised around a minority class and its pursuit of profit.

And the gap between the haves and have-nots continues to widen.

Animal rightists complain that hunting or trading commodifies wild animals. Yet we all commodify wildlife, no matter how we dress this up. Cell phone conservationists are perceiving wild animals as commodities that exist to gratify them and their needs – as something to see and enjoy while taking a holiday in the wilds. We all also derive status and self-worth from being part of a conservation network, whether our role is donating money, running a campaign or NGO, research or field implementation.

Or writing books about wildlife and conservation. We all yearn, at some level, to reach across the human–nature divide.

Namibia has built up a community-based conservation programme that, as imperfect as it is, shines as a bright light in Africa – and in many parts of the world. The country has played host to hundreds of groups from other countries across the world interested in learning about community conservation. It has also been useful in changing attitudes of communities in other countries who are resistant to living with wildlife.

A notable trip was to Norway. A few years ago, John K Kasaona, co-director of IRDNC, was invited by Melissa de Kock of WWF Norway to attend, among other things, a farmers' day in a part of Norway that has wolves. Here was the classic split between town versus country: most of the Norwegian farmers wanted the wolves killed because they take domestic stock; the conservationists who don't make their living from farming want to see the wolves thrive. John accepted Melissa's invitation on condition he could take two Namibian stock farmers with him. He chose Jantjie Rhyn of Torra Conservancy and Alina Karutjaiva of Sesfontein Conservancy.

They went to Norway and talked to Norwegian farmers about living with dangerous wildlife. Their stories of conflicts with lions, leopards and elephant no doubt amazed the Norwegians whose wolf problems could not compare. A frequent question: Why do Namibians put up with these animals? John and the others were able to explain how the conservancy programme is trying to add tangible value to living with wildlife – so that it outweighs the disadvantages. And that sometimes this meant some members of these species had to be shot.

While the Namibians talked about the economic value of wildlife they would also have conveyed its intangible value – how, as a Zambezi elder once said to me: 'We would be ashamed to show our grandchildren pictures of wild animals in a book and tell them these animals once lived here, but we killed them all.' Or as an old Herero woman explained: 'Wild animals are God's cattle. If you kill them all, He will stop sending rain and our cattle will starve.'

Melissa wrote to us about how well this south-north exchange of views had worked. And how it had broken a logjam which had been hindering true communication between farmers and WWF Norway. The farmers now felt that WWF could see and understand their position, and because they felt heard, they were more inclined to hear the conservation perspective.

Garth and I have won some international awards for our community-based conservation work over the last 30 plus years but in reality, it is the Namibian rural people who are prepared to live with wildlife who deserve the recognition.

Epilogue – Our future

*Overconsumption and overpopulation underlie every
environmental problem we face today* – Jacques Yves Cousteau

*When calling a person an animal – as indeed we are - is a
compliment, not an insult, then we will know we are on the road
to healing ourselves and our planet –* Margaret Jacobsohn

AMONG MANY PEOPLE I know, there is a sense of helplessness about
the mess we've made of our natural environment and the great and
growing divisions within human populations. Some of us worry
about the social upheaval that seems inevitable in the gap between
the increasing super-wealth of a minority versus the poverty of the
majority. And overarching it all, the inexorable increase in human
beings – born every minute, especially in countries where there
seems little hope of jobs for most of them.

Young people ask: What can I do to change anything? It's all
too big and complex. Even if I stop using plastic bags, I'm the only
one doing this in the queue. The supermarket manager says he's
waiting for the government to pass legislation against plastic – if
he goes it alone, he'll lose customers to other chains that give away
free plastic.

This is the ultimate tragedy of the commons – and of the cities, suburbs and slums.

And isn't it too late anyway? We are already deep into the sixth great mass extinction in the planet's history. Since the '70s we have managed to wipe out 60 per cent of global wildlife populations, according to a 2018 WWF report. Human activity is pushing the planet's natural systems that support life on earth – ours as well as that of other species – to the brink. If we needed more proof that our lives are inextricably linked to those of other species on our planet, this report, the work of 59 top scientists, provided it.

Far more than just being about losing the wonders of nature, desperately sad though that is, this is actually now jeopardising the future of people, Mike Barrett, executive director of science and conservation for WWF said. 'Nature is not a 'nice to have' – it is our life-support system.'

In countries that should know history better, there is a rise in nationalism. People are resisting globalisation. We have stepped back, even further away from the hope for what Carl Sagan called demographic transition – the flattening out of a population's exponential growth when grinding poverty disappears. Helping other countries become self-sufficient is thus not only elementary human decency but is also in the interests of richer nations – and the planet.

Decades ago, Sagan and others documented that the other most important factor to reduce birth rates is uplifting women. And, importantly, extending political power to them, as well as making safe and effective birth-control methods widely available. The population explosion in most poor countries as well as the migration crisis wealthy countries face now – with hundreds of millions seeking a better life – demonstrates the extent to which we failed to act on this information. Sagan also predicted that unless we curb population growth on this planet, some other process, less under our control, will do it for us.

It's not lack of knowledge about these challenges that render us and our governments ineffectual: it's our apparent inability to act in united and meaningful ways. We find it easier to oppose something than to help build something better in its place. Most of us, including the media, focus on the negative – what's wrong, rather than on possible solutions.

Take just one classic example from wildlife conservation: it's more exciting to try to catch poachers than to work towards stopping poaching – the latter involving a long, slow process of winning the apathetic or unknowing majority and getting them on-side. Community meetings under trees; building unity and creating coalitions of communities, conservancies, traditional leaders, NGOs and government who are able to act together; coordinating joint team patrols to monitor rhino ranges to prevent poachers being able to operate. All this is boring compared to chasing poachers and playing with drones and technology. It is the former 'boring' approach which, certainly in north-west Namibia, has stopped rhino poaching in recent years, as it did in the '80s.

Academic researchers – at least some of them – arrogantly assert their right to deconstruct and criticise with no idea of what it takes to effect positive grassroots change, as imperfect as it might be. Zimbabwe's Professor Marshall Murphy once famously called out a self-important young researcher at a common property conference to put up or shut up. The researcher offered no solutions, only attacked the work of field practitioners; so his research was impotent, the venerable professor suggested, to applause by scholar-practitioners like myself.

Then there is a pervasive belief that technology will somehow rescue us. Of course, our clever tools and technology, digital and otherwise, will assist us. But they can provide no lasting solutions to what is in essence a people problem, requiring attitude and behavioural transformations.

Community-based action can change our world. It may be all that can.

This is not just about wildlife conservation. The challenges associated with conservation in rural Africa differ from the other international problems we face only in scale and specific content – from plastic pollution of our oceans to family planning. They all require that *people* reach consensus, manage conflicts and, most important of all, are willing to change their attitudes – and then their behaviour. The people who can impact on a resource or challenge need to be directly involved in developing solutions. In addition, crucially such plans need to be put into action. Think global, act local.

The problem is *us* and it is *we* who need to change to ensure quality of all life and, indeed, a future for our children. Earth will recover in its own way after we have gone. Such distinctions – that it is humanity's crisis, not the planet's – are important so as not to give us a bolt-hole to avoid taking responsibility for human behaviour. It also implies we are separate from the natural environment as if we can distance ourselves from rivers we have killed with our waste, cows tortured daily by the conditions in abattoirs and feedlots or a rhino having its face hacked off for its horn.

So far social media has probably hindered us more than it has helped, even though its great potential to communicate and drive change for the better remains available. It could help us achieve critical masses of people across the planet agreeing that there are other ways to live, and who are prepared to change their lifestyles: to buy less and share more; to help build communities unsupportive of greed, dishonesty and corruption. If enough people stand up, politicians will follow.

So every positive act counts – which is what I tell any young person wanting to make a difference. Gather a community of like-minded people around you and use your different skills intelligently at different levels. Stop using plastic bags but also lobby government, the plastic factories and the supermarkets. One person can make a difference but a community is unstoppable, to quote a fellow Goldman Environmental Prize laureate.

Perhaps, it's all about respect as that Himba elder said when he stopped inept youth mishandling a frightened ox: Respect for ourselves and each other; respect for all species on our planet. Just think how our behaviour would have to change if we lived respectfully.

Although I read voraciously and travel widely, I often find

myself returning to rural Africa when I seek insights. Garth tells a story that for me epitomises how we need to change and see ourselves as part of the web of life, not in charge of it. Many decades ago, he was interviewing some Himba elders about plants and their uses. Their knowledge of their local vegetation was remarkable by any standards – the list topped 200.

Then, they got to one nearby tree. No one could think of anything that the people used it for. So, said Garth, this tree doesn't have any use?

Ayee (no) that's not what we said, a man intervened: 'We don't use it. But it's useful to the birds that sit on it and the insects that live in it. It's a very useful tree … just not to us.'

And there, in a nutshell, is the holistic, interdependent and respectful way we need to relate to our natural world if we hope for a decent future, or perhaps any future at all, for our grandchildren and theirs.

About the author

Dr Margaret Jacobsohn is a Namibian writer, anthropologist and community-based conservation specialist. The Namibian NGO and trust that she co-founded with Garth Owen-Smith in the late 1980s – Integrated Rural Development and Nature Conservation, IRDNC – pioneered successful community-based conservation and helped change the 'fortress' conservation paradigm.

MJ is an authority on the social organisation and cultural economy of the semi-nomadic Ovahimba people of Namibia and Angola. Her PhD thesis was based on more than five years of living and working with remote Himba and Herero communities. Apart from numerous articles and book chapters on aspects of community-based conservation, she is the author of *Himba, Nomads of Namibia* (Struik 1990). She has published short story fiction, including a story in Jacana Media's 2011 *African Pens* collection.

For the past four years MJ has helped mentor a small up-market mobile safari company, Conservancy Safaris Namibia, which is owned by five Himba and Herero communities through their conservancies in Namibia's far north-west. CSN pioneers a new model of socially responsible tourism in Namibia, which combines the key elements that underlie community-based conservation successes: community ownership, direct involvement and social as well as economic benefits.

MJ has received some of the world's top conservation awards for her work including the US Goldman Grassroots Environmental Prize for Africa (jointly with Garth Owen-Smith), the United Nations Global 500 award, WWF Netherlands's Knights of the Order of the Golden Ark and the Cheetah Conservation Foundation's Special Conservation award.